Literary Reading

PETER LANG
New York • Washington, D.C./Baltimore • Bern
Frankfurt am Main • Berlin • Brussels • Vienna • Oxford

David S. Miall

Literary Reading

Empirical & Theoretical Studies

PETER LANG
New York • Washington, D.C./Baltimore • Bern
Frankfurt am Main • Berlin • Brussels • Vienna • Oxford

Library of Congress Cataloging-in-Publication Data

Miall, David S.
Literary reading: empirical and theoretical studies / David S. Miall.
p. cm.
Includes bibliographical references and index.
1. Literature—Philosophy. 2. Books and reading. I. Title.
PN49.M445 801—dc22 2006019386
ISBN 0-8204-8647-7

Bibliographic information published by **Die Deutsche Bibliothek.**
Die Deutsche Bibliothek lists this publication in the "Deutsche Nationalbibliografie"; detailed bibliographic data is available on the Internet at http://dnb.ddb.de/.

Cover design by Lisa Barfield

The paper in this book meets the guidelines for permanence and durability of the Committee on Production Guidelines for Book Longevity of the Council of Library Resources.

29 Broadway, New York, NY 10006
www.peterlang.com

Printed in Germany

Contents

Tables and Figures

• CHAPTER ONE •

Introduction

Since the eighteenth century literary reading has enjoyed an elevated reputation. In the English tradition the names of critics such as Johnston, Coleridge, Arnold, or T. S. Eliot summon to mind a distinguished and influential range of arguments for literature's unique mimetic power, its ability to break the film of familiarity by which we view the world, or its importance for civilizing the mind of its readers. Such arguments no longer carry the conviction they once did. If we ask whether the modern literary theorist could point to any specific feature, process, or experience that would help distinguish literary from other kinds of reading, the standard answer is no. Although reader response theorists from I. A. Richards, through Wolfgang Iser, to Keith Opdahl have offered a range of proposals on this issue, the current consensus is that literariness is a social convention: the prevailing interpretive community—to borrow Stanley Fish's (1980) influential term—determines what counts as "literature." In the current postmodern view (if we can speak of such a fractured topic) the claims of literature to special status are subject to terminal suspicion. Yet many readers outside the academy who have never heard of Fish or his colleagues continue to value the experiences that literary reading offers and appear to find it distinctive. To cite one prominent example, on the Amazon website numerous readers' comments about novels they have read bear witness to the continued vigorous life of literature outside the classroom.

Yet literary studies seems to have abandoned its traditional post as the guardian and foster-parent of literature. A new genre of writing appeared in the last decade lamenting this phenomenon, bearing titles such as *Literature Lost* (John Ellis, 1997), and *The Rise and Fall of English* (Robert Scholes, 1998). In a recent review article Peter Berkowitz (2006) tells us that "The love of literature is endangered," in particular because "for more than three decades a large faction of professors of literature has contributed to extinguishing the flame." This seems unduly paranoid to me, as the Amazon example demonstrates. It is literary studies, rather, that may have written itself almost into oblivion, if the findings of a recent survey reported by Stephen Greenblatt (2003) are correct: when Americans were asked what image literary scholarship had in the public mind, the answer was a blank: the public gave no thought to it at all (see my more detailed reference to this issue in Chapter 3). But, I hasten to add, this book is not another lament for the decline of literary studies—far from it; although in several places I will make my own complaints about the treatment of literary reading by contemporary theorists (mainly in the next chapter, which will serve to get it out of the way).

The point from which I launch the present book is the following observation. I find it odd that almost none of the theorists in the debate about the fate of literature have considered examining the experiences of actual readers; several have remarked that such experiences are too idiosyncratic to be worth considering. But is that really so? Here is where the empirical project, the study of real acts of reading, can provide some new perspectives on old issues. Is there such a quality as literariness? What does it mean to engage empathically with a character in a novel? Do sound structures in literary texts systematically influence readers? Does reading literature perform some function for us that no other experience can provide? These are just some of the issues taken up in this book, but taken up in the context of empirical study: that is, what evidence we can gather for the reality of our proposals about literary reading from the experience of actual readers. Rather than speculating about the effect of reading, as traditional reader response studies have done (from Ingarden to Opdahl), the research discussed in this book is motivated by a continual two-way interweaving of theoretical proposal and empirical investigation. In my view theoretical statements are ineffectual without empirical support; empirical study without theoretical motivation is trivial. Both are required in order to establish any durable, significant insights into the nature of literary reading. This approach, I would add, constitutes the empirical study represented here (my own studies and those of many of my colleagues in the field) as the first meaningful and coherent scientific study of the literary phenomenon. (I will not attempt here to rebut the postmodern argument that the scientific claim is necessarily just another fiction.) As the empirical method will be unfamiliar for most of my readers, a detailed introduction to it is provided in Chapter 3.

So what is distinctive about the present approach? And what does it tell us about literary reading that we didn't already know? I can indicate the scope of the book overall by a brief description of some of its major themes and their empirical implications. Not surprisingly, some of the themes will be familiar; yet, the empirical dimension provides a new twist on some old insights. In summary (very cursory), this is the story of reading we will be pursuing in various ways throughout the book.

I will be concerned above all with *ordinary* readers, not academic ones. Even though, in our experimental work, we sometimes obtained the participation of students of literature, the issues they considered were of the kind that all readers would be likely to find relevant and interesting (I refer briefly to expert readers and their possible differences in Chapter 7). Second, in proposing an overall purpose or function for literary reading, I had in mind an evolutionary context, hinging on whether or not we can actually sustain a hypothesis for the adaptive value of literature. Thus the underlying concept for all the studies described in the book is that literature is *dehabituating*; that is, it invites us to consider frames for understanding and feeling about the world that are likely to be novel, or at least, unfamiliar. Thirdly, in contrast to the contemporary view that literary reading depends upon the acquisition of the appropriate conventions, the view I take here—while it does not dismiss the relevance of convention—asserts that through the reading process we can identity properties that are distinctive to *literariness*. This is not a modern version of the claim, fostered by the Russian Formalists, that literary texts can be objectively distinguished from other texts by a unique array of formal features (although we can identify some formal features that appear to be confined largely to literary texts); rather, literariness is manifested by the special nature of the interaction between reader and text.

Fourth, in accounting for the processes of literary reading my emphasis will fall in particular on the role of *feeling*. This will distinguish my approach from a recently developed school of literary scholars, that of cognitive poetics, which has been providing interesting accounts of how we read literary texts in the light of what is known about cognitive functions such as deixis, schemata and frames, figure and ground, theory of mind, and the like. While I find such readings plausible, I am surprised that a school that draws on an empirical science for its theory (cognition) has yet to see the need to carry out empirical study itself to help verify its proposals. More important, the restriction to a cognitive approach has almost entirely eliminated consideration of the role of feeling in literary response. The investigation of feeling, its roles, function, and consequences, is perhaps the key element in this book as a whole. Fifth, my approach emphasises *experiencing* literature rather than interpreting it. Given the attention to ordinary readers, it is clear that most readers most of the time are interested in the significance of the literature they read, not how to interpret it. Interpretation is the besetting preoccupation of literary scholars. The attention to experience also provides specifically for an empirical approach, since it prompts us to ask what experiences of literary reading actual readers have, and to what extent these are distinctively literary. As Tompkins (1980) pointed out some time ago, in criticism prior to the New Critics "the specification of meaning is not a central concern" (p. 201). The classical critics were concerned with effect, with the power of a text, not with its meaning (p. 203). Interpretation only becomes central with the advent of formalist criticism (p. 222). To focus on experience, therefore, is to move decisively beyond the formalism of the New Critics in a way that, as Tompkins observed, poststructural approaches were rarely able to do.

Lastly, the various theories about response canvassed and tested in the book can be related, as I suggested, to one master theory, that of the *evolutionary* implications of literature: I ask whether we can consider literary reading and its oral predecessors as adaptive, and, if so, whether, as some critics have claimed, literary response is shaped by some specific universals; that is, since literary culture is manifest in every human culture we know, do certain core features of it appear across literary cultures independently of outside influence (e.g., Hogan, 1997, 2003). Although few scholars have, as yet, made inroads on developing an evolutionary approach (e.g., Boyd, Carroll, Storey, Hogan), it is my judgement that the success of evolutionary theory in general in accounting for human development requires us to consider seriously how the evolutionary context will help us account for literary experience. Literary scholarship is in danger, otherwise, of receding into a quaint backwater, of little account to the readership still flourishing in the rest of the world that continues to generate insights about the self and our environment through the power of the literary text.

These six themes, then, motivate the discussions on offer throughout the book. The chapters are organized on somewhat varied lines, as might be expected of a book made up, as this one is, mainly of previously published articles written over several years. As might also be expected there is a good deal of interweaving of themes and topics, which means that readers will find themselves revisiting some topics several times when reading through the whole book. I have, nevertheless, revised some chapters to eliminate unnecessary redundancies; and I have also included some new material to bring certain chapters up to date, as well as providing two hitherto unpublished chapters (this one and Chapter 6 on feeling), in addition to another on neuropsychology that so far has been published only in Danish (Chapter 9). Individually the chapters represent a range of issues, whether primarily theoretical or empirical, or a balance of the two. However, the chapters in Part I are designed to provide a survey of the empirical issues and methods that I have found important in my work; the reader unfamiliar with empirical method might wish to start here by reading in particular Chapters 3 and 7, which provide an introduction to the field from my perspective. Part II broaches several other contexts for studying literary reading empirically, but ones that involve more speculative issues.

In the first main chapter, "On the Necessity of Empirical Studies of Literary Reading," I begin by arguing against the idea that the nature of literature must be decided by literary theorists, since this both gives rein to individual scholarly inventiveness (literature can be anything I say it is), and disregards the experiences of actual readers. I point to several postmodern conceptions that are held *a priori* by some empirical researchers, then advocate an empirical approach to such questions. I point to three issues in particular that merit empirical study: the role and place of the canon (where I cite historical evidence provided by Jonathan Rose, 1992) and the self-renewing power of canonical works; dehabituation, which enables us to perceive and feel the world with fresh eyes, and which can be exemplified in studies by Russell Hunt and Doug

Vipond (1986) of "evaluations" in narratives, or the studies of Will van Peer (1986) or our own of foregrounding (Miall & Kuiken, 1994a); and decentering, apparent in the power of empathy which invites us to adopt different identities as we read, and which seems to involve greater personal implication in literary than in non-literary texts.

In the next chapter, "Experimental Approaches to Readers' Responses to Literature," I question the emphasis given to interpreting literary texts, and suggest that most ordinary readers pick up a literary text in order to gain the experience it offers, not to determine its meaning as a literary critic would. The main body of the chapter is devoted to outlining experimental design and methods, including a caution against the manipulation of literary texts for experimental purposes (as is frequently done). I describe several alternative research designs, involving study of intrinsic features of texts, or conditions which influence reading, and show how these bear on the issue of literariness. I go on to raise some questions about the design of empirical studies, including the need to remain open to the possible distinctiveness of literary texts.

In Chapter 4, "Interpretation, Cognition, Feeling," I consider in some detail the problem of interpretation, and appeal to the evidence of one of Henry James's short stories. In "The Figure in the Carpet" the search for a specific "figure" embedded in the literary text is shown to be an illusion. Yet, as I go on to point out, the approach of cognitive poetics, which its proponents have hailed as a new literary discipline, continues to analyse texts in the service of interpretation, as well as overlooking the role of feeling; and despite specifying cognitive processes of reading in exemplary detail, no attempt is made to check such proposals empirically with real readers.

In the opening sections of Chapter 5, "Feeling in the Comprehension of Literary Narratives," I return to the problem of cognition. As another way of debating the issue, I point to the achievements of schema theory as an approach to reading, but show its limitations in accounting for literary meaning. Literary texts often contain a good deal of indeterminacy, which creates a problem for the schema theorist attempting to categorize textual elements. I introduce some of the roles that I hypothesize are played by feeling: its cross-domain, anticipatory, and self-referential functions, and illustrate these with analysis of a short story by Virginia Woolf. This is followed by an account of an empirical study designed to contrast a schema-based understanding with one based on feeling: I show how readers of the Woolf story shifted from the first to the second, leading to a feeling-driven revaluation of several aspects of the story, as signalled both by readers' ratings of story elements and their comments after reading. The study indicates the prevailing role played by the readers' feelings from the beginning of their response, a feature of response that I refer to as "feeling controls." I argue that literary reading involves not only schema instantiation but, more distinctively, schema creation.

Chapter 6, "Feelings in Literary Reading: Five Paradoxes," offers the most detailed account in the book of the relevance of feeling to literary experience. While in the previous chapter I considered the power and flexibility of feelings as a vehicle for literary reading, here I elaborate those aspects of feeling which seem especially likely to underpin the shifts in understanding that occur during reading, in particular, the creativity of the reading process; and I ask whether literariness, the aesthetic distinctiveness of literary reading, might be due to certain specific configurations of feeling. The aspects of feeling I review can be considered paradoxical: empathy for fictional characters, suspense and other feelings re-experienced when reading a text again; our pleasure in negative feelings; the relation of feeling to action; and how feeling can be either time-bound or timeless. I demonstrate the relevance of these conceptions of feeling to a short story by Kate Chopin (the text of which can be found in the Appendix), and provide examples drawn from readers' comments in response to the story.

In the last chapter of the first part of the book, "The Empirical Approach: A Survey and Analysis," I stand back and provide a selective survey of the field of empirical studies as a whole. I point out some of its links with mainstream literary scholarship and the reader response tradition, as well as its links to psychology, and discourse processing in particular. Among the questions considered, I mention literariness, the role of convention, and the effect of literary training or expertise on reading. In the main part of the chapter I review a range of empirical studies in an attempt to portray the field as a whole: this touches on such issues as polyvalence (the convention that literary texts are considered to support more than one meaning), anticipation, the nature of literary meaning, the role of personal concerns and feeling, and some of the formal components of literary texts (foregrounding, sound patterns).

Part II provides an introduction to several additional contexts that expand on the implications of the empirical study of literary reading. These involve considerations of narrative structure in the chapter on episodes; a study of some of the neuropsychological correlates of reading; an analysis of one contribution to cognitive linguistics, as it has been called—the structuring role of metaphors in everyday thought; the role of sound patterns in literary response; and, finally, an attempt to place literary reading in an evolutionary context.

In Chapter 8, "Episode Structures in Literary Narratives," I develop the idea of the episode as an overall organizing feature for the coherent development of narrative; this is presented as a literary alternative to the situation model of discourse processing theory. An episode is usually some half to a whole page in length; it presents a new perspective in the ongoing narrative, often by representing a shift in place or time, or a change in character; and it may culminate with a particular twist that intrigues the reader and motivates her to continue to the next episode. Episodes are thus another aspect of the formal structures of a literary text that act to defamiliarize the reader's understanding. I discuss some previous writers, such as Eco, Barthes, and Iser who have offered conceptions similar to the episode, but in order to elaborate the technical aspects of the episode I devote the most attention to an analysis by a Russian Formalist critic of a story by Maupassant. Finally, I report some evidence from readers that helps validate the conception empirically, in which I show the significance of feeling in binding together the elements of the episode and creating expectations beyond the episode boundary. The more effective readers were those who appeared sensitive to the episode structures of the narrative.

Chapter 9, "Literariness: Are There Neuropsychological Indicators?", confronts the question, what is literariness and what are some of its components. After some discussion of this issue, I examine three aspects in particular by reviewing evidence from brain research that tends to support them: first, the defamiliarization-recontextualization cycle in response to foregrounding; then the dynamic structure of narrative episodes in prose and poetry; and lastly the feelings of empathy we experience in response to characters in narrative. I finish by considering the nature of aesthetic experience more widely and how far neuropsychological discussion of the visual arts is compatible with the view of literature I present.

An influential development in philosophy, linguistics, and literary studies has been the metaphor theory of Lakoff and Johnson. In "The Body in Literature: Metaphor and Feeling" I undertake a critical analysis in particular of one contribution to this field, the book by Johnson, *The Body in the Mind* (1987), and consider to what extent Johnston's account provides a basis for understanding literary reading. While his account of metaphoric structures in thought is helpful, I suggest that the role of feeling is overlooked, that the presence of the body in thinking is notional, and that his concept of imagination fails to distinguish literary from non-literary types of thinking. I put forward some proposals from Coleridge that I suggest provide a better basis for understanding literary reading.

The next chapter, "Sounds of Contrast: An Empirical Approach to Phonemic Iconicity," represents one attempt to probe the contribution of foregrounding more deeply by considering the contribution of sound patterns to literary reading. I discuss the history of attempts to relate sound and meaning, then outline a new approach of my own that enables systematic comparisons of sound patterns in verbal materials, including literary texts. I validate the method with several examples drawn from literary and non-literary materials, then make a closer analysis of the influence of sound patterns on readers of one short story.

The final chapter, "An Evolutionary Framework for Literary Reading," takes up the observation that every culture known to us has a special mode of verbal behaviour that we can call literary. Thus I introduce the question whether literary reading can be considered an adaptation. If so, what specific problems did the evolution of literary experience help our ancestors to solve? After considering existing approaches to this question, in which critics have confined themselves mainly to the mimetic capacity of literature, I offer discussions of two aspects of literature: first, I discuss foregrounding and its apparently innate features, then look at the dehabituating role of literature, where my argument focuses on the power of literature for tuning our everyday schemata and enabling us to rehearse potentially problematic situations in imagination. I also ask whether one important function of literature is to ameliorate our experience of negative emotions. I end by considering the implications of an evolutionary perspective for empirical studies of literary reading.

In putting this book together I have become increasingly aware of how much more there is to learn: there are many problems with understanding the Protean nature of literature and its effects on readers. I hope that some of my readers will be motivated to enter this field for themselves and join the small, but growing, community of scholars dedicated to developing this challenging field.

In the meantime I would like to acknowledge the support and stimulation I have been given by a number of colleagues, including the communities of IGEL (the International Society for the Empirical Study of Literature and Media) and REDES (Research and Development in Empirical Studies), the graduate students who have come to Alberta to engage in empirical studies in our lab, and especially my research partner Don Kuiken at the University of Alberta, who has worked with me in this area over the last fifteen years (our joint research will be the topic of a separate co-authored book), and whose influence, as might be imagined, is evident at many places in the present volume. I also acknowledge with gratitude the Social Sciences and Humanities Research Council of Canada, whose grant support to Don Kuiken and myself facilitated several of the empirical studies discussed here. Finally, I thank the editors and publishers of the journals and books in whose pages most of the chapters of this book first appeared, who have graciously allowed me to reprint the materials: separate acknowledements will be found on the first page of each chapter. Further information about our empirical research programme is available from my website: http://www.ualberta.ca/~dmiall/reading.

•PART ONE•

Becoming Empirical

• C H A P T E R   T W O •

On the Necessity of Empirical Studies of Literary Reading

2.1 Why Empirical Studies?

Empirical studies of literary reading have not yet appeared over the horizon for most mainstream literary scholars.* Involved as most now are in theoretically self-conscious practices of historicist or deconstructive research, the very assumptions of empirical research would, if they came to attention, seem irrelevant, or even improper. This point has been made several times, for instance, by Jonathan Culler. When enquiring about literary competence, he argues, "The question is not what actual readers happen to do but what an ideal reader must know implicitly in order to read and interpret works in ways which we consider acceptable, in accordance with the institution of literature" (1975, pp. 123–4; cf. 1981, p. 129). Similarly, Culler refers to "the dangers of an experimental or socio-psychological approach which would take too seriously the actual and doubtless idiosyncratic performance of individual readers" (1975, p. 258).

Such statements reveal two common assumptions: first, that the nature of literary reading is necessarily decided by the theorist, who determines in advance what is to count in "the institution of literature"; second, that actual readers are too wayward in their readings to justify serious attention. Both these assumptions deprecate the value of an empirical approach, yet both presuppose the answers to questions that call for empirical study. Are readers idiosyncratic? How are we to decide what qualifies a reading to be "literary"? At the moment we have almost no attempts to examine these questions. But I will suggest that empirical studies have the capacity to take the primary place in defining literary

---

* This chapter first appeared as "On the Necessity of Empirical Studies of Literary Reading," *Frame*, 14, 2000, 43–59.

studies, and that this is an approach that would help to clarify the aims and unify the divided nature of current scholarship.

Thus at the present time empirical studies might be seen as the Cinderella in the family of literary disciplines. Mostly disregarded, and deprecated when noticed at all, as the example of Culler shows, no prince will arrive to exalt her at the end of the day. But by her own efforts empirical study will come to dominate the literary field by providing a matrix for evaluating theoretical proposals and for rethinking the nature of literary reading and its cultural place. It is destined to play this role in literary studies, just as over the last two centuries the sciences have emancipated themselves from theological control or superstition by subjecting themselves to validation by empirical methods. As astrology was replaced by astronomy, or alchemy by chemistry, or as evolutionary theory has replaced creationism, despite last ditch defences in several jurisdictions in the United States, our understanding of literary reading will be recast in the light of evidence gathered from real readers. Rather than debate the (often conflicting) assertions of reader response theorists such as Wolfgang Iser or Stanley Fish, literary scholars will formulate their claims as hypotheses and set out to design empirical studies to assess their validity. As Colin Martindale (1996), one critic of the conflicted state of literary studies has argued, "Literary theorists, for whatever reason, often take as axiomatic what are really empirical questions" (p. 349). While the place of theory will remain central, it will become possible to arbitrate between alternative positions; theory will no longer remain the interminable and inconclusive mode of debate that we currently witness; nor will it remain divorced from the interests and concerns of those outside the academy who continue to be engaged in reading literary texts. Such readers are currently excluded by the irresolvable conflicts that rack the discipline, and the excessive claims being made by its most prominent exponents. As De Beaugrande (1989) has put it, "Only empirical studies can resolve this state of affairs by freeing these claims from their absolute dependence on the personal eloquence or effrontery of the individual theorists and by providing progressively more reliable and intersubjective grounds for preferring any set of claims over any other" (p. 10).

One major shift in perspective will be required of literary scholars in order for this development to occur. The last thirty years has been dominated by what, following Ricoeur (1970), has come to be know as the hermeneutics of suspicion (p. 32). As Ricoeur's way of characterizing Freud (his other examples were Marx and Nietzsche), it was intended to suggest that the evidence of consciousness, whether the recollection of a dream or a slip of the tongue, was not to be taken at face value; the mode of suspicion is a way of understanding the aims of Freud's forensic approach. As an approach to literary texts it has been generalized to become the predominant paradigm: all texts are considered to conceal latent content at odds with their surface claims. Whether this is approached in the light of Derrida's *différence*, Foucault's *epistème*, or Barthes's intertextuality, a text is not what it seems; moreover, it has designs on its readers. A particularly clear example is provided by a recent issue of an online journal for Romantic studies, whose editor (Kooy, 2000) refers to the influence of the aesthetic of Wordsworth or Shelley on the critics of thirty years ago. There is, he says, "a recognition shared more broadly by many in the profession who can now only regard with irony the claim (did anyone really believe this?) that poetry 'can set one free of the ruins of history and culture', to borrow McGann's famous phrase." Advocating a renewal of historicist methods, he suggests that, on the contrary, "history will save us from poetry."

Suspicion is thus directed at the text, at whatever effects, feelings, or insights the text may be designed to elicit. One critic has renamed this approach, with some justice, "the hermeneutics of disparagement" (Grob, 1998). As a departure point for literary studies, it precludes attention to readers' modes of engagement. Whether or not a given aesthetic response should be called into question -- and this itself is an empirical question -- the reader's experience of that response is precluded as a focus for study. In fact, it is more likely, as I will argue in detail below, that a literary text stands in relation to its reader as Freud to his client, and that to read appropriately is to have one's own assumptions and way of life called into question. The reader, in other words, is invited by a literary text to place her experiences under the aegis of suspicion, to reconsider or modify her attitudes, feelings, and conceptions. This does not eliminate literary studies under the sign of Derrida or Foucault, but it displaces them from their current central place and turns each critical thesis generated by their approach into an empirical question: i.e., what, given sufficient evidence, can we trace of this supposed property of the text in the responses of actual readers. To continue otherwise, allowing the present hermeneutics of suspicion to assert its domination of literary studies, is to leave out of account the most important question of all: why do people read? It is like studying food in terms of its appearance, customs, and history, while failing to pay attention to its nutritional function.

In this chapter I will offer three more specific reasons for this claim (each, by the way, being empirically testable), drawing on the work of our research group and other published research studies. I will discuss the canon, stylistics, and empathic identification in narrative. Empirical studies have already reinvigorated some areas of research that had become largely disregarded, such as stylistics, or emotional aspects of reading; it has also broached some new ways of thinking about literary reading, from its inroads on discourse processing (e.g., Zwaan, et al., 1995) to the electrophysiological studies of Hoorn (1996). It has led to some rethinking over what literature is, and how we might delimit it. In these and other ways empirical study represents a significant alternative framework for understanding literature, but it is one that in itself has yet to achieve paradigmatic status. There is no consensus among its practitioners what its theoretical framework should be, or what would count as exemplary experimental methods. I will next indicate briefly what some of the main causes of dissension are that must be resolved before empirical study becomes coherent and programmatic.

Overall, not surprisingly, some of the same theoretical problems that have energized mainstream debate have preoccupied a number of empirical scholars. Several typical postmodern claims appear rather often in the empirical literature. For example, Bürger (1989) has argued that after Duchamp (with works such his urinal) we cannot argue that there is an essential nature to works of art: "What seemed to be an incarnate 'nature' turns out to be a pure construction." We now know that "the institution of art is, in the truest sense of the word, groundless" (p. 52). The canon of esteemed literary works is decided institutionally, says Shavit (1991): the dominant institution gains the mandate, which "has nothing what-so-ever to do with 'poetic justice' nor with the question of the value of the texts. . . . A text gains a high status not because it is valuable, but because . . . someone has the political-cultural power to grant the text the status they believe it deserves." (p. 233). Similarly, literature has no defining elements distinguishing it from what is non-literary. While conceptions of literature play a role in enabling readers to perceive and name the textual elements of their reading, according to Verdaasdonk (1982), "The normative and imprecise nature of conceptions of literature rules out, however, that the labels readers attach to textual elements have descriptive value" (p. 89). The programme of research initiated by Siegfried Schmidt, the Empirical Science of Literature, is based on two foundational conventions, the aesthetic and polyvalence conventions which, once again, are said to be institutionally determined. Other parallel examples could be indicated. Each such position must be confronted by the question that Elrud Ibsch (1989) puts to Schmidt: "Does this construction permit empirical testing or is it used as a hard core which does not need corroboration?" (p. 399). In this mode of argument, she points out, such theorists seem unreceptive to Popperian scientific procedure, since they have no place for "the ethical impulse inherent in the search for the counter-example." Assuming validity, rather than demonstrating it, a theory of this status calls for "immunization procedures instead of a strengthening of methods for testing" (p. 402).

The testing of such claims must be at the heart of the empirical programme. So far, however, we have no unequivocally accepted paradigm of empirical method, no foundational studies. The problems facing the empirical scholar have been well stated by Graesser and his colleagues (Graesser, Person, & Johnston, 1996). First, there is no agreed essential defining property of the aesthetic experience of literature: this could reside in good form, prototypical aspects, novelty, formal devices, or somewhere else; second, the components of response are relatively inaccessible to consciousness, thus hard to track empirically; and third, we lack agreement on a set of theories or mini-theories that would direct our research. Thus, in the three domains I discuss below, I try to show how the problems of the field identified by Graesser and his colleagues might be addressed. Taking issues that have commonly been debated in mainstream scholarship, I show how each has been amenable to empirical study.

2.2 The Renewal of the Canon

A qualitative basis to the canon has been called into question by most recent literary theorists, who now take the view that it is a sociological construct. But I will suggest that this is properly an empirical question. The institutional perpetuation of the canon is one possible explanation for the survival of eminent works such as those by Homer, Shakespeare, Wordsworth, or Dickens; but other explanations should also be considered. In particular, the canon appears to be subject to renewal: the canon renews itself through being re-experienced and reinterpreted (the main feature I examine below), and the canon is itself renewed by the appearance of new works that gain canonical status.

In the first case, the literary academy itself gives evidence of the power of the canon: it does so by its continual provision of new interpretations of the notable canonical works. This has been seen as unfortunate by some critics: "Each new generation feels the urge to produce new interpretations, new evaluations, new concepts of literature and new literary histories," remarks Fokkema (1988): "is it necessary to start time and again from scratch?" (p. 532). Moreover, new interpretations generally compete with extant rival views, suggesting widespread disagreement over what a given literary text "means." This phenomenon argues against institutional determination of the literary canon (since no institution worthy of the name would tolerate such an array of incompatible readings), but the renewal of interpretation itself points to the need for continual repositioning of a given text in relation to contemporary historical and social conditions; our *Hamlet* is not that of the 1960s, and this in turn differs from that of the nineteenth century. Reinterpretation is thus a sign of the inexhaustible vigour of the canonical texts at issue, not of our weakness as critics. It is, on a large scale, a parallel to the dehabituation requirement that I will mention below in the context of literary language.

The canon also seems to be renewed in another way that falls outside institutional control. While standard histories of reading argue for the emergence of the literary canon in the eighteenth century as a vehicle for the rising bourgeoisie to identify itself and its interests (e.g., Terry, 1997), there is a small but growing volume of evidence for the impact of canonical works on readers outside this class. Jonathan Rose (1992), summarizing his research on British working class readers of the nineteenth century, reports that such workers frequently discovered classical texts for themselves, picking them up from trash heaps or buying them from penny bookstalls, but were then influenced by them to imagine different or new worlds. Moreover, as Rose puts it in the case of Dickens, who appears to have had a particularly pervasive influence, "Dickens provided working people the inspiration and the generic literary conventions they needed to tell their own stories" (p. 61), an impact that intentionally popular fiction writers of the time failed to achieve. Rose's evidence shows repeatedly that the texts that genuinely influenced their working class readers were those we now regard as canonical. Far from being instruments of social control, as critics such as Eagleton have asserted, Dickens or Hardy were avenues to emancipation for many of their working class readers: they saw new worlds, recognizing their common humanity in the figures of David Copperfield or Tess D'Urberville, and were empowered as a result to change their lives and the lives of those around them (p. 64). Thus, rather than theorizing about the impact of the canonical text, or supposing it to be an instrument of social control, Rose has collected empirical evidence from the autobiographies or comments of the working poor, evidence that seems to provide strong support for the central values of the canon (see also Rose, 2001).

A contemporary example of the power of reading is a programme for sentencing criminals called "Changing Lives through Literature." Now available in a few jurisdictions—Massachusetts, Texas, and imitated in Manchester, England—the programme is an alternative to jail time. Offenders are required to read novels and short stories, and texts by Plato and Shakespeare, and attend discussions of them at regular intervals. According to one study, reoffending rates of those in the programme were 19% compared with 49% in a matched group of offenders (Fitterman, 1989). Again, most of the texts being read are canonical. These are texts with the power to make a difference in their readers' lives.

Jack Gold (1990) offers a personal view of such an experience. Reading a novel by David Lodge that describes air raids in London during the war, an experience Gold lived through as a child, he reports "I was strongly moved by it, but more, I was grateful for it. The expression, the novel, sometimes gives a shape, a form, to experience that we recognize as our own. The novel is then a gift, a creating of the reader's reality, existence, history. The pieces of my past, my life, that were lying around in a puzzling mess—unexpressed, unformed, vaguely felt—are gathered together and given recognizable and storable shape. This is a priceless gift . . ." (pp. 176–7).

In this way, the canon renews itself in the experience of individual readers. While this process may of course be assisted (or endangered: Miall, 1996) by the institutions in which most of us learn to read—the family, school, college—it seems improbable that the canon would be perpetuated if readers had to be persuaded of the value of the literary texts they read, rather than discovering it for themselves at first hand. That experience seems to matter, in the first place, because it often appears to be as vivid as our lived experience. Janos Lászlo (1990), for example, made a study of image production in readers. He found that images generated in response to literary texts were as strong as those derived from experience, whereas images generated in response to a newspaper article were generic in nature, similar to images of social categories. In the second place, literary reading can often be a powerful emotional experience. These two features are linked: as Goetz and Sadoski (1996) have shown, imagery in response to literary reading is usually associated with emotion, suggesting that imagery may provide a matrix for representing emotions. Through imagery and emotion, in other words, a literary text engages with the reader's own experience and, as Gold suggests, helps the reader to think about it afresh, even to reconfigure it and understand it in a new light. The two principal features specifically responsible for this process appear to be the dehabituating power of literary forms, and empathic projection into the lives of others through narrative.

2.3 Dehabituation

Everyday experience is governed largely through standard and familiar concepts that provide economical and efficient ways of dealing with the world. Cognitively speaking, this aspect has been enshrined in schema theory (other common terms being scripts, or frames): schemata are those stereotyped processes of behaviour by which we orient ourselves and know what to expect—as, for example, when we enter a restaurant. However, it is also critically important to be able to question our familiar, everyday behaviours; literary reading provides one vehicle for going beyond the customary, familiar world, and for reconceiving our role within it. Through literary reading we dehabituate, that is, we are enabled to contemplate alternative models for being in the world. Such reading prepares us for being more adaptable: it is an "offline" way of experimenting with emotions or experiences that might have dangerous or unpleasant consequences in the real world, gaining insight into their implications so that we know better how to act when similar situations occur in reality.

The dehabituating aspect of literature has been described in several ways. For the British Romantic writers it was a central part of the theory of imagination: for Coleridge (1983), writing in 1817, the imagination at its most powerful "dissolves, diffuses, and dissipates, in order to re-create" (I, 304). Among empirical scholars, several terms have been used. John Harker (1996) calls attention to the "reattentional" activity required of the literary reader: this is because "The literary text does not simply distort or blur reality; it refocuses it, instructing the reader in the new ways of knowing that to its author are more authentic and real" (p. 650). Similarly, De Beaugrande (1983) argues that the most important trait of literary communication, "the only one that seems to apply to all cases—can be termed the ALTERNATIVITY PRINCIPLE: that the world-model evoked by a literary text is free, though not obliged, to present or imply alternatives to the socially established model of reality." (p. 91).

A predominant way of achieving this is through special uses of language. Vipond and Hunt (1989) studied what they termed "evaluations" in narratives, defined as elements that depart from the local norm of the text. These might be discourse evaluations (the way something is told), story evaluations (an event that is surprising), and telling evaluations (that something is mentioned at all or that moment)—such evaluations are likely to be noticed by readers and prompt particular forms of attention. These are all connected with "the idea of incongruity, distinctiveness, or surprisingness" (p. 157). Other research, such as that of Van Peer (1986) and our studies (Miall and Kuiken, 1994a), has seen literary language as distinctive in comparison with the uses of language in everyday discourse, as in a news report. In this respect, following Mukařovský, we and Van Peer described such features as *foregrounded*, since they stand out against a background of common usage. Such features as assonance, metre, syntactic inversion, or metaphor, are effective in attracting attention; they serve to defamiliarize the reader, who (as our studies showed) lingers a little more over such features, and usually appears to attribute greater feeling to them; they may also provide the germination point of alternative interpretations that will emerge later during reading (Miall and Kuiken, 2001); or, in De Beaugrande's (1983) account, "Deviations act as intermittent cues to apply the alternativity principle to the *entire* text, including elements that could occur in the same form in ordinary discourse" (p. 92). In our studies we have found a high degree of consistency among readers: most readers notice and are influenced by the same set of foregrounded features, even though their individual interpretations might then vary widely.

The "literariness" of foregrounded language raises the question whether this is a defining characteristic of literature, as an earlier generation of scholars appeared to believe (e.g., Jakobson). The recent consensus among empirical scholars has been against this position. De Beaugrande (1983), for example, argues that literariness can be defined "only as a *processor disposition*, rather than as a *text property*"; there is "no one manifest property" than is necessary for a literary text (p. 91–92). Similarly, Halász (1989) rehearses the arguments for defining literariness in terms of the formal qualities in texts, but concludes "There is no literary *object*, there is only literary *function* that any sort of written text can have" (p. 31). This is to claim that literariness is an outcome of a reader's cognitive operations, opening the door to the claim that any text can be considered literary and that any interpretation is valid. But Halász stops short of such total relativism; a literary text is not a projective test, and possible interpretations are constrained by certain characteristics of the text. In this respect, the differences between readers appear to be less salient than the commonalities, and such agreement (as with foregrounding) appears to be due principally to the text.

The issue remains unresolved (and is perhaps unresolvable), but the question of the background against which foregrounded features would be perceptible is broached by at least one supporting study. Frey (1981) found that at in the case of word frequency, people show a high degree of accuracy in judging how often a set of words occur, and that their rank orders agreed closely with word norm data from several sources. Participants also gave different but consistent ranks when invited to consider the frequency of the same words in different situations (e.g., among workmen building a house; on the evening TV news, etc.). This provides evidence for the existence of a "background" against which deviations in a literary text will be perceived (i.e., the use of an unusual word in a given context); and if words are amenable to such judgements, then we might also expect a similar capacity for discrimination of sound patterns (a question I pursue in Chapter 11), the background against which metre, assonance, and alliteration are perceived. In the absence of further studies, it seems premature to claim that "literariness" is definable in terms of objective features in texts; but neither should this possibility be prematurely dismissed. What is clear from existing studies, is that dehabituation is a prominent, perhaps even the most significant, aspect of readers' responses to literary texts, and that as an agent for initiating this response identifiable formal features of the language of texts often play a key role.

2.4 Decentering

Another major component of literary reading is our interest in the fate of the characters we encounter in narrative, especially the protagonist in whose predicament we come to empathize. While a novel or short story often draws us to view the world from the protagonist's perspective, that character is not us, and does not share our experience; thus, in addition to the close interest evoked by our reading, we may also experience a decentering, a shift away from attending to our own daily concerns. As Birkerts (1994) puts it, during such reading the self is "suspended in the medium of language, the particles of the identity wavering in the magnetic current of another's expression" (p. 78); and, he adds later, "Our awareness, our sense of life, gets filtered into the character, where it becomes strangely detached from us" (p. 93). To emerge from the absorbed state of such reading can seem a distinct change of state, like awakening from a dream; there is a momentary and disorienting sense of engaging the gears of our own daily life once again. Yet, perhaps our interests are reflected at some deeper, transmuted level during reading.

Halász (1996) examined the how far personal meanings were invoked by a literary in comparison with a non-literary text. His studies employed two texts, Kakfa's "The Vulture", and an expository text called "The Peregrine Falcon"; these were presented to readers without information about their authors or that one was literary. During reading participants were asked to pause three times and to comment on the "accepted" (i.e., impersonal) meaning and the personal meaning of the text. In counting the frequency of impersonal and personal meaning units, Halász found that the expository text produced three times as many impersonal to personal meaning units; the literary text produced almost the same number in both categories, showing that the literary text enabled readers to generate a much higher proportion of personal meanings. Among the personal meanings, the predominant types were actions, feelings, evaluations, and what Halász termed "cognitive qualities" (intuitions, imaginative or day-dream-type responses).

Similarly, a study by Sielman and Larsen (1989) explored the kinds of memories that occurred to readers while reading a literary and a non-literary text. They proposed that when comparing responses to a literary and an expository text, the literary text would involve more memories of the reader as an actor than as an observer. Using two texts, a short story and a text about population growth (each of about 3000 words), they found that although a similar number of remindings was elicited by both texts, twice as many actor-perspective remindings were elicited by the literary text, while the expository text elicited more receiver remindings (memories of things read or heard about). Thus, they suggest, literary reading "seems to connect particularly with knowledge that is personal in the sense that one is an agent, a responsible subject interacting with one's environment" (p. 174). This seems to evoke the possibility of readers' complicity with the actions of the characters in a narrative, or more radically, as we have been finding in our own recent studies, an emerging convergence between the interests of the reader and that of the main character (cf. Miall & Kuiken, 1999).

Just as literariness at the level of language has been a focus for dispute, however, so too has the nature of fictionality and its effects. According to Siegfried Schmidt (1980) fictionality belongs to the level of discourse not text, and is attributed to texts "by judgements of agents according to conventions regulating fictional discourse" (p. 539); "whether a linguistic event is or can be treated as fictional cannot be decided except on the level of discourse and using information provided by the non-verbal social context of discourse" (p. 540). Similarly, Richard Gerrig (1993) has rejected the notion that our encounter with fiction causes us to "suspend disbelief"; the cognitive operations involved in reading literary and non-literary texts are the same, in his view, and judgements about fictionality follow later. This is questionable, however, when the devices available to the fiction writer are considered. These are precisely the devices capable of eliciting the decentering response of empathic projection. At the sentence level, for example, it is possible to demonstrate the so-called omniscient (or limited omniscient) narrative style that provides privileged information about a character's mind; since this is unavailable in any non-fictional mode of discourse, it is necessarily fictional (cf. Cohn, 1999, pp. 117–123). For example, the use of free indirect discourse enables us to be an intimate witness of the thoughts and feelings of a fictional character. As with foregrounding, then, omniscient narratives contain unequivocal marks of literariness at the level of language, although these are not defining features of all literary texts. If this is accepted, it is evidence against Schmidt's claim that "a concept like 'literariness' must primarily be defined *pragmatically* and historically" (Schmidt, 1980, p. 544); rather, it is another indication that we may be able to define literariness, at least in some respect, formally.

2.5 Conclusion

The concept of literature has been called into question, either through a hermeneutics of suspicion that attempts to forestall the effects of literature on readers, or by a dismissal of literariness except as a construct of recent (and unacceptable) ideologies. In contrast, I have tried to show that on three grounds literature appears to have innate powers: it renews itself through canonical texts whose effects are discoverable regardless of class or education, and it exerts local effects at the level of foregrounding and narrative through features that are probably objectively demonstrable and available to all readers. These claims, however, are not the outcome of purely speculative consideration, as has been the case with the positions they oppose. They are based on empirical evidence gathered from readers, whether Rose's historical witnesses or the participants in experimental studies of reading by scholars such as De Beaugrande, Halász, or Van Peer. This work is not yet well known, and so far lacks paradigmatic status; yet, as I have tried to show, it has the potential to reorganize our understanding of literary studies root and branch. Hence, I argue, empirical studies of literature are necessary. They are, perhaps, even inevitable, although only time will show whether in the present state of our discipline this prophecy is capable of being fulfilled.

• CHAPTER THREE •

Experimental Approaches to Readers' Responses to Literature

3.1 Why Experimental Approaches?

The question I pursue in this book is, at first sight, an obvious one to ask.[*] What are readers doing when they read a literary text? Despite several decades of work on reception, however, including such notable theoretical books as Wolfgang Iser's *The Act of Reading* (1978), few literary scholars have thought of asking ordinary readers what occurs when they read. To ask a student in a literature class what occurs is, of course, likely to be a biased question, given the asymmetric balance of power created by the expectations and the assessments that govern classroom discourse (see, however, Steig, 1989). Yet plenty of anecdotal evidence suggests that readers are influenced or moved by the literary texts they read. Why is this apparently common and important experience so little studied? In this chapter I discuss how systematic, experimental approaches to literary reading have been developed, and consider some questions raised by an empirical approach to understanding literature.

The paradigms within which literature is typically studied and taught have ruled against an experimental approach. Literary theorists, despite extensive theorizing, have been content to remain at what we might regard as a pre-theoretical level: literary theories cannot be right because they cannot ever be wrong. There is no evidence that could confute a literary theory, thus such writings are strictly speaking no more than interpretations. Literary theorists, like Galileo's inquisitors, refuse to examine evidence for literary reading in the empirical sense; offered a telescope, they rule that such an instrument cannot exist,

[*] This chapter first appeared as "Experimental Approaches to Reader Responses to Literature." *New Directions in Aesthetics, Creativity, and the Arts.* Ed. Paul Locher, Colin Martindale, & Leonid Dorfman. It is reprinted here by kind permission of the Baywood Press.

or that it exists only as an ideological construct rather than a tool to aid perception. Thus Jonathan Culler (1981) argued:

> there is little need to concern oneself with the design of experiments, for several reasons. First, there already exist more than enough interpretations with which to begin. By consulting the interpretations which literary history records for any major work, one discovers a spectrum of interpretive possibilities of greater interest and diversity than a survey of undergraduates could provide. (p. 53)

No doubt the study of published interpretations has its own merit, but it is no answer to the question of how texts are actually read. Filtered out of printed interpretations are details of how a reader arrived at her understanding of the text; printed accounts are also likely to be subject to distortions and repressions of various kinds that misrepresent the act of reading. Above all, what is usually given in print is an interpretation, but this is not necessarily what a reader reading "non-professionally" is aiming to produce; thus a reliance on printed interpretations for a study of literary reading has little ecological validity (although it offers an interesting approach to the history of criticism: e.g., Zöllner, 1990).

The question of interpretation is, itself, a troubled one. Whether readers typically generate interpretations is, of course, an empirical question. Yet for academic study, it still seems to be the case, as Stanley Fish (1980a) asserted over twenty years ago, that "like it or not, interpretation is the only game in town" (p. 355). Is this one reason why literary studies has lost its public role in the U.S.A. (and perhaps elsewhere)? Stephen Greenblatt (2003), when President of the MLA, commenting on the state of his profession, remarked that "in the public perception, it is as if we were cut off from the rest of the world, locked in our own special, self-regarding realm." At the same time, enrolments in literary studies have been steadily declining, whether in the U.S.A, in Canada, or in Europe. Moreover, surveys of literary reading in the United States by the National Endowment for the Arts over the last two decades have shown a steady decline in the number of people reading literature. According to their report *Reading at Risk* (released on July 8th 2004), over the two decades from 1982 to 2002 literary readership at all ages has declined by 10 percent, with the steepest drop in the younger ages (18–24) of 28 percent; and the rate of decline has been accelerating. Whether this is related to "our society's massive shift toward electronic media for entertainment and information," as the NEA chairman suggests in his preface, is not clear from the survey.

If a decline in reading and in literary study is indeed in progress, then literary scholarship may in part be driving it. In our classrooms we may too persistently have called on readers to marginalize their personal experience of literary texts in order to participate in the game of interpretation. A survey I carried out ten years ago (Miall, 1996) showed that for student readers the requirement to interpret literary texts was often a major disincentive to further study. Thus, experimental research on reading, as a way of finding out what occurs during literary reading, can be regarded as an essential step to reconsidering our approach to literature, in particular, towards rethinking the emphasis given to interpretation.

The evidence against interpretation being an aim of the ordinary reader is rather strong. For Vipond and Hunt (1984), for example, literary reading was best characterized as "point-driven," in contrast to reading for story, or reading for information. But when they turned to empirical study, it proved quite difficult to detect point-driven reading. In their main study of the issue, a questionnaire survey of over 150 student readers of John Updike's story "A & P," only about 5 percent were found to be engaged in a point-driven form of reading; readers were more likely to adopt a story-driven approach, that is, to read for plot. While Vipond and Hunt note that a point is not an interpretation, it is clear that it represents a step towards interpretation. So it is important to bear in mind that student readers, who are likely to be closer to the ordinary reader outside the academy, do not usually derive points from their reading when reading normally. When we are reading for pleasure, we might aim to form a relation with the author, as Vipond and Hunt suggest, but this is not because we expect the author to make a point, but because we expect a literary author to offer a certain kind of experience.

Supporting evidence against interpretation comes from one of our studies (Miall and Kuiken, 1999). Thirty readers were asked to think aloud after reading each segment of a story that we had divided into 84 segments (the story was "The Trout" by Sean O'Faolain). The comments readers made were analysed in detail and grouped into 14 types. Among these the most frequent type of comments (33.6 percent) related to explaining a character ("Julia will do it again for the excitement"); next came quotations from the text (21.5 percent), which we found to correlate highly with the presence of foregrounding in the quoted passages, suggesting that readers were savouring the quality of the writing and mulling over how to understand such passages; next were queries about local meanings in the text (10.1 percent), ("I wonder if Julia is afraid"); other types of commentary referred to style, expressions of surprise, or to the reader's emotions. One of the smallest categories, a mere 2.1 percent of all comments, was what we called "thematizing," e.g., "Again we have the symbolism of the trout in a prison." It is these comments that come the closest to what Vipond and Hunt mean by "point": they represent the moments when a reader is beginning to work out an interpretation of the story. In this example, the reader is elaborating her sense that the trout is like the main character, Julia, who is trapped in a prison of her parents' expectations; both will have broken free by the end of the story. But this analysis shows that during the course of reading such comments are quite rare. Readers appear to be engaged in a rather different set of activities: contemplating what characters are doing, experiencing the stylistic qualities of the writing, reflecting on the feelings that the story has evoked.

In this particular study we also asked readers to make comments about their responses to the story as a whole after they had read it. Here, as might be expected, there were more comments consisting of points. Interestingly, though, these comments tended to refer to the personal meaning of the story for the reader, such as insights into aspects of the reader's childhood, or their enjoyment of the character. One reader, for example, says: "I can really respond to how the little girl must have felt . . . I think it's neat that she can show that kind of compassion." Almost no readers began to offer interpretations of the story for its own sake, apart from any personal interest they might have in it.

Experimental studies, then, are unlikely to provide evidence for particular interpretations. But they do provide insights into what readers are able to tell us about their responses to literature, and in the next section I discuss some of the main types of research design employed in such studies. In the last section I will take up several issues raised by the experimental study of literature.

3.2 Research Design and Some Findings

In considering experimental approaches to literary reading, the first main difference in experimental methods to note is between studies that manipulate a literary text in order to isolate a particular effect, and studies with an intact text. The first approach is derived from the concept that different experimental conditions (i.e., different versions of the same text) will reveal how a particular aspect of the text influences readers. For example, in the studies by Vipond and Hunt I referred to earlier, the notion of "point" was made specific by identifying it with a specific type of feature that Vipond and Hunt (1986) termed "evaluations." They proposed that the narrator indicates how he or she "feels about an event, character, utterance, or other story element" by creating unexpected text elements, such as figurative language, an unusual word, deviant syntax, and the like. For the reader these evaluations are "deliberate invitations to share a meaning with the storyteller" (p. 58). In an experimental study they presented one group of readers with the original version of a short story, and another group with the same story but with evaluations rewritten in neutral prose: e.g., the evaluative phrase "they camped around the room" was replaced with the more neutral expression, "they sat around the room." Shown a list of phrases taken from the story after each page and asked to indicate what they had particularly noticed while reading, readers with the original version chose the evaluation phrases significantly more often than readers with the rewritten version chose the equivalent neutral phrases (Hunt and Vipond, 1985).

Bortolussi and Dixon (2003) argue that "the careful manipulation of the text . . . allows one to identify covariation between features of the text and corresponding reader constructions and . . . allows much stronger and more precise inferences concerning causes" (p. 24). Although their own studies show the value of this approach, textual manipulation can also introduce unexpected, secondary side-effects that, while unrelated to the variance that the experimenter hopes to isolate, also influence readers. The elicitation of information from readers must be designed so as not to be confounded by the secondary changes in the text. In the Hunt and Vipond example the passages that are rewritten lose the connection they had in the original, where an aura of disorder and implicit violence, as in "they camped around the room," primes response to a series of of "evaluations." To rewrite the passages introduces a series of questions about what literary qualities of the story may have been lost, not only the evaluative function. Although the general question to readers, what was noticed, provides an index of reader differences that is informative, it is not clear from this study what readers were noticing.

A study of a similar literary concept that we carried out (Miall and Kuiken, 1994a) involved experiment without manipulation. Readers notice evaluations because they stand out from the local norm of the text. Similarly, we argued that the various stylistic features known as foregrounding also attract readers' attention. Foregrounding includes features such as alliteration or assonance, metrical effects, or metaphor. Our hypothesis was that paying attention to foregrounding during reading requires more time, and that readers would find passages rich in foregrounding both more striking and more evocative of feeling. To test this we analysed a series of short stories for the presence of foregrounding, and developed an index of foregrounding in each segment of the story (usually one sentence) based on the presence of foregrounded features at the phonetic, syntactic, and semantic levels. Instead of manipulating a text, each text itself provided a naturally varying level of foregrounding from low to high. If readers pay attention to foregrounding, then we can expect their reading times per segment to show covariance in line with its presence; and when asked to rate the segments for feeling or strikingness, higher ratings should correlate with elevated levels of foregrounding. In a series of studies with three literary short stories, these are the effects we found in each case. In addition, whether our participants were experienced senior students of English literature or beginning first year students of Psychology with little commitment to or experience of literary reading, our results were virtually the same, suggesting that response to foregrounding occurs regardless of degree of literary training—a finding that challenges the standard view that literary response depends on acquiring the relevant conventions and genre knowledge (e.g., Rabinowitz, 1998).

This study is an example of the use of single texts in which we hypothesize that intrinsic features of a text influence the reader. A second type of study involves finding or creating extrinsic determinants that can be supposed to influence the reader. For example, Zwaan (1991) theorized that readers deploy "particular cognitive control mechanisms" specific to the genre they are reading. He proposed that literary reading would invoke a different set of "controls" from reading a newspaper. He chose six short stories taken from either newspapers or from novels that could be read in either a newspaper or a literature condition, and participants were told either that they were reading from a newspaper or from a literary text. Participants read the texts on a computer which recorded reading times. As Zwaan predicted, the "literature" condition readers read more slowly than the "newspaper" readers—about 10 percent more slowly; in addition, when asked about their memory for the texts, it was found that literary readers had formed a stronger sense of the surface features of the texts, that is, of their stylistic features.

Another example of a frame approach is a supplementary study by Vipond and Hunt (1984). While looking for "points" among readers of a short story, they created a condition in which readers first read a supposed letter from an East German reader (this was in the 1980s) who claimed to find that the story illuminated understanding of his own position. Readers who received the story preceded by this frame generated more "points" in their comments.

While the studies I have mentioned suggest the existence of a specific literary form of reading, they leave open some important questions. Is reading in a literary mode (however we might define that) driven by the frame in which we encounter a text or by features of the text itself? Zwaan's study seems to point to the first possibility; the studies by Miall and Kuiken (1994a) and Hunt and Vipond (1986) seem to point to the second. Given the rejection of literariness by recent literary theorists, the question is a critical one for empirical study. Terry Eagleton (1983) expressed a now common view: there can be "no 'essence' of literature whatsoever. . . . any writing may be read 'poetically'" (p. 9). Thus given the right frame we would read a railway timetable as literature. It follows, says Eagleton,

> that we should drop the illusion that the category 'literature' is 'objective,' in the sense of being eternally given and immutable. Anything can be literature, and anything which is regarded as unalterably and unquestionably literature—Shakespeare, for example—can cease to be literature. Any belief that the study of literature is the study of a stable, well-definable entity, as entomology is the study of insects, can be abandoned as a chimera. (pp. 10–11)

We read a text as literary, in other words, only because we find it in a literary frame (e.g., the back cover of a book tells us it is literary). The materiality of the book has also been held to influence reading. For example, N. Kathleen Hayles (2002) insists that "the physical form of the literary artifact always affects what the words (and other semiotic components) mean" (p. 25; cf. Genette, 1997). These views challenge the power of the literary text to preserve its meaning regardless of context: whether we find *Hamlet* in a leather-bound folio or on the computer screen, does *Hamlet* remain essentially the same? The question calls for empirical study.

A third kind of study involves comparison of two or more texts. A simple but effective method developed by Seilman and Larsen (1989) was applied to comparing a literary text (a short story) with a non-literary, or expository text (an essay on population growth). Their method required what they termed "self-probed retrospection," one of a class of methods that depends on the reader's self-report (such as the collection of ratings from readers in Miall and Kuiken, 1994a) rather than an "objective" measure such as reading times. Larsen and Seilman (1988) argue that their method is less disruptive than the think-aloud method that requires readers to make comments after each sentence (a method I describe below). Their study asked readers to make marginal check marks while reading whenever a passage reminded them of something they had experienced. After the reading participants were given a short questionnaire to complete about the experience related to each marked passage: its age, concreteness, perspective (from what position was the experience viewed), etc. On average they found that readers were able to remember 95 percent of the experiences. Although a similar number of "remindings" was elicited by both the literary and expository texts, twice as many "actor-perspective" remindings were elicited by the literary text, while the expository text elicited more "receiver" remindings (things read or heard about). Thus literary reading, they remark, "seems to connect particularly with knowledge that is personal in the sense that one is an agent, a responsible subject interacting with one's environment" (Seilman and Larsen, 1989, p. 174). Other measures of remindings (age, vividness, etc.) showed no significant differences. Interestingly, remindings were found to occur more frequently in the opening section of each text, and more frequently with the literary than the expository text. This suggests that readers initially need to mobilize specific personal information to contextualize the world of a literary text.

Readers of literary texts thus appear to draw more explicitly and frequently on their active personal experiences, a process that might be held to distinguish literary from other kinds of texts. Rather than attempting to define what is literary by a text's formal features (stylistic deviations, narrative form, or generic features), this points to an interactive process underlying literariness: a literary text is more likely to speak to the individual through its resonances with the individual's autobiographical experiences. To learn more about such resonance and what it means for the reader, however, we must turn to the think-aloud method, despite the well-known problems that have been supposed to render verbal protocols questionable (Nisbett and Wilson, 1977; but see also Ericsson and Simon, 1980, 1984).

Thus, in a fourth kind of study, readers are asked to think aloud about a text during or after reading it. Either the text is presented section by section and readers comment after reading each section; or, in another model based on the "self-probed retrospection" of Seilman and Larsen (1989), readers make marginal check marks while reading whenever they find a passage striking or evocative; after reading they return to each passage and comment on what they were thinking while they read each marked passage. Both methods tend to generate lengthy protocols which must be transcribed and analysed. Here, two alternative strategies for content analysis are (1) to apply a previously designed category system to the protocols, or (2) to develop categories from whatever is found in the protocols themselves.

An example of the first type, the application of pre-prepared categories, is a study of Andringa (1990). Readers of a Schiller short story were instructed to "think aloud" about all that came to mind after each of nine sections of the story; an interviewer was present to prompt and to question participants. Readers in the study ranged from beginning students of literature to professors. Two levels of analysis were applied when categorizing responses: first, speech acts (acts, metacomments, emotions, evaluations, arguments, references to text); second reception acts (emotive reactions, (re)constructive, forming bridges between constituents, elaborating, identifying). Among her findings, most notable was a sequence she found often among the less experienced readers: emotion, evaluation, then argument. This "seems to be a regular sequence": the emotion, as she put it, "initiates, selects, and steers the way of arguing" (p. 247). To refine this view of emotion has been one important aim of an alternative method that we have developed, called Numerical Phenomenology (Kuiken and Miall, 1995, 2001).

In this method categories of analysis emerge from the readers' statements. Also, unlike standard psychological studies of reading, which are "laden with presuppositions appropriate to the study of reading comprehension rather than reading experience" (Kuiken and Miall, 1995), the method is designed to be as open to readers' descriptions of their reading experiences as possible.

The process involves a systematic comparison of statements made in all the verbal protocols (typically, we will collect responses from at least thirty readers) in order to identify similar expressed meanings; these are paraphrased, producing what we term "constituents." No preconceived categories are employed. The constituents, we argue, are natural kinds, not presuppositions brought to the study by the researcher. The constituents are then re-expressed at three different levels, from close to the original statement to the most general category. For example,

Level 1: Dogs do not say "bark bark"
Level 2: I negatively emotionally respond to literary style (phrase/word)
Level 3: I emotionally respond to a literary device

At the most general level, this enables us to count the proportion of responses that are made in a given category (here, emotional response to an aspect of style). But the method has at least two further analytical benefits.

First, the resulting categories can be used to create matrices of occurrences of constituent by reader, amenable to cluster analysis. These allow for the discovery of distinctive types of reader response based on similarities in occurrence of a range of different types of constituent. In one study, for example, we found four distinctive types of reading that we termed: 1. Reading resistance; 2. Emotional engagement; 3. Story-line uncertainty; and 4. Aesthetic coherence (Kuiken and Miall, 2001). Second, the development of meanings across a set of responses can be studied and their determinants examined. We have, for example, recently focused on the impact of reading on the reader's self-concept and how this manifests through what we term "self-modifying feelings." In several studies we have adopted the "self-probed retrospection" method in which readers are asked to choose several passages from the text they had marked and to think aloud in response to each passage. In a study of readers of Coleridge's "The Rime of the Ancient Mariner," comments by one group of readers were characterized by what we termed "expressive enactment." Here we found the emergence of comments involving resonance of the reader's feelings with the world of the text. In particular, "there was evidence of blurred boundaries between the reader and narrator, as though they were temporarily identified as members of the same class." This feature often takes the form of the use of the pronoun *you*, as in this commentary: "So in a way you would be feeling kind of cursed and haunted" (Kuiken, Miall, and Sikora, 2004, p. 187). In a number of readers' comments we find the expression of an affective theme that is re-expressed and modified across the course of their commentaries on successive passages. We also found that readers in the expressive enactment group cited autobiographical memories less often in relation to the poem than readers in other groups, a finding that, in part, helped us distinguish two kinds of identification with the narrator of the poem: similes of identification (e.g., this emotion is like something I have experienced), and metaphors of identification (e.g., this experience in the poem is my experience—as with the use of the pronoun *you* to speak inclusively).

The fourth type of study, especially the phenomenological method I have just outlined, is at a considerable distance from the more typically "experimental" models, especially those involved in manipulating a literary text to create two or more experimental "conditions" that are expected to elicit differing responses from readers. The liability of this latter kind of study is the possible loss of what is distinctively literary when the variables influencing a reading are thus strictly delimited. The liability of the phenomenological type of study, in contrast, is its dependence on a degree of connoisseurship in categorizing and interpreting verbal protocols, and in the problem of its generalizability, i.e., what it would mean to attempt to replicate it with different texts and different participants. At the same time, the complexity of literary response, and the extraordinary variability in the texts that have usually been deemed literary, suggests that only a wide range of experimental methods will suffice to capture what, if anything, is distinctive to literary reading.

3.3 Issues for the Empirical Study of Literary Reading

In my survey of experimental methods I have already mentioned several issues that face research in this field. In this section I will single out four for specific discussion.

3.3.1 What is Literary?

An ambivalence over literariness has influenced a number of scholars of reading. For example, in his recent book *Cognitive Poetics*, Peter Stockwell (2002) tells us that since "there is nothing inherently different in the form of literary language, it is reasonable and safe to investigate the language of literature using approaches generated in the language system in general" (7). Whether literature can be distinguished is, properly, an empirical question; thus to develop experimental tools likely to elicit a specifically *literary* response must be a primary aim of research in this field. If "high" literature, as we might call it, calls upon characteristically different modes of reading, then it should be possible to demonstrate this (without, of course, disparaging the role of readers when reading popular fiction, which has its own values).

3.3.2 Delimiting the Literary

A separate question is how literature stands in relation to other forms of language, other media, or advertising. Since younger readers in particular are now likely to be exposed to such media from an early age, we must ask what influence these media may have on the skills or aptitudes required for literary reading. (So far, it appears to me, almost no research has yet been done on the literary aspects of other media.) Little is known about how ordinary readers choose their reading, what different kinds of media they choose, how they respond to it, how it compares in their view with other forms of leisure activity such as video gaming or going to the movies, what difference it makes to their lives, and what cultural or historical processes impact the activity of reading (Mackey, 2002). Better information on this is important in its own right, but might also enable us to develop a more effective classroom environment for literary studies.

3.3.3 Normative Assumptions

We must ask whether in our studies of literary reading our research designs embed hidden assumptions about the kind of reading we think should be occurring. Should we, or even can we, avoid such assumptions? For example, in the phenomenological work I described, when comparing similes and metaphors of identification, it is tempting to pay closer attention to readers demonstrating metaphors of identification since these appear to involve a more radical commitment of the self to the text being read. But is this to argue that such readings are to be preferred, or are better than those of other readers whose protocols cluster in our other groups? This issue raises larger questions about the place of literary reading in society that are ethnically and historically inflected, and which have been little studied outside the troubled domain of literary theory.

3.3.4 Empirical Studies Require History

It could be argued that by studying readers now, and by studying only those narrow aspects of reading amenable to experimental study in particular, we have neglected to consider not only how reading may be influenced by history, but have overlooked the possibility that reading in the past may have been experienced differently (Darnton, 1990). Here two additional contexts seem required, although neither so far has had more than a marginal influence on empirical studies of reading. First, we should attempt as far as possible to recover reading experiences from the past and subject the evidence to as much empirical rigour in our analysis as we do to verbal protocols collected now. For example, the recent work of Rose (2001) has provided rich information on numerous working class memoirs from the previous three centuries in which acts of reading and their effects are described, often in considerable detail. Second, developments in cultural analysis by evolutionary psychologists suggest that the evolutionary determinants of literary reading must now be seriously considered as a framework for understanding its present significance. What underlying, species-specific proclivities have led to the emergence of a literary culture in every human society in the world? Findings on this issue would lend stability and direction to the field of empirical studies of literary reading (Boyd, 1998). I return to this question in the last chapter of this book.

3.3.5 Beyond Empirical Research

How, finally, might we make evident the relevance of empirical research and its findings, and how can we invite debate on its significance from our colleagues who teach literature in schools and universities? What difference might awareness of empirical findings make to how one teaches? As empirical study matures and takes account of a wider range of literary experiences and historical contexts, perhaps it will begin to influence the thinking of literary scholars in the mainstream. But at the present time of writing the likelihood of such a development is by no mean clear, especially as the field of empirical research is itself a mosaic of different methods and incompatible assumptions. To begin to resolve the declining status of literary studies and even of literary reading itself, however, empirical study seems the most promising candidate: it undertakes, after all, to give central place to the experience of real readers, placing on the agenda for the first time the richness, range, and personal significance of reading in our culture.

• CHAPTER FOUR •

Interpretation, Cognition, and Feeling

4.1 Interpretation

In this chapter I return to the question: What are literary texts for?* I look at the emphasis given to interpretation in the professional and educational discourse about literature, focusing in particular on the recent emergence of cognitive approaches. Cognitive literary scholars have begun to develop some powerful new tools for formal analysis of texts but, as I will point out, the work needed to validate them empirically has not yet been done. Two other limitations of the cognitive program will also be considered here: first, without an empirical approach with its study of real readers, cognitivism risks becoming merely another vehicle for arriving at interpretations of texts; and second, the cognitivist perspective has largely neglected the domain of feeling, which is central to the experience of literary reading. At the end of chapter I provide a short sketch of the properties of feeling that give it a distinctive role in literary reading, and I suggest that if we wish to understand the processes of reading then feeling must be given as much consideration as cognition.

Interpretation has been the main aim of literary scholarship, particularly since its widespread acceptance as a university discipline in the days of T. S. Eliot and F. R. Leavis in England and the New Critics in the U.S.A. While interpretation has, no doubt, many significant achievements to its credit, especially in contextualizing literary texts historically, it is questionable whether interpretation is, or ever has been, the primary aim of reading literature. To interpret a text is to invoke what Rabinowitz (1996) terms "the Rule of Abstract Displacement": a literary text is always understood as being about something

* This chapter first appeared in part in "Beyond Interpretation: The Cognitive Significance of Reading," in Harri Veivo, Bo Pettersson, and Merja Polvinen (Eds.), *Cognition and Literary Interpretation in Practice*. University of Helsinki Press.

else (p. 139). The ordinary reader, however, is more likely to stay close to the text itself, its character predicaments, plot turns, and stylistic textures; her aim is to experience these rather than ask what the text might mean.

This contrast between interpreting literature and experiencing it is illuminated by one of Henry James's short stories. In "The Figure in the Carpet," James (1937) shows us the responses of two critics to a distinguished author of several novels, Hugh Vereker. The narrator, a writer for a literary journal, produces what he thinks is a clever review of Vereker's latest novel. He believes he has "got *at*" him, unveiled his mystery (p. 224–5), and he looks forward to hearing Vereker confirm his cleverness when he meets him at a house party shortly after his review is published. To his dismay, Vereker, not knowing who the reviewer is, during dinner calls the review "the usual twaddle" (p. 226). Later that evening, Vereker visits the narrator to apologize for his insulting comment. He goes on to explain that no reviewer has ever understood his work, his "little point," "the particular thing I've written my books most *for*" (p. 230), the "idea in my work without which I wouldn't have given a straw for the whole job" (pp. 230–1). Hearing this fires up the narrator to find out what the mysterious point is. "Is it a kind of esoteric message?" he asks. But Vereker dismisses this idea as "cheap journalese" (p. 233). In a second (and last) meeting with Vereker, the narrator seems to come closer in his description: "It was something, I guessed, in the primal plan; something like a complex figure in a Persian carpet. He highly approved of this image when I used it, and he used another himself. 'It's the very string,' he said, 'that my pearls are strung on!'" (pp. 240–1). But the narrator, despite a month's intense labour, fails to discover what Vereker's secret is: "it proved a dead loss. After all I had always, as he had himself noted, liked him; and what now occurred was simply that my new intelligence and vain preoccupation damaged my liking" (p. 236). As he puts it later, because of his failed quest, "Not only had I lost the books, but I had lost the man himself: they and their author had been alike spoiled for me."

Meanwhile, however, the narrator has revealed Vereker's account of the secret to his colleague, Corvick. Now Corvick, with his fiancée Gwendolen, sets himself to go through Vereker's work in pursuit of the secret. Some months later, Corvick is obliged to leave for a journey in India to write articles on the country for a London paper. After several months of absence, Gwendolen receives a telegram from Corvick: "He has got it!" she tells the narrator. All the cable says is "Eureka. Immense." She reports that Corvick had not been working on it, had in fact left the matter strictly alone; it "has simply sprung out at him like a tigress out of the jungle" (p. 251). Corvick then returns from India via Rapallo in Italy, where Vereker is now living, in order to check his insight with the author. He writes in another telegram, "Just seen Vereker—not a note wrong. Pressed me to his bosom—keeps me a month" (p. 255). On his return to England, Corvick divulges the secret to no one, saying he will publish it in a long article, but before he can even start this he marries Gwendolen and on their honeymoon is accidentally killed. This leaves only Gwendolen. The narrator supposes Corvick must have confided the secret to her. When he writes to ask her if, during her brief time with Corvick, she heard the secret, she writes back, "I heard everything, . . . and I mean to keep it to myself!" (p. 263). He falls to wondering "if I should have to marry Mrs. Corvick to get what I wanted" (p. 265). The narrator hopes to see Vereker again, but he and his wife are soon dead too. Gwendolen marries again after several years, another critic called Drayton Deane. But after Gwendolen herself unexpectedly dies, the narrator eventually asks Deane if he had been told the secret, and finds out that he hadn't. Thus the secret dies with Gwendolen. The reader of the story is left in the dark about the supposed "figure in the carpet" just as much as the benighted narrator.

The story has, as one might expect, aroused a good deal of interpretive commentary. Despite the warning that the story appears to hold, that looking for the figure is a fruitless or dangerous enterprise (all those who learn it die prematurely), explanations of the "figure" have often been offered. Thus Tzvetan Todorov (1973) claims that "The Figure" and other "James's tales are based on the quest for an absolute and absent cause" (p. 74)—a reading which is best exemplified by his ghost stories. Robert White (1992), building on the erotic hints in the story itself and in James's preface to it, claims that the story conceals James's celebration of sexuality, drawing in particular upon the Indian symbol of the lingam, the male organ (remember that the secret breaks in on Corvick in India). He points out that James had recently read a book on travel in India by Chevrillon that discusses Indian temples in some detail. Such readings, however, appear to violate the warning that the story itself contains, and which is emphasized in a short discussion by Wolfgang Iser (1978).

Interpretation, as Iser remarks, is understood by the narrator of the story "as the very heart of the work, [that] can be lifted out of the text" (p. 4). Such an approach, says Iser, is fatal both for literature and criticism, "for what can be the function of interpretation if its sole achievement is to extract the meaning and leave behind an empty shell?" (p. 5). Literary criticism, Iser says, "frequently proceeds to reduce texts to a referential meaning." In this way, criticism repeats the model of mastery and domination that Michel Serres (1995) has identified in our use of technology and science: the critic claims mastery over the literary texts being analysed; but, as Serres has shown, just as such technical mastery leads to what he calls ecocide (pp. 31–2), so the exercise of mastery over literature leads to its death. The narrator of "The Figure," even though he strikes on a metaphor for the secret that Vereker approves ("a complex figure in a Persian carpet"), seems never to realize that the secret, whatever it is, cannot be enunciated and handed over, and as a result, the significance of Vereker's work dies for him.

Iser (1978) goes on to infer that James's figure must be "imagistic," the product of an interaction between the textual signals and the reader's acts of comprehension" (p. 9); thus "meaning is no longer an object to be defined, but is an effect to be experienced" (p. 10). Instead of interpretation, Iser argues, "Far more instructive will be an analysis of what actually happens when one is reading a text, for that is when the text begins to unfold its potential" (p. 19). This seems helpful, but Iser doesn't go far enough. When the narrator asks Vereker for a clue, he is told "My whole lucid effort gives him the clue—every page and line and letter. . . it chooses every word, it dots every i, it places every comma" (James, 1937, p. 233); and a few moments later he compares it to the heart, remarking that "What I contend that nobody has ever mentioned in my work is the organ of life" (p. 234). In this light, interpretation would not only be reductive and beside the point; it would be impossible. This is why Vereker is so impatient with the narrator's blundering attempts to name the secret—an "esoteric message," "some idea *about* life," "a preference for the letter P!" (pp. 233–4)—when his real intention for his work is to "tease us out of thought," as Keats put it ("Ode on a Grecian Urn" l. 44).

James provides other hints about the clumsiness of criticism in his preface to the volume of the New York edition in which the story appeared. In the novelist's work, he says, we take account of nothing "that hasn't passed through the crucible of his imagination" (James, 1962, p. 230). Thus, in referring to the characters in "The Coxon Fund" (which echoes the situation in later life of Coleridge), "let us have here as little as possible about its 'being' Mr. This or Mrs. That. If it adjusts itself with the least truth to its new life it can't possibly be either" (p. 230). Hence (he concludes the preface), the interest in the question "of how the trick was played" (p. 231). We can take this comment together with what James claims to remember about the impulse behind "The Figure in the Carpet": it was "to reinstate analytic appreciation, by some ironic or fantastic stroke, so far as possible, in its virtually forfeited rights and dignities" (p. 228). Since James also refers to the case of "Hugh Vereker and his undiscovered, not to say undiscoverable, secret" (p. 228), we can infer that "analytic appreciation" means no more nor less than a feeling for the intrinsic structure of the literary text in all its details, whatever particular virtues in this respect Vereker's work can be supposed to have had and that Corvick is said to have discovered. James's plot in this story, which shows us first Corvick, then Gwendolen dying shortly after they gain possession of the secret, is perhaps his indication that the secret is really undiscoverable, or at least impossible to communicate. Perhaps it can only be experienced, not enunciated. Vereker suggests as much in his odd comment when he learns from the narrator that Corvick and Gwendolen are likely to be married and are to pursue the secret together, "That may help them, . . . but we must give them time!" (p. 240), as though the intimacy of marriage might help bring into view the "organ of life" in his writing (p. 234).

"Analytic appreciation" is not, for the most part, what is offered in critical discussions of James's story. There is widespread recognition of the unknowability of the "figure," particularly as a representation of the act of reading. The figure in the carpet, writes M. A. Williams (1984), "is to be traced out through the very act of reading which engages the responsive consciousnessness with the text" (p. 108); it is "a kind of fictionalized parable of the reading process" (p. 112). Dorothea Krook (1988) claims that the real reader must be either like the narrator or like Corvick, either believing the figure is not there or that it is (p. 307), and that the point of the story is that we are invited to find the figure in James's other works (p. 312). Hillis Miller (1980) suggests that the story represents the "uncanny blind alley of unreadability encountered ultimately in the interpretation of any work" (p. 112). These views, like that of Iser, fall short of pointing to the impossibility and danger of interpretation, and they generalize beyond the details of the story as interpretations typically do. I believe we can understand from "The Figure in the Carpet" itself that James places an interdiction on such critical activities, while leaving open a rich domain for appreciation.

4.2 Cognitivism

The latest and most promising literary discipline to appear in recent years, cognitivism, has been providing rich grounds for indicating how and why we appreciate literary texts; but the warning offered by James's story has been disregarded. As I will now discuss, the cognitive approach has not yet worked out a framework for considering the literary field as a whole, and by this I mean in particular reception issues, what it means to read a literary text. As a result cognitivism is at risk of making two other disabling mistakes: blurring the distinctiveness of literature, when the issue of literariness should be pursued not only theoretically but as an empirical question; and failing to inquire into the reader's experience of literature, in particular the processes of feeling that are central to literary reading. Moreover, since the cognitivist approach has positioned itself as a model for a new kind of educational engagement with literature, this development appears to place interpretation back at the centre of the literature classroom, with potentially unfortunate effects.

The problem of focusing on interpretation is evident from its effect on literature students. Asking students what a literary text means distracts them from the experience that the text offers, and may lead to dispiriting games in the classroom where the student is supposed to guess what the teacher or examiner has in mind (Miall, 1996). This might help explain what has been called "the precipitous decline in 'literature majors'" in the United States (Fitts and Lalicker, 2004, p. 427). Evidently fewer students are seeing the relevance of a degree in literary studies. The decline may be due to the problematic question, what *is* an appropriate approach to literature nowadays, given the decline and fall of deconstruction and the lack of any other paradigm to significantly determine the field. The title of a review article by John Rouse (2004) in a recent issue of *College English* helps to frame the issue: "After Theory, the Next New Thing." Rouse reviews three new books, each of which, it emerges, recommends a turn to the scholarship of teaching: this, it seems, will be the next "new thing" (p. 452). "As the dark of night slowly descends on literary studies" (p. 465), says Rouse, what will come to dominate teaching is the pedagogy of composition, the teaching of writing, which is to say, that literature as an academic study is fated to disappear.

As the review by Rouse indicates, several books about the decline and fall of literary studies have been published recently, leaving us in no doubt that the crisis is a real one, although by no means everyone agrees on the causes. But one witness, Daniel Green (2001), also writing in *College English*, puts his finger on a central problem. As he entered the profession he found that the very idea of literature as an academic discipline "seemed a contrivance designed expressly to destroy all interest in the actual writing that brought the subject into being in the first place" (p. 273). Green is not advocating a return to older methods of teaching, as though these had been quite unproblematic before the new theories took over, as if teaching had been "an entirely transparent affair, simply a matter of making available the intrinsically valuable qualities of literary works through the methods appropriate to the task" (p. 274). He suggests that the academic study of literature has not enlarged its audience, rather "it has instead done the opposite, discouraging more potential readers than it has encouraged" (p. 286). Moreover, he argues that no change in teaching methods will rescue literature: "its intrinsic usefulness cannot be served by the practices of the academy," because "its benefits are ultimately and unavoidably personal" (p. 287). In the light of such a comment, we must ask: Has the classroom practice of insisting on interpretation in one form or another finally alienated student readers, driving them away from literary studies into other disciplines?

Thus we might attribute blame for the present crisis to literature faculty themselves—the turn to various types of postmodern theory, the arguments over political correctness, the loss of commitment to literature as a distinctive form of art. If the public at large is turning away from reading, as recent surveys show (e.g., *Reading at Risk*, 2004), if literary scholarship has lost public support, if it is losing its students, and if literary studies has lost a sense of what its aims are as a discipline—then we may well ask what is next.

Is the cognitive approach to literature likely to remedy some of the problems we now face in literary scholarship? This is the claim of Peter Stockwell, for example, in his recent book, *Cognitive Poetics* (2002). He argues that cognitive poetics "has the potential to make the discipline and the institution of literature more accessible and more connected with the world outside university and college life"; he emphasizes repeatedly throughout his book that the focus of cognitive poetics is on the reader: "It is all about reading literature" (p. 11). To this, Gerard Steen and Joanna Gavins (2003) add that cognitive poetics "sees literature not just as a matter for the happy few, but as a specific form of everyday human experience" (p. 1), which would place us back in the world from which literary scholarship has largely excluded itself.

Given the current state of literary studies, then, is cognitive poetics the way forward? First, as I indicated above, its focus on *interpreting* literary texts is unfortunate, and a liability that opens it to becoming simply another orthodoxy as a literary school. Second, it often isn't really about the *reader* as a real entity, just as earlier reader response theories only made suppositions about the processes thought to be engaged in by readers. Third, it has adopted a model of cognition that, surprisingly in the present stage of psychological research, is restricted almost entirely to information processing issues: in other words, the role of *feeling* has been neglected. I will consider these issues at various points in the remainder of this chapter, but my main purpose will be to put forward several additional perspectives which I believe cognitive critics should now consider if the new discipline is to flourish.

4.3 Beyond Interpretation

Cognitive poetics claims to draw on our understanding of cognitive processes to examine what occurs during literary reading. The question here, then, is what role interpretation of texts might play. While the introduction to *Cognitive Poetics in Practice* (Steen and Gavins, 2003) endorses the marginalizing of interpretation proposed by Jonathan Culler in 1975 (p. 5), and repeats Mark Turner's objection in 1991 to interpretation (p. 7), interpretation does keep creeping back in. The issue is posed clearly by Peter Stockwell's book *Cognitive Poetics* (2002). The opening pages illustrate the problem, as almost from the beginning we find a slippage in the key term "reading."

Stockwell cites four lines from Browning's poem about Wordsworth, "The Lost Leader." He then urges that we need to reflect on what happens when we are reading it. He refers to "understanding what we do when we engage in reading literature"; a couple of sentences later he says that we need "many different readings," and that "Particular readings are important for us." This could be an introduction to study of actual readers' responses to the poem. But this is not what concerns Stockwell, since his discussion turns next into a question about Browning's lines: "What are they about? What do they mean?" (p. 2). We have moved from the experience of reading the lines to interpreting them. "Reading" a poem considered as a cognitive process is not the same as a "reading" of the poem that accounts for its meaning (Stockwell slips from the verb to the noun form of the word).

The cognitive processes that underlie reading, analysed by Stockwell and others, should not, therefore, be considered to lead necessarily to readers' interpretations. This is a question for empirical study. At the same time, it should be pointed out that some empirical studies of reading have biased their findings by assuming that readers read for meaning, that is, that readers are point-driven. The instructions they give readers may in this way deselect those features that are most characteristic of literary reading. For example, the readers studied by Olson, Mack, and Duffy (1981) were told before reading that "later we would explore how well they understood each story" (p. 299). Imagine a reader hearing this: consider how it would change her approach to reading a literary text, making it into a kind of classroom exercise. But this, of course, has been one of the overt aims of cognitive poetics: to provide new, alternative methods for classroom discussion of texts. As Elena Semino (1997, p. 225) puts it, for instance, in a chapter entitled "Suggestions for further analysis": consider a particular poem by Seamus Heaney. "What main schemata need to be activated in order to interpret the text?" As Susan Sontag told us a long time ago, what we need is not more interpretations of literary texts but an erotics of art, an attention first and foremost to its sensuous, formal qualities. In Sontag's challenging words (1983, p. 98), "interpretation is the revenge of the intellect upon art."

Thus the promotion of cognitive poetics for classroom use that we are now seeing, might be regarded as anomalous and perhaps premature. In addition, given the origin of its cognitive models and processes in an empirical science, why would cognitive poetics take no steps to examine its hypotheses empirically? The models are, after all, not uncontentious. As far as literary reading is concerned, for example, as long ago as 1982 Rand Spiro (1982) called into the question the adequacy of schema theory to literary reading (and I will make a similar point in the next chapter). In fact, a major strength of books such as those of Stockwell or Semino is that they specify in considerable detail the supposed contribution of a particular cognitive process to reading, which should make it possible to devise empirical studies of their role during reading. Do readers interpret a text in terms of figure/ground relationships? Does cognitive deixis position a reader in relation to the points of view on offer in a narrative? In this context, we might consider the finding of Seilman and Larsen (1989) that during reading of a literary text compared with an expository text, the memories prompted by the literary text contained twice as many actor-perspective memories as the expository text, which mainly prompted observer memories. This suggests that the deictic indicators function differently in a literary text, inviting the reader to cast herself as an agent, as (in their words) "a responsible subject interacting with one's environment" (p. 174). Deictic indicators, in other words, may be taken up differently according to the genre of the text being read.

Such research, whether or not it develops an empirical dimension, is based on a hypothesis drawn from cognitive science: the proposal that reading is shaped by figure/ground contrasts, or by the instantiation of schemata. In this sense it can be seen as a top-down strategy. Much empirical research is of this kind. The earlier work on foregrounding I carried out with Don Kuiken (Miall and Kuiken, 1994a) provides an example. Here we made the assumption that literary texts are characterized by variations in density of foregrounding (an idea that we adapted from an earlier study by Willie van Peer, 1986), and then set out to test this using such indicators as reading times per segment of a short story, and reader's ratings of the same segments. But research on literary reading should also be conducted using bottom-up methods, where we do not set out to test a previously developed hypothesis. Here our approach is "To find, not to impose," as Wallace Stevens puts it ("Notes toward a Supreme Fiction"). We have conducted several such studies (e.g. Kuiken and Miall, 2001; Kuiken, Miall, and Sikora, 2004): these involve asking readers to think aloud while reading a literary text, to mention any thoughts or feelings that they have. The analysis we conduct on this material is a content analysis, but of a rather unusual kind: we allow the protocols themselves to suggest the categories. On the basis of our analysis of such think aloud protocols we not only gain insight into classes of response and their relationship to the features of the text being read, but we can also follow individual responses through the story, tracing the emergence and development of reader's feelings, their imagery, empathy with a main character, queries about story meaning, and many other features. And in this way we position ourselves to discover features of response which have not yet been described, and are not predicted by cognitive poetics. On the basis of such research, we may be in a position to formulate a specific hypothesis that we can then set out to test using more familiar experimental methods.

4.4 The Neglect of Feeling

Given that literary reading is so often imbued with feeling, it is surprising that feeling has still received so little attention from cognitive poetics. Of the major scholars in this field, only Reuven Tsur and Keith Oatley have made significant contributions. Tsur's work has largely been at the level of sound structures and metre in poetry (e.g. Tsur 1997). Oatley's earlier view of emotion (Johnson-Laird and Oatley, 1989) can be classed with several other influential views of the time as an interrupt theory. Here emotions are situated within a story grammar approach, explained in relation to plans and goals; as Stockwell (2002), who adopts this view, puts it, "emotions follow upon the maintenance of plans, the achievement of goals, their frustration or failure"; emotions arise "when there are variations in plans or goals which are being monitored" (p. 172). In other words, emotion occurs primarily when the functioning of a plan is interrupted (Oatley's more recent work goes well beyond this model: see Oatley, 2002). This would make emotions secondary, after-effects of a cognitive appraisal (the issue is related to the longstanding debate in psychology over whether emotions have "primacy" or not, begun by a paper of Robert Zajonc in 1980).

While these approaches to emotion are of value, more recent work on emotion, especially on the neuropsychology of feeling (Damasio, 1999; LeDoux, 1996; and see Chapter 9), demonstrates the need for a comprehensive framework for understanding the role of feeling in literary response. This would suggest a more balanced approach to feeling, in which it might at times take precedence in response, at other times follow upon some prior cognitive processing. Our own theoretical work on feeling (Miall and Kuiken, 2002) proposes a four-part framework for the feelings involved in literary response. First, *evaluative* feelings such as enjoyment, pleasure, frustration, or satisfaction in reading are reactions to a text, and provide an incentive to sustain reading or consider it afterwards. Second, *narrative* feelings such as suspense, curiosity, and empathy with an author, narrator, or narrative figure are involved in the processes by which a representation of the fictional world is developed and sustained. Third, *aesthetic* feelings (called "artefact emotions" by Kneepen and Zwaan, 1994) of fascination, interest, or intrigue may constitute the initial moment in a readers' response to the formal components of literary texts (narrative, stylistic, or genre-based). While serving to capture and hold readers' attention (Miall and Kuiken, 1994a), these aesthetic reactions may anticipate a fourth level of feeling: the *modifying* powers of feeling. We have found that, at times, aesthetic and narrative feelings interact to produce metaphors of *personal* identification that modify self-understanding. We have suggested (Miall and Kuiken, 2002) that the concept of catharsis (the conflict of tragic feelings identified by Aristotle) identifies one particular form of a more general pattern in which aesthetic and narrative feelings evoked during reading interact to modify the reader's sense of self.

Cognitive poetics has touched at various times on each of these levels of feeling: for instance, Tsur's primary interest has been in the realm of aesthetic feelings prompted by the sound textures of poetry; Bortolussi and Dixon (2003), whose theoretical framework involves the reader's representation of the narrator in fiction, discuss the various possible feelings that may occur when identifying with a narrator; Semino (1997) implies self-modifying feelings when considering the more radical processes involved in schema-refreshment (that is, the creation of a schema), although she gives little space to considering the reader as such; similarly, Oatley (2002) in a recent paper tells us that "the reader may reach an insight, and build a new piece of his or her model of the self and its relations. In other words, some cognitive transformation may result" (p. 54). What is missing from these accounts is an overall theory of the role that feeling plays in the process of literary reading: feeling is largely treated as a subsidiary effect, an epiphenomenon occurring in the interspace of the cognitive processes being described.

In attempting to go beyond this in our account of feeling, we have also postulated three properties of feeling that are independent of the kind of processes described by cognitive poetics. In brief, we suggest that feeling facilitates border-crossing, that is, feelings enable us to relate concepts in unrelated fields. Second, feeling prompts us to take a certain stance towards events, preparing us to interpret incoming evidence in a specific way; anticipation of this kind seems to be one of the fundamental properties of feeling. Third, a more common claim, feeling is generally self-implicating; it occurs when some issue of our self-concept is in question. These processes may not only cut across cognitive processes, reshaping them in ways not allowed for by cognitive accounts, but even take over the primary role in literary understanding, perhaps derailing such processes (at least for a while). In several publications we have pointed to this possibility and provided empirical examples showing the crucial role of feeling during literary response (see e.g., Miall and Kuiken, 2002; Kuiken, Miall, and Sikora, 2004; and Chapter 5). But this work is only at a preliminary stage and needs developing and elaborating in a number of ways. What is required, in part, is a more focused attempt to integrate feeling into the structures of response already laid out in cognitive terms by cognitive poetics, and to do so in a way that allows for the priority of feeling where appropriate; then to develop hypotheses that are amenable to empirical testing, so that the theoretical claims we make can be arbitrated in the light of responses from actual readers.

4.5 The Question of Literariness

To review these three aspects of literature, interpretation, cognition, and feeling, is to suggest that the significance of reading is wider than the interpretive issues that cognitive poetics has so far studied. There are a number of other processes involved in literary reading that need not, and in the case of the ordinary reader outside the classroom, probably do not eventuate in an interpretation. The perspectives I have suggested would also, I believe, bring coherence to the research questions involved in the cognitive study of literature. One feature of cognitive poetics as it now stands is the impression of a mosaic of various processes, among which it would be hard to say why a particular process should determine reading in a given situation. For example, even in the case of Bortolussi and Dixon (2003), whose overall thesis proposes that the relation of reader to narrator determines the reading process, this breaks down into a number of subprocesses whose relative significance cannot be decided on the evidence they provide (that is, how would we decide between the different claims of plot structures, character construction, or different discourse styles, or the relation between them).

Given the pre-eminence of feeling when we are thoroughly engaged in literary reading, perhaps we should look here for the overall determining process during reading—if there is one overall process waiting to be found. This seems a tenable claim, worth pursuing, as our previous empirical research has shown. But we don't yet know enough to be sure. One important issue also requiring clarification is that of literariness, where cognitivist scholars have been ambivalent. Bortolussi and Dixon (2003), for example, indicate their acceptance of "the assumption [of discourse analysis] that literary language is not distinct from, but rather an instance of, ordinary language, and that consequently it is processed as such by readers" (p. 29). This assumption, that the methods of literary analysis drawn from cognition will be adequate for all tasks, forecloses the possibility of establishing what may be distinctive to the experience of literature. Similarly, while Peter Stockwell (2002, p. 92), in a discussion of discourse worlds, suggests on one page that good literature is able to seem universal, reinstating a context that is not closely tied to particular historical conditions, two pages later also argues: "It is a principle of cognitive poetics that the same cognitive mechanisms apply to literary reading as to all other interaction" (p. 94). Here, I suggest, feeling may make all the difference, showing us what is unique in the literary interaction. If so, then the case for interweaving our understanding of feeling into the claims of cognitive poetics is an urgent and important one.

This is to argue that while cognitive poetics fails to take feelings seriously under consideration, and to conduct empirical studies of the experience of reading, it may also be missing what makes literary reading distinctive. This too is, of course, an empirical question. Until cognitive poetics is grounded upon a body of research with real readers, we will have only ambiguity on this important question, or we will dispute over the contentions of rival theories, which will only reproduce in a new form the inconclusive debates of the last thirty or forty years. The choice facing cognitive poetics now is whether to continue with a limited and perhaps limiting focus on interpretation, or seek to situate literary study within an explanatory scientific framework in which the phenomena of interpretation form only one corner of a much larger field.

• CHAPTER FIVE •

Feeling in the Comprehension of Literary Narratives

5.1 Schema Theory

Literary narratives are often indeterminate, exhibiting conflicts between points of view or ambiguities in the status of narrative elements.* In this chapter I will begin by suggesting that an account of the process of comprehending such complex narratives is beyond the reach of purely cognitive models. I will suggest that during comprehension response is controlled by feeling, which directs the creation of schemata more adequate to the text—that is, literary texts call our existing structures of knowledge into question and require us to formulate new structures. I will point to several properties of feeling that contribute to developing this model of narrative understanding. To examine and test the model I examine in some detail a short story by Virginia Woolf (1944) and describe an empirical study with readers of the story: shifts in the relative importance of story phrases during a rereading of the story, and comments made by readers point to a process of schema creation under the control of feeling.

Within psychology, the analysis of narrative has been directed by an information processing approach, in particular by different versions of schema theory (Rumelhart & Ortony, 1977; Graesser, 1981) or by related models, such as story grammar or propositional analysis (Mandler, 1984; Van Dijk, 1980). The models of narrative analysis these authors proposed, including those that incorporated feeling, assigned narrative elements to categories, such as propositions, goals, or plot units. Story structure was then generated by mapping connections between elements according to specific rules of inference.

---

* This chapter is a revised version of "Beyond the Schema Given: Affective Comprehension of Literary Narratives." *Cognition and Emotion*, 3, 1989, 55–78. It is reprinted here by kind permission of The Psychology Press, http://www.psypress.co.uk/journals.asp.

These first models possess a degree of predictive power, indicating that they captured some of the salient features of the reader's comprehension process (e.g. Black & Bower, 1980; Yekovich & Thorndyke, 1981). Their limits are suggested by the relatively simple narratives that have been explicated by their means, either folk tales or elementary stories for children, or specially devised narratives. Although some authors claimed that the principles of their model would extend to encompass any narrative, in practice, the narratives that are amenable to their methods of analysis are comparatively simple. None of the models seemed adequate to the analysis of such literary narratives as short stories or novels. As Spiro (1982) argued, reviewing these approaches, a schema based analysis of complex literary narratives is inherently unlikely to succeed, as the comprehension of such texts goes beyond the schemata activated during comprehension. More recently, other versions of schema theory have been developed (Cook, 1994; Semino, 1997) that are more adequate to understanding the structures of literary texts, and which have considered the extent to which literary reading involves processes of schema creation rather than instantion. As I will suggest, however, despite the impressive achievements of these approaches, the indeterminacy of literary texts seems to indicate another important factor is involved in literary experience, that of feeling.

Because the elements of a literary text do not exhibit stable meanings, and variations in individual response play an essential role, no network of relationships and inferences will capture the indeterminacy of a literary text, its complex of shifting and continually developing meanings. Under these circumstances the reader must necessarily have recourse to an alternative principle for guiding the comprehension process: feeling provides the necessary criteria for such a principle. I postulate three main criteria: (1) feeling is self referential: It allows experiential and evaluative aspects of the reader's self concept to be applied to the task of comprehension; (2) feeling enables cross domain categorization of text elements; and (3) it is anticipatory, pre structuring the reader's understanding of the meaning of a text early in the reading process (I will discuss these features in greater detail later). At the highest level the goals and beliefs of the self are instantiated in the feelings; thus it seems likely that feeling plays a determining role in cognitive processing (perception, memory, and reasoning) when this is performed in the service of the self. An analysis of the structure of literary narratives, together with empirical studies of response, provides an important source of information about this process, as I will show in the case of responses to a short story by Woolf.

First, however, I will briefly consider two contributions to schema theory, one older and one more recent example (Graesser, 1981; Semino, 1997), as a way of suggesting the limitations of a cognitive approach to literary experience.

Schema theory was well developed in Graesser's (1981) model, which he described as "Schema Pointer Plus Tag" since it addressed the implications of processing typical schema based elements of a narrative together with elements that are atypical of the schema. Each statement within a narrative is assigned to one of six categories: An event or a state, which must be either physical or internal to a character; or the statement represents a goal node or a style node (that is, how something was done). A statement can be assigned to only one of these categories. Statements are then related to each other structurally by one of six types of directional arcs, such as "reason," "consequence," or "property." In terms of the "reason" arc, which is the most common connection between statements in the narratives studied by Graesser, it is a rule that only one reason can emanate forward from one goal statement to another. For example, *A person buys the plant* is connected to its superordinate goal by a reason arc, *in order to have the plant.* Through these and related methods of analysis, Graesser and his co workers devised a theory of narrative structure which has strong predictive power in accounting for how readers comprehend and remember simple narratives. It is Graesser's claim that "In principle, passages in all prose genres should be accommodated by the system" (p. 116).

The limitations of this model of analysis, however, quickly become apparent when it is applied to a literary text. Literary narratives cannot easily be accommodated to these categories and rules. For example, the rule that only one reason arc can emanate forward from a goal is contradicted by the existence of dual or multiple goals, in which characters have several motives or perform actions which are "overdetermined" (to use Freud's useful term), a phenomenon which is rather common in literary texts. Is Jones going to town to buy a gift for his wife, or is he buying a gift for his wife so that he can go to town? More fundamentally, knowledge about causes and goals, which is basic to a schema model of analysis, is often ambiguous, withheld, or becomes a focus of narrative interest. Thus, a cause that is an assumption or default of a given schema may be modified or displaced; a character's goals may be unknown, illusory, or mistaken. Literary narratives typically pose schemata in a critical framework in order to suggest their inadequacy or to show their inapplicability. This makes literary narratives much less determinate than the relatively simple narratives studied by the schema or story grammar proponents: The principles on which such models are built are thus unlikely to account for comprehension of literary narratives.

This point can be turned around: The indeterminacy itself may be a primary agent in the reading process, driving other systems that control and modify schemata with their apparatus of causes and goals. The argument presented in this chapter is that such indeterminacy points to feeling as the primary process underlying comprehension. This contention is compatible with other research findings on feeling, but also goes beyond the functions generally assigned to feeling in most theoretical accounts.

A specific example can be given of a phrase from a literary narrative which presents problems for the schema view of Graesser. This narrative, which is the focus of the empirical study of response I will discuss below, is a short story by Virginia Woolf (1944), "Together and Apart." The section that follows is the beginning of the opening paragraph:

> [1] Mrs Dalloway introduced them, [2] saying you will like him. [3] The conversation began some minutes before anything was said, [4] for both Mr Serle and Miss Anning looked at the sky [5] and in both of their minds the sky went on pouring its meaning [6] though very differently. . .

The phrase which presents particular difficulties is No. 3. The first two phrases indicate a social setting, probably a party. Given that an introduction has just taken place, initiating a conversation would seem to be a standard goal. Is this goal being met or not? Because the conversation takes place "before anything was said", the status of the phrase as a goal statement is ambiguous. Although this remains unresolved, the indeterminacy it involves is also likely to transfer to other elements of the narrative. But perhaps the statement should be categorized as an event? If so, another difficulty awaits us over deciding whether the event is an internal or an external one. Does the statement indicate non verbal communication, such as a meaningful exchange of glances, or a reciprocal sense of empathy? Or is a character conversing in imagination, fantasizing a conversation? Is it an *event* at all? As the "conversation" began "before anything was said," it might signify a *state,* such as mutual indecision or embarrassment. At least the *cause* of the "conversation" seems clear: It follows as a result of the introduction. But, in terms of a cause, this is perhaps the least interesting aspect of the statement, as a cause of a more interesting kind appears to be implied in the next phrase, through the conjunction "for": "for both Mr Serle and Miss Anning looked at the sky . . ." The operation of this cause is, however, left unclear: the sky "went on pouring its meaning," which may indicate some cause for the conversation; but the phrase is itself a metaphor, and thus only compounds the indeterminacy.

Perhaps enough has been said about this phrase to show the scope of the problem. The subtlety of Woolf's prose makes such an analysis seem particularly clumsy. The conclusion to which it points is that the process of comprehension is driven by an indeterminacy over causes, goals, the status of events as internal or physical, and other uncertainties. It is a process that frequently serves to unsettle the schemata of the reader at just the moment that the schemata are being identified.

From the point of view of schema theory, therefore, a literary narrative will often be found not to be "well formed," whether in terms of overall plan, coherence, completeness, or conventions (Olson, Mack, & Duffy, 1981). The difficulties of the schema approach so far can be summarised as follows:

1. Schema identification is necessary to allow the work of understanding to begin, but the application of schemata is likely to be thwarted or disrupted in a variety of ways by a range of textual features.
2. Providing a causal account of states or events is often problematic, due to uncertainties about how text elements relate or to multiple potential relationships within the text. The status of narrative elements as states or events may itself be indeterminate.
3. A goal directed account of characters is often inadequate. Goals may be multiple, ambiguous or conflicting, so that their status becomes a focus of narrative interest.

The outcome of a literary narrative, therefore, may include the following: Causes are not what the reader might have believed (a cause may be more complex, profound, or obscure); goals may be ineffective or turn out to have been inappropriate, so that the story becomes a critique of the goals as such. Thus, the reader's effort after meaning is directed towards developing a schema for the narrative that transcends the more simple schemata with which she started. The aim of comprehension can be described as the creation of schemata, rather than their application. It is notable, however, that few attempts to examine the creation of schemata are available in the research literature (Vosniadou & Brewer, 1987).

One outcome of studying the comprehension of literary narrative may be a better purchase on the elusive process of schema creation. In more recent developments of schema theory, schema restructuring, or creation, is said to characterize the experience of literary reading (Cook, 1994). As Elena Semino (1997) points out, however, when analysing the ways in which schemata can change, it is the process about which schema theorists have been the most vague (p. 132). It is the basis of Cook's (1994) theory of literariness: according to Cook literary texts involve "discourse deviation," challenging the reader by causing schema disruption, followed by schema refreshment (see Semino, pp. 153–4). Semino disagrees that this must be a defining feature of literariness, however: she points out that literary texts may often reinforce schemata rather than challenge us to engage in schema refreshment. One of Semino's examples of such a text is Seamus Heaney's poem, "A Pillowed Head" (reprinted, pp. 162–3), which she puts forward as an example of a poem that calls for no radical reconception of the schemata on which it relies. She suggests that the poem "presents, from a male perspective, a fairly conventional view of childbirth" (p. 162), hence it can be regarded as schema reinforcing. The poem effectively relates the description of dawn, during which the husband and wife drove to the hospital, to the new birth (their second child), while concluding with a reminder of the earlier dawns spent waiting for the birth. In the context of the argument presented in this chapter, however, the missing factor in Semino's analysis is feeling: not only might schemata themselves arouse feeling, but feeling unrelated to the poem's schemata may occur in response to particular words or phrases yet play a leading role in shaping a reader's understanding.

Semino's analysis in support of her schema-based interpretation is detailed and plausible, but it cannot, of course, account for the possibility of individual responses that would contravert her overall claim for the unchallenging nature of the poem. Semino's emphasis on the relation of dawn and childbirth in the poem (the poem's two principle schemata) seems to provide a context for much of what she has to say about the poem. At the same time, this overlooks an important component of the poem, the emphasis on the birth being the second for this mother—hence her confidence now, compared with "The first time, dismayed" (p. 163). Thus a second, less obvious metaphoric meaning of dawn offered by the poem is that of the mother's maturing beyond "bride" into "earth-mother," an insight that seems to provide a good deal of the optimism and assurance of the poem. The mother is now felt to be aligned with the natural forces alluded to in the references to dawn.

Semino's analysis also includes "Emotional Associations," but these are conventional associations of the main schemata of Dawn/Birth—hope, joy, optimism, etc. (p. 174). In the alternative view presented here, feelings may come from other sources in the poem, and these may invoke literary associations or personal, idiosyncratic ones that have little or no relation to the main schemata of the poem. For instance, the repeated verb in lines 4 and 6, "To be first on the road" and "To be older and grateful," might remind some readers of Hamlet's famous soliloquy, leaving an ominous undercurrent of "Not to be" through the rest of the poem. Or take the final lines which refer back to the time waiting for the birth, "When your domed brow was one long held silence / And the dawn chorus anything but" (p. 163). Here, the literal meaning of the elliptical last phrase is surely "anything but silent"; but this broken phrase also leaves open other possibilities: anything but a chorus, something other than the benign image of birds greeting the dawn, perhaps a predatory gathering—which would complement other distant intimations of danger and death perceptible in the poem, overcome on this occasion but not eliminated (why would the poet end the poem on such a doubtful word as "but"?).

Thus there is scope here, in reading this supposedly schema-reinforcing poem, for feelings that challenge and undercut the main and apparently conventional schemata on which it appears to depend. For the reader who experiences the feelings I have mentioned, the poem may come to challenge standard conceptions of childbirth, that is, disrupt previous schemata and call for the creation of a novel schema more adequate to the data of the poem.

5.2 Beyond the Schema Given

Having suggested some shortcomings of the schema model, I will now outline an alternative approach to literary narrative. Readers instantiate schemata to interpret a text, but the text itself *defamiliarises* the schemata: that is, a familiar or usual schema that would have been applied automatically becomes questionable, and its adequacy may become a focus of narrative interest. Defamiliarisation is frequently cited by critics as a standard effect of literary texts, including narratives (Iser, 1980; Perry, 1979; Shklovsky, 1917/1965; Van Peer, 1986). In moving to a more constructive view of the role of the reader, the present approach also sees literary texts as "writerly" rather than "readerly," in Barthes' useful term (Barthes, 1970/1975, p. 4), that is, it places the main emphasis on the constructive role of the reader (noting, however, that the degree to which a reader constructs the text has been a subject of contention and ambiguity on the part of literary theorists: e.g., Culler, 1983, pp. 69 70).

One effect of defamiliarisation is to require the creation of a new schema adequate to the material presented by the poem or story. The initial schemata are likely to contradict each other in subtle ways, providing the reader with signals of their inadequacy and impelling her to recognise that they have only provisional status. The primary work of the reader is thus to interpret the unfolding sentences of the text for clues to a more adequate schema. It is the reader's feelings that appear to guide this process.

The term *feeling* has, of course, different meanings among psychologists, and a variable relationship with such terms as *emotion* and *affect*, which makes it difficult to define (Kleinginna & Kleinginna, 1981; and see Chapter 6). For present purposes I will understand *feeling* to denote a subjective experience without the overt signs and incentives to action of emotion, including (necessarily for my argument) feelings that have little or no cognitive content but which operate immediately as judgements, preferences, and the like. This is the dimension of feeling described by Buck (1985) as the internal, subjective readout of the current state of the emotion motivation system. It follows that feeling may have "primacy" in relation to cognition (Zajonc, 1984), but the study of literary response indicates a complexity of feeling beyond the limitations of Zajonc's earlier account of "preferences" (Zajonc, 1980). As will be seen from readers' responses cited below, the intensity of feeling experienced by readers ranges from slight (e.g., a vague unease) to strong (e.g., "an unbearable intensity"). Regardless of intensity or cognitive context, however, I suggest that feeling plays the primary role in directing the reading of literary narratives. I discuss three properties of feeling which make it appropriate for this task: feeling is self-referential, cross domain, and anticipatory.

While reading a story a reader will judge that not all phrases are equally important. Some carry more weight, acting as the main focus for the reader's developing view of the story; some carry less weight, acting as support or background, or conveying supplementary information. Phrases can be categorised for their salience to evaluating text meaning, as Hunt and Vipond (1986) showed. But as the schemata for the story are called into question the reader must turn elsewhere for clues to make a more adequate interpretation. In addition to processing new phrases, the reader also reassesses her understanding of phrases initially seen as less important. The feeling valency of such phrases, which may have been peripheral, now becomes a central resource for construing the meaning of the story. Old schemata gain new feelings and are developed or undermined by the implications that the feelings bring with them. In this respect, feeling is cross domain: It can transfer from schemata in one domain (such as those concerned with a story's setting) to those in another (such as the relationship between two characters). The ability of feeling to cross domains has been noted previously (Bower & Cohen, 1982, p. 329; Bruner, 1966, pp. 12 13), although the potentially productive role of this process in cognitive functioning appears generally to have been overlooked. I have suggested elsewhere (Miall, 1987) that it may underlie a number of processes that have been difficult to explain, such as the comprehension of metaphor, dream formation, and bisociation in creative thought.

Feeling is also anticipatory. Given the indeterminacy of the reader's experience of a literary story such as the Woolf, the reader must develop some representation of the outcome of a narrative to keep the comprehension process on line. Because the schemata are defamiliarised, and causes and goals cannot reliably serve to represent the outcome, a representation will be constructed instead from the felt implications of the narrative. For example, given the inadequacy of the introduction schema in the opening of the Woolf story, it is probable that the reader draws on the implications of the phrases about the sky as an alternative source of feeling. If this story is to develop a more adequate meaning, it may (perhaps must) be one that is consonant with the weight and resonance of the sky metaphor, for which (at this stage) no clear cognitive meaning is available. Thus, the sky metaphor, together with the connotations of the non verbal "conversation" create a feeling which anticipates one or more potential outcomes. In this sense, feeling offers a pre structuring of the meaning of the text as a whole. It has been shown empirically that anticipation is common during the reading of narrative; when reading expository prose it is rather uncommon (Miall, 1988; Olson, et al., 1981).

Finally, feeling is self referential. The most obvious self referential effect is the frequent experience of readers that they empathize with the experience and motives of the main character or characters in a narrative; that is, the reader comes to share a character's feelings and goals. But feeling has a wider scope in narratives than this: Any feeling response involves self-concept issues. This provides the interpretative process with a range of potential contexts for attributing meaning to text elements, drawn from the reader's prior experience and concerns.

Evidence that feeling signifies the activation of self concept issues was provided by studies of the self reference effect. It was established that when material is judged in relation to the self, this leads to better recall than if the material is related to a relatively unknown person, or judged during a semantic task; but material was remembered best when it not only referred to the self but was coloured by feeling (Miall, 1986b). Thus, feeling during reading not only causes schemata to be reconfigured, but also constitutes the route of access to motives for reading derived from the reader's self concept. Of course, the implications of a text can reflect back on the issues it has activated. Reading is potentially capable of transforming the self (Kuiken, Miall, and Sikora, 2004), although the extent to which it actually does so will depend upon the concerns that emerge from the reader's prior experience, or, to put it another way, the extent to which the reader's imagination is seized by the text.

The reader's response to literary narrative may rehearse on a symbolic stage the current concerns (Klinger, 1978) of the self, enabling implications for the self to be anticipated in isolation from the world of action. Readers of narrative are typically more conscious of themselves as readers than readers of expository prose (Miall, 1990), which indicates an awareness of implications for the self in the feelings generated by reading (although self reference need not always imply self awareness—degree of access to private self consciousness is an established personality variable: Fenigstein, Scheier, & Buss, 1975). Because the self is directly implicated in anticipating the outcome (the meaning that will be attributed to the narrative as a whole), different readers are likely to project different self related concerns onto the narrative. As teachers of literature are aware, there are often as many "meanings" to a literary text as there are students in the class.

The main features of the comprehension process I have been describing can now be illustrated through an analysis of the opening section of the Virginia Woolf story, shown in Table 5.1 (the empirical study I go on to report was focused on this section). In particular, I point to the process of defamiliarisation that may take place in response to a literary narrative, and indicate the role played by feeling.

5.3 Theoretical Analysis of Woolf's "Together and Apart"

The opening section, which represents one fifth of the story, is shown in Table 5.1. The story describes the introduction of two characters at a party, and follows their halting attempts to start a conversation until the mention of

Table 5.1 Opening Section of Virginia Woolf's "Together and Apart" (Woolf, 1944)

[1] Mrs Dalloway introduced them, [2] saying you will like him. [3] The conversation began some minutes before anything was said, [4] for both Mr Serle and Miss Anning looked at the sky [5] and in both of their minds the sky went on pouring its meaning [6] though very differently, [7] until the presence of Mr Serle by her side [8] became so distinct to Miss Anning [9] that she could not see the sky, simply, itself, any more, [10] but the sky shored up by the tall body, [11] dark eyes, grey hair, clasped hands, [12] the stern melancholy . . . face of Roderick Serle, [13] (but she had been told 'falsely melancholy') [14] and, knowing how foolish it was, [15] she yet felt impelled to say:

[16] 'What a beautiful night!'

[17] Foolish! Idiotically foolish! [18] But if one mayn't be foolish at the age of forty [19] in the presence of the sky, [20] which makes the wisest imbecile [21]—mere wisps of straw—she and Mr Serle atoms, motes, [22] standing there at Mrs Dalloway's window, [23] and their lives, seen by moonlight, [24] as long as an insect's and no more important.

[25] 'Well!' said Miss Anning, [26] patting the sofa cushion emphatically. [27] And down he sat beside her. [28] Was he 'falsely melancholy', as they said? [29] Prompted by the sky, [30] which seemed to make it all a little futile [31]—what they said, what they did—[32] she said something perfectly commonplace again:

[33] 'There was a Miss Serle who lived at Canterbury [34] when I was a girl there.'

[35] With the sky in his mind, [36] all the tombs of his ancestors [37] immediately appeared to Mr Serle in a blue romantic light, [38] and his eyes expanding and darkening, he said: 'Yes.'

[39] 'We are originally a Norman family, [40] who came over with the Conqueror. [41] That is a Richard Serle buried in the Cathedral. [42] He was a knight of the garter.'

[43] Miss Anning felt that she had struck accidentally the true man, [44] upon whom the false was built. [45] Under the influence of the moon [46] (the moon which symbolized man to her, [47] she could see it through a chink of the curtain, [48] and she took sips of the moon) [49] she was capable of saying almost anything [50] and she settled in to disinter the true man [51] who was buried under the false, [52] saying to herself: 'On, Stanley, on' [53]—which was a watchword of hers, a secret spur, [54] or scourge such as middle aged people

often make [55] to flagellate some inveterate vice, [56] hers being a deplorable timidity . . .

Note. Phrases 12 and 13 in the original read: "the stern melancholy (but she had been told 'falsely melancholy') face of Roderick Serle".

Canterbury (phrase 33) appears to offer the possibility of communication. The remainder of the story alternates between the perspectives of Miss Anning and Mr Serle. We learn that for Mr Serle Canterbury represents "the best years of his life, all his memories." Prompted by Miss Anning's interest he seems on the point of offering genuine information about himself. But the challenge of intimacy is too much, and both withdraw, waiting in paralysed silence until another guest interrupts them and they are able to part. The cause of the failure in communication is not explained in literal terms, so that the reader must depend on figurative, symbolic, and other indirect references to it scattered through the story. Only the opening of the story will now be analysed in detail.

At the outset it seems likely that the reader will identify with the characters' situation, and wish to see some communication which would allow them to move closer. The potential for this is reinforced by Miss Anning's resolve to "disinter the true man" and by Mr Serle's animation at the mention of Canterbury. There are cross currents in the opening part of the story, however, which are likely to cause the reader to have reservations about both the ability and the understanding of Miss Anning. Against the background of the sky, which is twice associated with Mr Serle, Miss Anning senses that what they say or do may be "a little futile"; and the two characters respond "very differently" to the sky, although at this stage we are not told why. Thus, in the foreground (to use Iser's terminology, 1978, p. 92) is the reader's positive response to the possibility of genuine communication; in the background are a set of inferences which may cut across this possibility. Two opposing currents of feeling are initiated, in which the more negative (but less prominent) implications of the second are available as a potential re reading of the hopes represented in the first.

The cue to the more negative reading of the situation which will be made later is already present in the phrases about the sky: For example, the sky makes "the wisest imbecile," and the moon "symbolized man" to Miss Anning. But at a first reading these phrases seem permissive rather than threatening: that is, under the sky the characters may come to share a sense of their littleness, in which what is said matters less than the act of communication itself. The moon which symbolises man also gives Miss Anning the feeling that she can say almost anything. These phrases offer one felt meaning if it is seen that communication can take place, but another when that possibility has been withdrawn. On reading the story again with hindsight, it is the negative feeling inherent in the situation which is more apparent in these phrases: They establish the sense of human insignificance, and point to the male principle as a primary cause of the failure in communication. The negative feeling also transfers to other key phrases in this section, such as the "blue romantic light" of Mr Serle, and Miss Anning's resolve to "disinter the true man," both of which had seemed to promise communication but which now seem illusory.

Although the actual cause underlying the failure of communication is not described directly, the reader is able to grasp a cause at the level of feeling. The cause is inherent in some deficiency in both Miss Anning and Mr Serle, some lack of alignment in their vision of the situation which calls into question the possibility of communication itself. This schema, which must be created by the reader, is signalled by references to the sky and setting which occur through the story, and by perspectives on the inner self of each character. By the end of the story it is clear that the sky symbolises the negative implications of the failure of communication, making available to the reader her pre existing feeling in response to the sky, such feeling acting as a catalyst for transforming understanding of the relationship postulated in the opening of the story.

The role played by feeling is thus critical: Successful understanding of the story, which involves the creation of a new schema, could not progress without the properties of feeling which I have postulated. Whereas a schema is domain-specific, feeling can transform the meaning of a schema by transference of inferences across domains, as in this ease the feeling induced by the "sky" phrases transfers to the relationship schema. But feeling also appears to be self referential, thus readers are motivated to seek a resolution to the critical implications of such a story for their own concerns (the value placed on relationships, the need for communication). In that the phrases at the opening of such a story are ambivalent and no single schema will account for the range of meanings being felt, several possible outcomes are (at least in a preconscious form) probably entertained by the reader. In this sense, feeling anticipates the schema that will be created by the reader, and signals the points in the story at which the new schema begins to be formed. Feeling keeps subsequent processing of the story on line, and provides a reference point by which to judge whether the eventual interpretation is adequate.

Understanding of the opening section of "Together and Apart" thus depends in several ways on the role of feeling: Feeling enables a wider, self referential resource of contextual information to be brought to bear on the story, it transfers feelings across domains, and it provides the main vehicle for anticipation. Despite the existence of considerable differences that occur between readers who are reading the same text (another problem for schema based approaches), some consistent pointers to the anticipatory role of feeling seem likely.

Figure 5.1 Feeling Controls on the Comprehension of the Opening Section of Virginia Woolf's "Together and Apart."

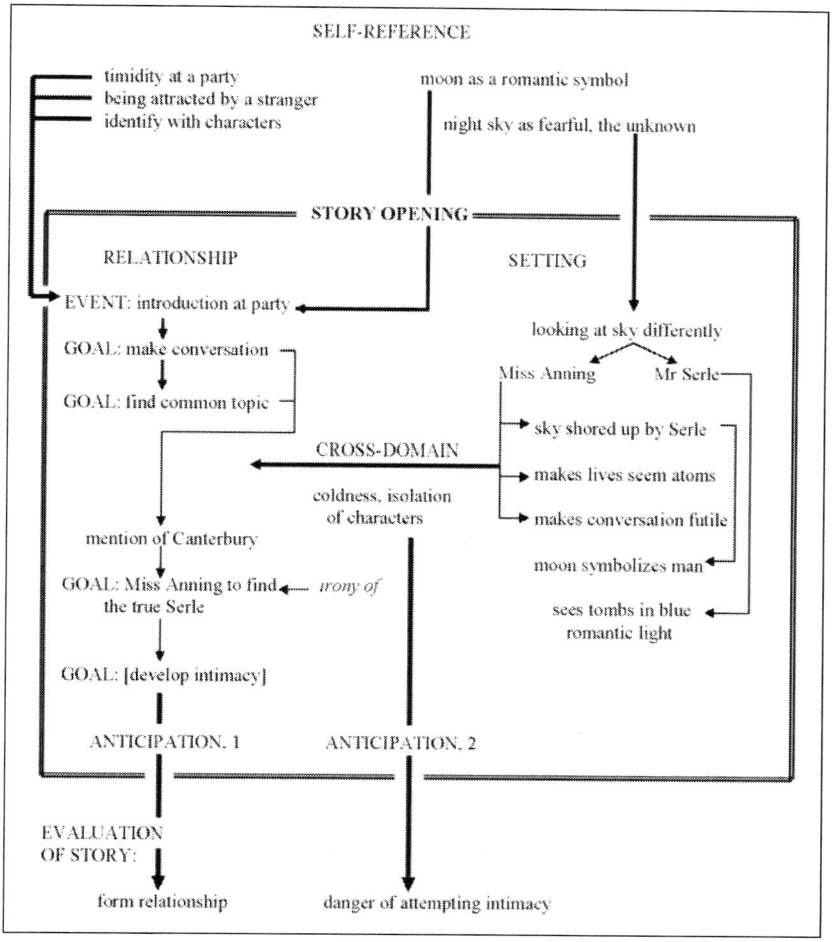

The two main schemata relevant to the opening of Woolf's story are shown diagrammatically (and somewhat simplified) in Fig. 5.1, with schema elements linked by thin arrows. Thick arrows show the influence of the three feeling controls that determine the development of the schemata. For example, a set of possible self referential feelings are shown as influences on the two main groups of phrases concerning the relationship schema and the sky and setting. Two potential (described later) suggests that the "form relationship" anticipationis the stronger one at a first reading. It is also worth noting that the sequence of "relationship" phrases is easier to fit within a conventional schema model, as the use of EVENT and GOAL descriptors indicates. The cross domain effect of the setting phrases is likely to have its full effect only later, either further on in the story or at a second reading (when, for example, the irony of postulating "the true" Mr Serle becomes clearer).

5.4 A Study of Readers' Responses to "Together and Apart"

If the account of the story summarised in Fig. 1 is correct, then several predictions can be made about readers' responses to the opening section of the story. Readers will attribute *felt intensity* to the more salient phrases concerning both the relationship schema and the sky and setting. In judging the same phrases for *importance,* however, readers will initially see the phrases referring to the relationship as the more important. At a second reading it will be the phrases indicating the distance between the characters, especially those which refer to the setting of the sky or moon, which will be seen as the more important. Thus, a reversal in importance can be expected between "relationship" and "sky and setting" phrases: what was foreground will recede into the background, and the phrases which appeared as background will now come into the foreground.

It can also be predicted that because readers exposed only to the first section will construe the story as primarily about a relationship between the two main characters, asked to recall the phrases, such readers will recall more frequently those which offer evidence for a relationship. These hypotheses were examined in the study I will describe. Ratings and recall data was supplemented by eliciting readers' free comments about the meaning they saw in the story, both on reading the first section only, and again after having read the whole story. Such comments provided additional evidence of shifts in interpretation and the creation of new schemata. While a number of other hypotheses could also be formulated on the basis of the theory of response I have put forward, the design of the present study is limited to illustrating how readers go beyond their initial schema.

Participants were 28 undergraduate students of English literature. The study was run with the students in several sessions, during which the 56 phrases shown in Table 5.1 provided the main focus for collecting response data. The opening section of the story was presented typed normally on a page, with the name of the author and story title as the heading: participants read the story in this form first. They then received a version in which each phrase was printed on a separate line, for the purpose of rating.

One group of 12 participants rated the phrases for feeling intensity on a scale of 1 to 6, where 1 signified strong feeling; they then attempted to recall as many phrases as possible. Another group of 16 participants read the first section and rated the phrases for importance (scale 1 to 6, where 1 = very important), then rated the phrases again after reading the story as a whole. Both groups provided written comments on their responses to the story before undertaking the ratings. In the second group, four of the participants left a significant proportion of the phrases without ratings, due to a misunderstanding of the instructions. For the numerical analyses to be reported these participants were omitted, and the results are thus based on the ratings of 12 participants. But the written comments are taken from the protocols of all 16 participants.

The participants in the first group who rated for feeling recalled an average of 14.65 phrases, but "relationship" phrases were recalled significantly more frequently than "sky and setting", as shown by a biserial correlation, $r = 0.257$, $t(49) = 1.86$, $p < 0.05$. This finding indicates that for these readers, who rated for feeling, the relationship aspects of the story were more salient, as the phrases referring to this schema were more memorable after reading only the first section. Most of the participants, for example, recalled the phrases in which Miss Anning and Mr Serle are introduced, in which Miss Anning invites Mr Serle to sit next to her, and where the theme of Canterbury is taken up by both characters (phrases 1 3, 26, 33, and 41). In contrast, the sky and setting phrases were generally recalled by half or fewer of the participants.

Thus, the main factor influencing recall appears to have been the relationship schema. It is worth noting that feeling ratings show no significant correlation with recall. Yet examination of the mean ratings for feeling shows that a number of the sky and setting phrases received ratings for feeling as high as those for the relationship phrases: The mean feeling ratings for the relationship and sky and setting phrases is 3.31 and 2.88, respectively (there is no significant difference between these means). It seems likely that the salience of the feeling in such phrases becomes available to readers subsequently: As the relationship schema is found unsatisfactory, so readers will draw upon the sky and setting phrases for their felt potential in re construing the meaning of the story. The strong feeling attached to such phrases, in other words, tends to predict their subsequent importance in understanding the story. An example is phrase No.46, "the moon which symbolized man to her." This obtained a mean feeling rating of 2.25, indicating strong feeling; its importance increased from 3.09 to 2.64 at the second reading. Several other sky and setting phrases show a similar pattern.

The ratings for importance were examined for evidence of shifts between first and second readings. Overall, the relationship phrases declined in importance whereas the sky and setting phrases increased: A biserial correlation of the mean shift of each phrase against its classification (51 of the phrases were assigned to one of the two groups) showed the shift to be significant, $r = 0.419$, $t(49) = 3.23$, $p < 0.025$. A more detailed study of the 24 phrases receiving the highest ratings for importance at the first reading was carried out, as shown in Table 5.2. The table shows how the phrases shifted in importance at the second

Table 5.2 Woolf's "Together and Apart": Mean Rank Order of Phrases for Rated Importance at First and Second Readings

No.	M	Ordl	Ord2	
r 3.	1.67	1	1	The conversation began some minutes before anything was said
r 43.	1.67	2	3	Miss Anning felt that she had struck accidentally the true man
r 50.	1.67	3	6	and she settled in to disinter the true man
r 44.	1.91	4	16	upon whom the false was built.
s 5.	2.0	5	2	and in both of their minds the sky went on pouring its meaning
r 30.	2.2	6	24	which seemed to make it all a little futile
r 56.	2.25	7	13	hers being a deplorable timidity . . .
s 45.	2.33	8	9	Under the influence of the moon
s 6.	2.55	9	4	though very differently,
r 13.	2.55	10	23	(but she had been told 'falsely melan choly')
r 37.	2.55	11	32	immediately appeared to Mr Serle in a blue romantic light
s 35.	2.58	13	15	With the sky in his mind,
r 51.	2.58	14	12	who was buried under the false,
s 29.	2.64	15	5	Prompted by the sky,
s 9.	2.83	16	17	that she could not see the sky, simply, itself, any more,
r 49.	2.83	17	33	she was capable of saying almost anything
s 21.	2.91	18	11	-- mere wisps of straw -- she and Mr Serle atoms, motes,
s 23.	2.91	19	8	and their lives, seen by moonlight,
r 2.	3.0	20	10	saying you will like him.
s 24.	3.0	21	18	as long as an insect's and no more impor tant.
s 46.	3.09	22	14	(the moon which symbolized man to her,
r 7.	3.18	23	38	until the presence of Mr Serle by her side
s 4.	3.25	24	7	for both Mr Serle and Miss Anning looked at the sky

Key. r, "relationship" phrases; s, "sky and setting" phrases; *M*, mean rating for importance at first reading; *Ord1*, rank order of phrases at first reading; *Ord2*, rank order of phrase at second reading.

reading. In this set of phrases 13 refer to the relationship schema and 11 to the sky and setting. The shift downwards in importance of the relationship phrases at the second reading is accompanied by a shift upwards in the sky and setting phrases. Comparison of the mean ratings showed that both shifts were significant ($p < 0.02$). The shift in mean ratings for these groups of phrases (based on the data in Table 5.2) is shown graphically in Figure 5.2. The predicted reversal in importance of the schemata at first and second readings thus appears to have taken place.

The nature of the shifts among the key phrases in each group can be seen by comparing the order data in Table 5.2. For example, the phrases suggesting that Miss Anning will set herself to know the true Mr Serle were originally seen as being almost the most important phrases in the opening of the story. At the first reading these phrases, "[43] Miss Anning felt that she had struck accidentally whom the false was built", occur in positions 2, 3, and 4; but at the second reading they have moved to positions 3, 6, and 16. The questioning of Miss Anning about Mr Serle's "melancholy" (phrases 13 and 28), declines from positions 10 and 12 down to 20 and 23. The promise of communication contained in Miss Anning's sense that "[49] she was capable of saying almost anything", slips from 17 to 33. Most dramatically, the romantic potential of Mr Serle, whose ancestral tombs "[37] immediately appeared to Mr Serle in a blue romantic light", is relegated from position 11 to 32.

By contrast, the importance of the sky as an influence on the characters comes to be seen as perhaps the dominant aspect. The most important phrases indicating this, "[5] and in both of their minds the sky went on pouring its meaning", "[6] though very differently", "[29] prompted by the sky", and "[24] for both Mr Serle and Miss Anning looked at the sky", move up in importance from 5, 9, 15, and 24 to 2, 4, 5, and 7 respectively. Several other phrases mentioning the sky and the moon and their effects (numbers 21, 23, and 46), also move from positions 18, 19, and 22 up to 11, 8, and 14. Thus, the major shift that takes place in the interpretation of the opening part of the story is the reversal in importance of the relationship and the sky and setting schemata. This gives only a first approximation to the nature of the interpretative processes involved; more subtle methods of tracing readers' responses are required to investigate the role of feeling in the process of schema formation (such as the use of a think aloud method: Kintgen, 1983; Kuiken and Miall, 2001). Readers' written comments, however, show a process of anticipation based on the schemata prevailing at the outset; they also reveal how responses change when the whole story had been read.

Most readers anticipated a story about a relationship, whether this was to be satisfactory or not (the numbers preceding the comments refer to the different readers):

Figure 5.2 Mean Ratings for Importance of Phrases at First and Second Readings

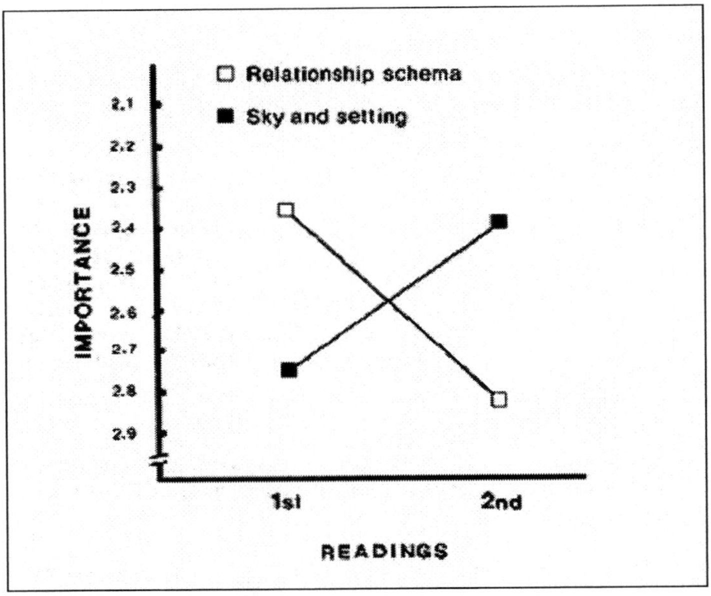

Rating of 1 = most important.

> 1. The story may continue with a more in depth conversation between the characters, perhaps culminating in the discovery that they have a lot in common. 5. The phrase 'the conversation began some minutes before anything was said' is important as it shows an affinity 'the together bit' between two people. 4. Raises expectations of how story will progress and how the relationship between Miss Anning and Mr Serle will develop.

But some readers were also aware of an undercurrent created by references to the sky and setting, which may either support or cut across the relationship schema. These comments provide one example of the indeterminacy of the sky and setting phrases.

> 8. They will probably continue to talk and either drift apart or recognise some kind of connection and become closer. Sky and moon will somehow influence how they relate to one another. 7. I sense an exploration of appearance, perception, opposites, apparent contradictions which may or may not be truly so. There is also the introduction of the idea of futility, insignificance. Although only shown so far in relation to the vastness of the sky, I feel the author may well take this further, bring it down to a more internalised level with all its attendant dangers.

The last reader quoted here is anticipating one possible schema which the story as a whole serves to create, concerning the limits of communication. After reading the whole story it is a schema of this kind which the readers note:

> 2. A waste! Neither character wants to be at Mrs Dalloway's, both seem to force themself into social polite comments, although under this is an unbearable intensity. 16. Story is about communication and the rejection of it, or inability to accept it and its implications. Love akin to dislike—preconceived notions being destroyed. 7. 'ultimate' communication is transient, comes in flashes and, perhaps, would not be altogether desirable . . . This is seen clearly in the internalization of the narrative, the isolation of the characters even in a social setting, and ultimately, their rejection of, sliding away from true relationship.

Several readers also point in retrospect to the 'sky and setting' aspects of the story. This is seen to symbolise the source of the problem over communication, as in the following comment:

> 5. Moon and sky—awesome, tend to show the unimportance of people's lives. They are not particularly romantic symbols—emotion is stunted and undeveloped. They could be symbols of the unconscious having an important effect but one which is difficult to pin point.

Through these and other comments it is apparent that readers worked towards a more adequate schema for comprehending the story. The author herself provides only figurative language for transcending the primary schemata of interpretation, thus it is not to be expected that among a group of readers one schema will emerge, or that readers will be able to give a clear description of what schema has been created in response to the story as a whole. Rather, the power of a literary text such as this lies beyond the sentences of the text itself, in activating vectors of concern within the reader that are likely to continue resonating for some time to come. In this sense the overall schema which is being created by the story constitutes a part of the reader's continual creation of the self through the work of the emotions. To put it another way, a schema (in the formal sense) is only a part of what the story brings into being.

5.5 Narrative, Cognition, and Feeling

The evidence I have analysed suggests that the cognitive approach to representing narrative inherent in schema theory is not adequate to representing literary texts. It cannot account either for the indeterminacy of literary texts or for the variety of different and often conflicting readings that result from the same text. Such models of narrative imply that the feelings that arise in the reader are an after effect of reading, playing no role in the comprehension process itself. But the responses to the Woolf story show significant differences in comprehension from the outset which can be traced in part to distinctive differences in readers' feelings, to prior value systems concerning communication, relationships, parties, and the like. In this respect, a reader is primed to respond in characteristic ways, to read the environment for signals that impinge on issues of current concern. At the outset of a narrative the reader is thus ready to put into operation a set of feeling controls to manage the self relevant issues she has identified. It is these controls, I argue, that direct subsequent decoding of the narrative, resolving indeterminacies or conflicts between schemata and similar failures at the cognitive level of comprehension. Above all, as literary narratives defamiliarise standard schemata, the feeling controls must negotiate the production of new meaning, that is, they manage the process of schema creation.

Clearly, more research is needed to relate this model of feeling to existing approaches to narrative, which have convincingly accounted for a range of cognitive features of comprehension in the case of simpler, non literary narratives. Some major revisions would be required, however. For example, what readers recall following the processing of a literary text is probably reconstructed in part from states of feeling and their implications. Thus feeling provides a higher order control over memory than the narrative summary or gist proposed by Kintsch (1998). Individual differences in response must also be accounted for by showing the relation of schema knowledge to individual concerns. Put most simply, schema relationships of the type analysed by Graesser (1981) or Semino (1997) provide certain building blocks of narrative structure that are independent of any reader, but readers then colour the structure according to their own feelings, and each produces a higher level structure for the whole story that is more or less unique.

Perhaps the most challenging issue is the problem of schema-creation, which none of the cognitive models tackles. As literary narratives tend to defamiliarise the schemata that the reader brings to them, a process which in itself is likely to arouse feeling, the reader must have recourse to an interpretative level which is prior to schemata. The reports of readers show that in response to narrative a reader often becomes self aware, conscious of entertaining hopes or fears for the characters; readers feel curiosity, and respond to the challenge to understand (this includes the readers of the Woolf story reported above, despite the somewhat artificial framework imposed on their reading). In conditions of uncertainty, when narrative elements cannot readily be assigned to existing schemata, the reader's current concerns (Klinger, 1978) are activated. Thus, to read a literary narrative is to rehearse the implications for the self of the situations and events portrayed. Out of the feelings of self reference, therefore, emerge the schemata which will be adequate to understanding the narrative. But understanding this process better undoubtedly forms one of the most difficult problems confronting empirical research.

The present model of response to literary narrative suggests several approaches to understanding the relation of emotion to cognitive processes. It may be true that emotion often functions as an appraisal mechanism or stimulus evaluation check (Leventhal & Scherer, 1987), or coordinates switches between cognitive plans in changing circumstances when behaviour is interrupted (Oatley & Johnson-Laird, 1987). But these models of emotion seem less able to account for the feeling components of the response to complex narratives of the kind I have outlined in this chapter. Although the ambivalence or disfunctionality of schemata may be a cause for anxiety in normal experience, leading to withdrawal or pathological behaviour, it must be assumed that the readers of literary texts seek the experience of defamiliarisation. Narratives allow us to redefine, modify or suspend schemata, but through this process it seems likely that the primary goal of reading is to explore the feelings of the self through engagement with the text. The feelings invoked by narrative episodes and their outcomes allow the reader to enact symbolically various implications for the self. One effect may be to alter the felt valency of existing schemata, and thus their relationship to other elements within the cognitive system, as well as to bring into being new (and possibly more adaptive) schemata.

Of course, literary texts have a variety of functions. At this point psychological analysis must be supplemented by the resources of the critic, able to reflect on the ways in which readers and texts are situated within a culture. What feelings are drawn upon during response, and what potential schemata are actually realised will be the result of complex interactions between the text and the previous experience of the reader (including experience with other texts of the same kind). The purpose of the present chapter has been to examine one text in detail in order to demonstrate psychological processes of response not accounted for by the schema based models of narrative structure. In this analysis, the primary focus has been on the constructive role of emotion in going beyond the initial schemata of response.

• CHAPTER SIX •

Feelings in Literary Reading: Five Paradoxes

6.1 Feelings and Literary Reading

Well, my feelings changed a lot during this passage. At first, I was thinking of times when I get really frustrated and cry and scream. I feel like something else, some kind of spirit is possessing me. It sort of reminded me of that kind of feeling. And, I guess, it's sort of like a feeling of death, like something must be happening beyond the world that is just unexplainable. And the way that she was yelling, "Free! Free!" reminded me of just a desire to get away sometimes and escape from the world.

This is one reader's response to the climactic episode of Kate Chopin's "The Story of an Hour" (see Appendix for the text of this story). At this point the protagonist believes her husband has been killed, and she is overwhelmed quite unexpectedly by the realization that she is now free. Almost all the readers we have studied, encountering the story for the first time, are surprised by this turn of events; quite are few are shocked by it. The degree of feeling shown by this particular reader, then, is not unusual, although her response is more detailed and expressive than many.

In the study of reading that enabled us to elicit this response, we presented readers with the Chopin story in four sections, and asked readers to stop after each section in order to think aloud about their responses. Readers' commentaries were tape-recorded and later transcribed. Our readers were recruited from senior courses in English at the University of Alberta. This reader is reflecting on her experience of the story after the third section (which ended: "'Free! Body and soul free!' she kept whispering").

The story by Chopin is often anthologized and has been praised for the feminist implications of its critique of conventional marriage, daring for its time (it was first published in 1894). This is not what our readers saw in the story, however, although most realized that the marriage in the story was being called into question. Whether any of our readers would have gone on to formulate an understanding of the story consistent with the feminist perspective we cannot know. Notably, however, readers tended to figure out what the story meant to them as they went along; even the few who began with a preliminary thesis after reading the first section were usually obliged to change their minds while reading the third section, and certainly by the time they read the last sentence of the story; and, typically, it was the reader's feelings occurring while she read that tended to shape her understanding.

This brief account of how readers responded to Chopin's story contrasts with the widely current view that readers bring meaning to the literary texts they read. According to Stephen Mailloux (1982), for example, "literary texts and their meanings are never prior to the employment of interpretive conventions; they are always its results. Texts do not cause interpretations, interpretations constitute texts" (p. 197). For the reader cited above, on the other hand, the succession of feelings that she reports appears to play the major role in constituting the text, beginning with her comment "my feelings changed a lot during this passage." The feelings, in turn, appear to be driven by her immediate engagement with the details of the text. While feeling may be driven by convention (some of our readers were clearly influenced by their feelings for the sanctity of marriage), I suggest that feeling also provides a forum for questioning or transcending convention. Feeling provides an important, partly text-driven source for literary understanding. Insofar as feeling drives interpretation, then, the text itself plays a significant role in shaping the meaning it comes to have for a given reader.

That feeling during reading plays a key role in representation has recently been pointed out by Keith Opdahl (2002, p. 23). Feeling, however, is a vehicle for more than the content of a text: it has distinctive properties that are responsible for the perspective-setting, the shifts or reversals, the surprises that occur during reading, the "affective shifting and sliding," as Susan Feagin termed it (1996, p. 74). As Noel Carroll (1997) suggests, emotions in response to fiction organize our attention to matters of plot, character, and the like, and help us anticipate or watch out for what may be to come (p. 192). These properties give feeling a role quite distinct from the cognitive schemas that also help sustain reading (e.g., Stockwell, 2002), a role that I will describe in what follows in terms of a series of paradoxes. Overall, feeling appears to enable a reader to "frame" a particular meaning, to register it for the time being as a possible component of the story, and to draw if necessary on the reader's prior experience when a feeling matches an occurrence or an issue from the reader's memory. But as feelings shift, or other feelings occur, a particular feeling can be framed in such a way as to call it into question, to place it in a critical context. In this way, the paradoxes of feeling can at times impel changes or reversals, or underlie ambiguities, that are important to the reader's developing understanding.

Some of the paradoxes can be detected at work in the reader's commentary I cited above. In temporal terms, feeling can either situate us within a moment of time ("I was thinking of times when") or outside time, which the reader may be evoking in her desire to "escape from the world." Feeling can also act as an inhibition to action ("I get really frustrated") or an incentive to action ("a desire to get away"). Inherently paradoxical, also—or so it has generally been regarded—is the reader's capacity to experience real feelings for fictional characters or their situations, as the reader here appears to do. Another paradox of literary reading is the experience of pleasure while reading of negative events (loss, suffering, death). Although this is not directly apparent from the reader's third commentary, her enjoyment of the story is shown by one of her concluding comments: "I feel that this is a very powerful story." I consider each of these paradoxes in more detail below.

The topic of feeling in literary response has been the occasion for a small but growing volume of research papers and books, and among these several of the paradoxes of feeling have been considered (e.g., Yanal, 1999), with empathy receiving the most attention (Keen, in press). In her recent outline of feelings in fiction, for example, Nussbaum (2001, p. 272) considers empathy, but also draws attention to three other possible realms of feeling: feelings for the the sense of life created by the implied author; a renewed feeling for one's own possibilities in response to fiction; and delight at coming to understand. Other taxonomies of the feelings that reading elicits have also mentioned empathy (e.g., Kneepens and Zwaan, 1994), alongside evaluative feelings, or the aesthetic feelings of response to literary form (Miall and Kuiken, 2002). A topic less often considered has been the processes of literary reading that may be distinctively embodied by feeling, as I discussed in the previous chapter; these include the anticipatory role of feelings, especially their capacity to guide the unfolding of response to aesthetic form (Miall, 1995), and the power of successive feelings to modify the understanding of the self (Kuiken, Miall, & Sikora, 2004). Another important scheme is Sternberg's (1978) account of the temporal dynamics of narrative, based on three cardinal narrative feelings: suspense, curiosity, and surprise.

No doubt there is much still to be explored in relation to this array of feelings in literary response, especially the question of how feeling relates to cognitive modes of understanding (given the recent emergence of cognitive poetics), that is, to what extent feeling takes control of the reading process, or complements the cognitive processes of reading, or perhaps only supplements cognition as an after-effect. No doubt empirical study could show feeling functioning in all three roles, depending on the context and on the reader.

A second question we have raised before (Miall and Kuiken, 1999, 2002) is whether literariness can be identified with some specific feeling processes in the reader, given that feeling plays many of the roles we have mentioned in ordinary life as well—we have empathy for real people; we experience suspense about how, for example, a political crisis will unfold; and we discover our own possibilities in circumstances other than the reading of fiction. In one critical tradition, that of Hindu poetics, it has been held that a unique aesthetic emotion, the *rasa*, is the aim of literary experience (see Hogan, 2003, pp. 47; Oatley, 2004, p 107; Reddy, 2001, p. 57). How far this concept can find an equivalent in western poetic theory or empirical study is not yet clear. To what extent the paradoxes of feeling I will discuss provide a distinctive *literary* mode of response is a question I defer until later.

In this chapter, then, I will present five dimensions of feeling that appear to be significant for literary response, especially as they offer avenues for developing responses that are probably distinct from normal cognitive processes. What distinguishes them is what I will term, rather loosely speaking, their paradoxical nature, a feature that has already motivated considerable discussion of the first three dimensions as I will point out. Thus one theme of the discussion will be the extent to which feeling provides the matrix for a switch of perspective, not unlike the familiar gestalt pictures of the young woman/old crone, or the vase/two faces profile. In addition to analysing its implications, I will show the dynamics of each dimension by referring to passages from the Chopin story, "The Story of an Hour"; I also consider additional readers' responses to the story in order to demonstrate ways in which readers appear to be aware of some of the dimensions I outline.

6.2 Feeling Real Feelings for Fictional Characters

This is undoubtedly one of the most frequently discussed issues raised by response to fiction or drama. How can I, knowing that the characters before me on the stage or described in the novel I am reading are purely imaginary, experience feelings for them, such as joy or fear, or a sadness so intense that I may actually weep. The debate goes back to the eighteenth century. Most prominently, Dr. Johnson asserted that when watching a play we are never deceived into believing the reality of what we see. Lord Kames, in contrast, described the illusion of seeing a play as a "waking dream" where the reason is suspended. This was followed by Coleridge's more nuanced claim, that literary reading calls for "that willing suspension of disbelief for the moment, which constitutes poetic faith" (Coleridge, 1983, II, 6; cf. Burwick, 1991, pp. 27–32). While it is Coleridge's phrase that has become the most frequently cited, it is not clear that is has always been well understood, nor is it clear whether it points towards an answer to the problem, except that included in Coleridge's will is the role of feeling. Among the scholars I discuss below questions of belief range from a Kamesian to a Johnsonian attitude.

In their discussion of the issue Livingstone and Mele (1997) propose that reader's feelings during fiction depend on two assessments: the reader's assessment of the coherence of the truth presented in the fictional world; and pragmatic aspects, that the feelings evoked by circumstances in the real world would apply in the fictional world (pp. 168–173). This seems to imply that readers make a prior cognitive assessment of truth and correspondence. But, as we have seen in some of our empirical studies, readers often experience feelings almost at once in response to a fiction, before such judgements have any evidence on which to unfold. They also consider Gregory Currie's supposition that we respond to fiction as if someone (the fictional author) were telling the story as fact. The emotions of the work provide evidence that the fictional author experienced them; the reader is thus capable of experiencing the same emotion, except that his state is one of "make-belief" (pp. 162–3). This seems to reaffirm Coleridge's suspension of disbelief.

Levinson (1997) also suggests that we imagine or make-believe in fictional characters in order to have emotions about them (p. 25; cf. Walton, 1990). Emotions toward fiction lack both belief and the motivational consequences of ordinary emotions, so such emotion is not *literally* an ordinary emotion (p. 26). He continues: "to classify our emotions for fictions as imaginary is to say that they are ones we *imagine* ourselves to be having, on the basis of experiences, contributory to emotion, that we are actually having" (p. 27). Levinson also proposes that the object of emotion is a surrogate object we are reminded of, such as the work itself or its parts, or real individuals for whom we feel care, resentment, or the like—this is known as the shadow-object proposal (pp. 22–3). This approach, however, is dismissed by Susan Feagin (1997) as not literary: "Explanations of art emotions in terms of beliefs, desires, or even ideas that a reader already has is a formula for philistinism" (p. 60). Yet it is the basis of another of Currie's (1997) proposals: that an answer to the problem of why we have a feeling of caring towards fictional characters should also account for real situations where we feel others' emotions, i.e., that empathy towards fictional characters should be amenable to the same explanation as towards real people (p. 57). This conflict, as I will suggest below, is to confuse the origin of emotions with their aesthetic consequences.

Oatley and Gholamain (1997) propose identification as one of the core components of reading fiction. We wish to become in part a character in the story, or wish to be elsewhere, to be a hero, etc. Thus we simulate a character's plans and goals with resultant emotions (pp. 268–9). Carroll (1997), on the other hand, argues that identification with characters is inadequate as a general account of emotion in response to fiction (p. 206); yet his account seems ambiguous. In his consideration of the paradox of feeling emotions while reading fiction, he notes that emotions do not always require beliefs; they may involve thoughts, or a pattern of attention: a thought can be held unasserted, yet raise emotions (p. 209). As a result "we may have emotional responses to fictions concerning situations, persons, objects, and things that do not exist. For we can imagine or suppose that they exist, and entertaining unasserted the propositional content of the relevant thoughts can figure in the etiology of an emotional state" (p. 210). But to "imagine or suppose" seems to take us once again towards the willing suspension of disbelief, Coleridge's phrase for "supposing."

While these discussions are informative, they make apparent that a convincing explanation of the paradox of fictional feelings is not yet available. The problem in the previous accounts, I suggest, comes from too narrow a focus on the immediate context of feeling. The arguments of Walton (1990) provide a transition to the larger view that I wish to put forward. Walton proposes that in experiencing feelings while reading fiction we are engaged in a game of make-believe and that our feelings are "quasi-feelings." Participation is key to the representational arts as well as to games: "imagining something . . . seems to involve, perhaps necessarily, imagining (oneself) believing or knowing it" (p. 214). At the same time, feelings in response to art or literature are not the same as real feelings: they are "fictional" feelings (p. 247). This is not to underestimate the power of such experiences, as Walton suggests: "having or expressing certain feelings in a dream or fantasy or game of make-believe is the means by which one achieves insight into one's situation, or empathy for others, or a realization of what it is like to undergo certain experiences, and so on" (p. 272). And, he adds, from within the experience, the world of the fiction seems real. This is his answer to why we should care about fictional characters: the function of the experience has some similarity to that of dreams and daydreams—the opportunity to rehearse feelings in particular situations; the purging of undesirable feelings, the working through of conflicts (p. 272).

What Walton's account suggests (although this is not discussed directly), is that the invitation of fiction is that we imagine being a particular kind of person, one with the requisite knowledge and feelings to act as an observer or participant in the unfolding narrative. To adopt this position is not necessarily to coincide with that of a particular character—the claim that is supposed to underwrite the experience of empathy. Rather, this position is close to that of the narrator (whatever type of narrator that happens to be); the basis of the fictional experience is that we share in the imaginative act of narrating, moment by moment, the unfolding fiction. This, I argue, is the basis for understanding the long-standing problem over the puzzle that we seem to experience real feelings for fictional situations and characters. It is important to understand this problem, since the underlying interaction effect is central to the role and meaning of literary experience in many instances: while we are reading we inhabit a different being from our "real" one, but that being draws on our conceptual powers, our memories, and, above all, our feelings.

The act of reading, as Walton reminds us (pp. 271–2), shares important similarities with the experience of dreams, daydreams, or reveries. To engage in a reverie is to become, however slightly, a different person (a possible person, if my reverie is a modest one; an impossible one, outside the realms of my character and endowments, if the reverie is an immodest one). If I anticipate, let us say, my next vacation trip, I populate my mind with the people I will meet, the hills I will walk, perhaps even the conversations I will have. While these mental events are (at this stage) fictions (what Moran, 1994, calls "modal facts": p. 78), they are powerful enough to absorb my attention fully and often to evoke strong feelings. The fact that, in reality, in a few weeks I will actually (if my plans work out) experience something like the events I have imagined, in no way detracts from the power of these imaginations now. While I engage in my vacation imaginings I become another kind of person, not very different from the one I am right now while sitting at home in my armchair or while riding the bus back home after a day at work, but different enough that if my reverie is interrupted there may be a perceptible jolt as I readjust to the current situation, not unlike being awoken from a pleasant dream. To imagine how things might or will be is a way of considering their implications or consequences, and to evoke in advance the feelings that we might experience. Mrs Mallard has such a moment of foresight in #13: "She knew that she would weep again when she saw the kind, tender hands folded in death." This is a capacity we make use of every day to assess potential or hypothetical situations. As Regan puts it after hearing King Lear curse her sister, to cite another example, "O the blest gods! so will you wish on me, / When the rash mood is on" (II.iv.142–3).

The experience of reading fiction is similar, except that the reverie is now directed largely (although not wholly) by the words we read on the page: now it is the author's characters that I imagine, his or her settings that I inhabit and traverse. And because I have lent my imaginative powers to the narrator it is my memories, my feelings that elaborate the fictional situation while I am having the experiences described on the page (in some accounts this is decribed as simulation: see Currie, 1997, p. 68; Oatley, 1999, p. 441). If the writer mentions a house in a secluded valley, it is my memories of houses and secluded valleys that flesh out the appearance and situation of the house. I am not exactly in the position of the author, because I have no power to determine what happens next, whatever my wishes in the matter; my role as reader is more that of a helper, a kind of stagehand, or perhaps a director realizing a sequence of events that have already been scripted. At times, when the fictional point of view is focused on one character (the limited omniscient point of view, or passages of free indirect discourse, or a first-person narrative) I may adopt the position of that character and become him or her, and experience the feelings of that character. As Walton puts it, the reader is "an actor, of a sort, . . . as well as object; he is a reflexive prop generating fictional truths about himself" (p. 242). But fiction, even first-person fiction, usually offers a much wider range of imaginative invitations than that of inhabiting one character, especially since modern fiction (from Defoe's period onwards) is often ironic, enabling the reader to perceive and understand more than the central character understands.

This view is more comprehensive than that of Walton, since it postulates a state of being as a reader as the basis for the experience of feeling (comparable to the states of being we inhabit in reveries). Just as the issue of belief is not relevant for a fully-realized reverie (I can envisage myself walking the hills on my vacation, even though I know my plans might change and I might never actually go there), so is it irrelevant for the reader of fiction: disbelief is not merely suspended (as Coleridge notably claimed: 1993, II, 6) or rendered inactive (as Yanal has argued: 1999, p. 102). This is because, as the case of the reverie demonstrates, feeling and its implications can be active independently of the existence or reality of its objects; or, to put it more precisely, feeling, by virtue of its context as the expression of our state of being and its possibilities, brings into play a reality of its own. Once fiction has instantiated the state of being proper to it (ideally, from the opening sentence of the current fiction), feeling follows its own inherent laws.

This does not eliminate the paradox: we can still be sensible of it at such moments as those when, interrupted in our reading, we surface to the surrounding reality and surprise ourselves that we have been feeling so much for a fictional character, such as Anna Karenina or Emma Bovary. Yet the paradox can also dissolve following such moments when we realize that the feeling of grief or frustration has its correlates in the real world, when we recall that friend X may be in love with an unworthy man like Anna, or we catch ourselves wishing that friend Y was less absorbed by romantic soap operas.

Yet, there is an important difference between the feelings of everyday life and those experienced during fiction, and this appears to be due to the aesthetic issue that, as I noted above, divides Feagin and Currie. Although the feelings of fiction must be amenable to the same explanations as ordinary feelings, as Currie argues, their fate in the fictional context may well differ: fiction does more than rehearse the consequences of feelings with which we are already familiar. As we have pointed out elsewhere (Miall & Kuiken, 2002; and see section 6.5 below), a notable effect of literary fiction is to subject a feeling to a critical context, to modify our understanding of it—a general process occurring in fiction of which, we argued, catharsis (with its modification of hubris by fear and pity) is a specific example.

Actual readers often demonstrate the power and critical significance of their feelings while reading fiction. To examine some fictional invitations to feeling and example responses, I turn to Chopin's "Story of an Hour." Near the beginning of the story, for example, we find successively what we could term situational and reflective empathy. In paragraph #3 we can readily understand the situation of Louise Mallard, hearing of the death of her husband, hence her response "She wept at once, with sudden, wild abandonment." It is not surprising that some readers already feel empathy for the character although we know little about her but her situation. Recognizing a typical impetus to grief, it is as if readers understand how they too could find themselves in that situation and project their own feelings onto the character. In the next paragraph the point of view shifts to that of Louise at the point where her internal state is described in the last clause: "a physical exhaustion that haunted her body and seemed to reach into her soul." A reader feeling empathy here is directly reflecting the feelings of the character. Feelings for characters also occur in other forms than empathy: for instance, rather than feel the grief that is attributed to Louise in #3 a reader may feel sympathy or compassion; and the last sentence (#23) with its ironic twist seems to call for compassion, although not all readers we have studied experience that.

Whether the feelings readers experience for fictional characters are similar to, or the same as, those they experience for real people, literary texts can use feelings to switch perspective in a way that seems less common in ordinary experience. Here, for instance, is the report of one reader responding to the unexpected shift she finds in #11:

> The combination of tension and sorrow is quickly contradicted when, in passage eleven, the threat of a heart attack turns to the realization of freedom, "free, free, free." I found this to be quite shocking as it unexpectedly changed my emotions of the previous occurrences of the story. [18]

At this moment the empathy for the character appears to have vanished, but it provides a potentially salutary experience for the reader, who now finds that the assumptions embedded in her feelings of empathy (as it would appear) were mistaken. A more positive example was reported in an earlier paper (Miall, 1990), where again a reader acknowledged being caught out in a feeling towards a character which seemed inappropriate (the reader says that the current phrase "makes me feel a bit insecure . . . about laughing"). In this way, because feelings for a character, especially empathy, are rather readily evoked, a literary text can situate such a feeling in an unexpected light, calling it into question either tangentially by showing its inadequacy, or by reversing it—possibly an informative experience for the reader.

The feelings discussed in this section, especially empathy, are perhaps the most widely discussed of those that inflect literary response, even though their status, i.e., how they relate to the "real" feelings of ordinary life, remains to be established. But one partial explanation of the readiness with which feelings are evoked by a text may lie in the evolutionary domain. In terms of responses that facilitate survival, it clearly pays to endow with animation what appear to be living entities, and to assess what feelings they may have. Thus we have developed a high sensitivity to the physiognomy of animate entities to the extent that facial or bodily stances emit signals of emotion, i.e., given an identifiable movement we project back from this the emotion state that would motivate it, which then allows us to predict what the organism (if that is what it is) may do next. In the ancestral environment to endow with emotion what later turns out to be a waving bush clearly offers better odds for survival, as Tooby and Cosmides (1990) put it: "Because the costs and benefits of false alarms, misses, hits, and correct rejections are often unequal, the decision rules may still treat as true situations that are unlikely to be true" (p. 411, n. 7). Given the salience of emotions to survival in the environmental and social domains, our readiness to perceive feelings in the literary context is perhaps less surprising: although what we perceive is no more than words on a page, we bring to bear the same "just in case" strategy, which, in this particular case, then allows us not only to educe feelings but also, given the complexities of the narrative context, to refine and educate them.

6.3 Anomalous Suspense and Other Repeat Feelings

The experience of suspense during reading normally involves possible plot events that we have been led to anticipate (does she agree to go to bed with him; does the murderer escape unseen; does the volcano erupt before the village is evacuated). When we reread a story we already know the outcome of all the plot events, thus suspense, which appears to depend on ignorance of such outcomes, should not recur. Yet it does. Richard Gerrig (1993), who has made the closest empirical study of it, has termed this anomalous suspense. For instance, even though the participants in his studies well knew that Charles Lindbergh was the first pilot to successfully cross the Atlantic, providing them with a story in which the facts were called into question led them to measurable delays in endorsing a statement about Lindbergh's success compared with other readers for whom no such questions were raised.

This is odd. But suspense is not the only feeling that can be reexperienced. So too can other significant feelings, which occur in us again when we reread a text. For instance, although we now know that the woman decides not to come to his bed, we experience again the desire of the man, perhaps even more poignantly. We experience again the sense of surprise and liberation of Chopin's character saying "free, free, free!", although we know this is implicated in shortening the time she has yet to live; and we feel again "the coursing blood [that] warmed and relaxed every inch of her body." Clearly, our knowledge of the outcome of the story and of the details yet to come influences our response, yet in central respects the feelings we experienced at the first reading seem insulated from this knowledge; only the secondary consequences or more remote implicatures of the feelings may have changed. Feelings, like suspense, appear to be anticipatory, projecting possible future states of our being (Miall, 1995); such anticipations, encapsulated by the feeling, replay as we re-experience the feeling, regardless of the knowledge we have acquired elsewhere that would influence their outcome. In this respect we can regard such feelings in the literary domain as cognitively impenetrable: they are immune to information that we might expect to change or forestall them, a feature that Frijda (1988) referred to as the Law of Closure. Keats describes this second-reading power of feeling in his sonnet, "On Sitting Down to Read King Lear Once Again":

> once again, the fierce dispute
> Betwixt damnation and impassioned clay
> Must I burn through

The "burn through" of feelings indicates that we take on once again the implications of a feeling, the agenda it presents in this context for understanding or action.

In accounting for the experience of suspense Gerrig argued that it involves a schematic expectancy that outweighs or suppresses the specific (or veridical) information that we possess about what happened (174). In this respect he is proposing a type/token distinction (172), which provides a basis for considering more widely the function of repeat feelings. In the Chopin story, one of the most powerful moments occurs as Louise envisages her future, #19: "Her fancy was running riot along those days ahead of her. Spring days, and summer days, and all sorts of days that would be her own." During a second reading the feeling of time to come at this moment again seems pervasive: it holds out a value that we recognize independently of its context. Louise's specific experience of it is the token through which as readers we experience the meaning and plenitude of all such future hopes, i.e., the type, a value that is not cancelled by our knowing that Louise will shortly be dead. Specifically, as we have noted elsewhere (Miall & Kuiken, 2002), in the literary context such an example of feeling creates an ad hoc class, what we are referring to here as the type. In hierarchical terms (to adapt Glucksberg and Keysar's (1990) account of metaphor) the feeling in most general terms proposes joy in prospect of future days of liberation and self-determination, with Louise's specific anticipations nominated as a specific instance of the class. In horizontal terms, the profusion of days is the central, prototypic feature; whether the days are summer or spring or other sorts is incidental. The power of the feeling lies in this structured ad hoc class, which carries a conviction for the sympathetic reader whether encountered during a first or subsequent reading (and in interpretive terms, invites that initial move of generalization that, for example, facilitates inferences about Louise's marital status).

6.4 Finding Pleasure in Negative Feelings

Literary texts, perhaps for most of their length, deal with feelings of discomfort, anxiety, dismay, loss, and other negative states. Chopin' story is no exception, with the initial reaction of the protagonist to the news of her husband's death and her own death at the end of the story. Clearly, one of the significant enigmas of literary reading is why we willingly turn to texts containing negative feelings and even appear to find pleasure in them. The classic example, of course, is presented by tragedy: why, we must ask, do we subject ourselves to the spectacle of the fall and destruction of an Antigone or an Othello?

Several explanations of this phenomenon have been offered. For example, Nussbaum (2001) locates her account in the cognitive yield of the tragic spectacle: we take pleasure in the negative emotions of tragedy because we come to understand something, and coming to understand is always a pleasure. A painful novel, she argues, "shows us the truth of our situation" (p. 244). Understanding, however, can never be entirely adequate in the case of tragedy: a non-human force, whether the gods, or fate, or blind chance, profoundly influences the course of events, making it clear to us that the protagonist is not in control of events and that understanding them necessarily remains elusive. As Gloucester puts it in *King Lear*, in one of his moments of despair, "As flies to wanton boys are we to th'gods—/ They kill us for their sport" (IV, I, 36–7). Thus, while a degree of immediate causal understanding is possible (of Antigone's obduracy, or the role of Iago's malevolence), tragedy seems designed overall to warn rather than enlighten, to suggest that we think we know more about managing our predicaments than we really do. Even in a story as short as that of Chopin, while the immediate cause of events is clear (including Louise's weak heart), the tragic outcome of her sudden death leaves us balked as readers, taking pleasure in the ironic twist of misunderstanding among the survivors, but wondering how such things can happen.

According to Morreall (1985), our enjoyment of negative emotions remains within certain limits: "we can enjoy negative emotions only when we retain our overall control of our situation" (p. 97), that is, when the situation involved has no immediate consequences for us, as when we have feelings about a past event—or about a fictional one (p. 101). But this seems unsatisfactory when we consider the place of tragedy in the life of the Greeks: it is the lesson about mankind's lack of control over fate that their major tragedies, such as *Oedipus*, are designed to teach, and this surely touches the audience watching as well as the characters on stage.

In a recent paper Hogan (2004) provides an indirect context for understanding the pleasure in negative feelings. His principle theme is the loneliness of human consciousness. He points out that literature not only treats loneliness as a theme, but that literature also interacts with the reader's loneliness. More specifically, "one of the primary functions of literature—along with a range of related cultural practices, prominently including religion—is to defend against or 'manage' loneliness" (p. 138). Through fiction or drama we become intimate, for the duration of the literary experience, with a group of others, sharing not only their lives but, often, their inner thoughts and feelings, giving us the illusion of breaching the barriers of our own loneliness. In this respect, literary reading allows us to recognize and live through the negative feelings in others—an experience relatively uncommon in daily life—and, more importantly, to experience their vicissitudes, consequences, and modifications, in intimate contact with a set of fictional situations. In one respect this is an argument (once again) for the role of empathy. But it has a wider implication. Literature assuages "existential loneliness," as Hogan puts it (p. 139), a central part of which, it can be assumed, is the experience of a range of negative feelings; it is characteristic of such feelings that they are generally socially unacceptable and remain confined to our individual consciousness. As I discussed in an earlier account (Miall, 1995), studies of daydreams have shown that they predominantly deal with negative construals of the self (mistakes, humiliations), states of disease, injury, or death, or unpleasant social situations. This points to the need for processing of such negative experiences. Reading literary texts, I argued, provides a context similar to the daydream, but possibly a more productive and demanding one, given the unfamiliar perspectives within which negative feelings may be presented.

The pleasure of literary reading may thus centrally implicate the re-experiencing of negative feelings from ordinary life, but within a context in which they can be developed, contextualized, and brought into relation with other feelings. The issue, then, is not experiencing negative emotions while we remain safely in control, as Morreall (1985) puts it, but gaining a degree of control through the aesthetic experience. As Nesse and Lloyd (1992) have pointed out, there may be adaptive value in attending to negative feelings that otherwise are likely to be repressed in the familiar social settings for self-expression. This points to an everyday therapeutic role for literary reading, in which the experience of negative feelings in a pleasurable context serves to lighten the allostatic load (the degree of dysregulation in the physiological system, involving blood pressure, the immune system, etc.; Ryff and Singer, 2003). In other words literary reading has beneficial effects for our physical as well as our mental well-being.

6.5 Feelings as Inhibition or Incentive to Action

Feelings, insofar as these are distinguished from emotions (e.g., Damasio, 2003), appear to unfold in bodily experience and processes of thought, hence they would seem to be a disincentive to action. Emotions, in contrast, as the derivation of the word suggests (from French, *mouvoir*) generally seem to indicate action. As Damasio puts it, "emotions are actions or movements, many of them public, visible to others as they occur in the face, in the voice, in specific behaviors" (p. 28). Feeling seems to consists of, or to call for, reflection. In literary response we see this in a local way in the response to foregrounding (Miall and Kuiken, 1994a), where as readers respond to a passage that they find striking stylistically, the pace of reading is slowed; readers often appear to savour the shape and sound of a sentence at such moments, perhaps giving time to allow the feeling to register. On a larger scale feeling may instill a state of inaction that is important in the light of the immediate situation. A fictional example is provided by Chopin's story. Louise is sitting in her room after the first storm of grief is over, #4: "pressed down by a physical exhaustion that haunted her body and seemed to reach into her soul." As the context goes on to make clear, her inaction here is a necessary prelude to the new feeling that will begin to manifest itself shortly, #9: "There was something coming to her and she was waiting for it, fearfully." This can be contrasted to the emotion she goes on to experience, the sense of freedom of the years to come that then impels action, #13: "she opened and spread her arms out to them in welcome."

While this seems consistent with Damasio's distinction of emotions from feelings, it is also incomplete. Some emotions instill inaction: Louise's "storm of grief" (#3) evidently precipitates her long moment of inaction in the chair in her room. On the other hand, the feelings that Louise experiences for the spring day outside her window seem implicated in the forthcoming sense of freedom, since this reaches "toward her through the sounds, the scents, the color that filled the air" (#9).

To leave emotion on one side, it seems too constricting to confine feeling to states of inaction. The agency of feeling as a prompt to action or inaction seems to depend upon local circumstances, which means, specifically, the current condition of the reader. This could mean something as simple as, during reading, coming across an account of a letter being mailed, which reminds the reader of her feelings about an unfinished letter, prompting her to get up, complete it, and put it out for the mail. In this context, it is worth recalling one of the principle findings of Seilman and Larsen (1989), who asked readers of two texts (a literary and a non-literary text) to make marginal marks when they were reminded of something they had experienced. They found that twice as many actor-perspective remindings were elicited by the literary text as with the non-literary text (which was more likely to evoke what they termed "receiver remindings," that is, things read or heard about). It seems quite possible that when such actor-perspective remindings occur to us, the feelings may involve unfinished concerns that call for action (either immediately or as soon as feasible). It seems unduly limiting to assume that literary reading must be confined to a purely aesthetic experience, excluding any interest of the self (as Kant, or the New Critical approach proposed).

Perhaps the most significant role of feeling in this context, however, is the possibility of one feeling confronting another during reading. The most striking example, which we have analysed in more detail elsewhere (Miall and Kuiken, 2002), is that of catharsis. Here the initial feeling of hubris or pride (propelling the actions of the protagonist, in a play such as *Oedipus Rex*) gives way at the tragic crisis to the feeling of fear, a process that includes hubris in the domain of fear and radically qualifies its meaning as well as its capacity to impel action. From the audience's point of view, as Nussbaum (1986) has suggested, for its original Greek audience watching the play was an education in the dangers of their besetting sin, hubris. In this case the propensity for action of a first feeling (hubris) is modified by a second (fear).

On a smaller scale this can be observed in responses we have studied to literary stories, such as Chopin's text. For instance, one reader (A228) was reminded of his own family position in contrast to Louise's sudden access of freedom, observing late on in the story (#16): "It's odd. I've said that a lot, but this woman's constant use of the word free, free, free. Free from her husband, and then, well, I guess that kind of resonates with me. Family obligations." Yet, as he considers Louise's celebration of her forthcoming freedom, his feelings shift dramatically, having seen the implications for marriage: "I find it just very off-putting. I guess just because I'm a guy and I don't think about such matters. But, still. It's weird to just be so drawn in and then to be put back by a movement of thought, ideas that's clearly in the writing." The implications for action in his earlier comments on the story, contemplating liberation from his "family obligations," are suddenly thwarted when he realizes the underlying basis of Louise's claim to freedom. However we might regard this reader's understanding of the story, this moment represents a real shift in his potentials for action, realized at that moment through a confrontation of feelings.

6.6 Feelings as Timeless or as Temporally Marked

In ordinary daily life it seems obvious that feelings, like thoughts or sensations, are subject to decay, change, or extinction within a limited time. As Damasio (2003) points out, feelings can change internally quite rapidly—within a few hundred milliseconds (p. 118). It seems probable, however, that one of the distinguishing features of literary reading is its ability not only to foreground feeling but to prolong our experience of it. This comment parallels the well-known remark of Shklovsky that "The technique of art is to make objects 'unfamiliar,' to make forms difficult, to increase the difficulty and length of perception" (1917/1965, p. 12)—a remark that is supported elsewhere by Shklovsky's reference to the role of feeling in response to literary devices (p. 9). In this way, literature gives feeling power to develop more pervasively, and to deepen its implications for the reader through prolonged consciousness of its presence in a revivified temporal framework.

Certain stronger feelings, on the other hand, seem to have another power, that of representing the timeless. Such a moment seems central to Chopin's protagonist, #18: "she was drinking in a very elixir of life through that open window"—her sense of the timelessness of her future expressing itself in a reference to the drink that makes one immortal. Such moments seem most evident in feelings occurring during a sublime experience. For example, Helen Maria Williams (1798) at the Rhine Falls in Switzerland, after referring to "emotions too strong to be sustained," contemplates "a scene on which, while we meditate, we can take no account of time! its narrow limits seem too confined for the expanded spirit" (I, 63). Coleridge (1957–2002), speaking directly to the issue, asserts that "intense passions have faith in their own eternity" (Vol. II, 2168).

While this phenomenon, of experiencing feelings as though they were timeless, speaks to the control precedence of emotion accounted for by Fridja's (1988) Law of Closure, the issue may be a qualitative one in addition to the degree of intensity of a given feeling. It seems possible that when evoked strongly a feeling presents itself as outside time, as an atemporal experience. In neuropsychological terms this may signal a role for the amygdala, in contrast to the hippocampus where we know that emotions are time-dated when they are recalled. The implications for the self can be profound, as Fridja's Law suggests; but, most indicative, the feeling instantiates a perspective on the meaning of the self that seems inescapable and totalizing, whether for good or ill. For Williams, celebrating her renewed sense of self at the Rhine Falls, the moment "will form an epocha in my short span." In contrast, for one of our readers (C12) commenting on a passage in Coleridge's "The Rime of the Ancient Mariner" where the Mariner is in a state of suspension in the middle of the poem, "this passage reminds me of the times when it seems everything in the world was against me, that I had nothing to look forward to." In other words, he was led to construe his whole life in the light of a negative experience of wrongness outside time. The atemporality of feeling, when sufficiently powerful, thus demonstrates our ability to experience altered states of consciousness in which the meaning of the self is radically modified, in which all that we are becomes translated into the terms of the new, comprehensive state that the feeling signifies.

6.7 Shifts in Perspective

In addition to the intrinsic interest of the five parodoxes I have outlined, and their potential significance for a better understanding of feeling in literary response, their role as vehicles for managing the shifts and ambiguities of a story such as Chopin's can readily be seen. In the summary below I reproduce the main features of feeling already attributed to the story, whether by direct reference to a story passage or by reference to a reader's response:

#3 storm of grief: induces inaction
-- switch from situational to reflective empathy for Louise
#4 inaction: Louise haunted by exhaustion, waiting
#11 reader shock at change in perspective at "free"
#13 action: Louise welcomes sense of freedom
#16 reader's prior feeling modified (obligation to family)
#18 elixir: timeless sense of freedom
#19 token / type of free days to come, resistant to rereading
#23 compassion at unexpected death; pleasure at tragic outcome (fate?)

This listing makes apparent how often feeling can act as a pivotal reference for a change in perspective or understanding. The comparison of #4 and #13 shows Chopin describing a feeling-induced state of inaction that is a necessary preparation for the pervasive feeling of freedom that will supersede it. This sequence of feelings guides the reader in attributing meaning to the protagonist's responses. We have found that for some readers the transition to the second active feeling of freedom is either unwelcome or incredible. One reader, for instance, remarked "I found this to be quite shocking." For another of our readers, as I mentioned above, the realization that the freedom claimed by Louise was problematic for him occurred later at #16. Perhaps a striking feature of the story for all readers is its foregrounding of temporality, again through feeling. While the timescale of the story is signalled by its title, the feelings experienced while Louise waits alone in her room clearly evoke a sense of the passage of time; in contrast, the feeling of joy, the "elixir" that Louise experiences, will last through "all sorts of days," including the day when Louise will weep again, underscoring its timelessness; it is a joy that "has faith in its own eternity." Finally, the sudden twist at the end in which Louise dies, offers its own distinctive pleasure like other tragic denouments, including the realization that those left standing have radically misunderstood the meaning of Louise's death. But this local irony is perhaps overshadowed by the larger irony that the strength of Louise's hopes that make her seem for a moment "like a goddess of Victory" should be so vulnerable to mere accident, a realization that obliges not a weakening of that central, timeless feeling of joy, but its radical recontextualization.

As this brief summary suggests, a number of critical moments in the story (although not all) are essentially managed by pivotal switches in the meaning of feelings inherent to the story, or by the feelings that story passages call up in readers. This is to propose a view of feelings that, as I pointed out in the introduction, lays out an alternative pathway for understanding and charting readers' responses. Such switches in meaning suggest a more dramatic role for feelings, arguing that we navigate a literary text through the shifting perspectives that feelings provide. In this respect we might regard a feeling during reading as an avatar. Feeling is an agent that we adopt (or it adopts us) in the role of a putative experiencer (in the first phase of the feeling process during reading), which, given the intimate relation of feeling to self-concept issues, enables us to experience specific subject positions in the form of characters, situations, settings, language devices, and the like. The term *avatar* was given its contemporary currency by Neal Stephenson's novel *Snow Crash*, where it represents an icon standing in for human presence in the virtual reality world of the *Metaverse*. In literary reading the reflective empathic response to a fictional character provides the clearest example: here we adopt the feelings and perspective of a fictional character in order to experience that character's world. The avatar of feeling is experiential and responsive, but it cannot interact directly with the fictional world. We might consider aesthetic disinterest as a function of the role of feelings as avatars in literary reading. For this reason we can call the feelings in question first order feelings: because feeling is an internal event, in itself it changes nothing outside the self. But it may provide the reader with opportunities to identify and implement an external change (driven by second order feelings), that is, to engage with a real experience in order to understand something or to act on the basis of a new perspective. The reader we cited above, who was led to contemplate his family obligations while reading Chopin, and then said "I find it just very off-putting," seems to have taken a step outside the story. At such a moment the avatar drops out or is put on hold, while the feeling evoked by the story becomes a premise in a real-world issue for the reader. This is another major switch accomplished by feelings: from first order (intrinsic to the text) to second order (extrinsic to the text), where on the basis of a feeling evoked by the text we reconnect to the world around us in order to consider the implications of the feeling for the real self.

This has been an argument for the importance of feelings in literary reading, a discussion that continues investigations begun more than fifteen years ago when it seemed more urgent that it does now to assert the identity of feelings as distinct from cognitive processes (Miall, 1989; Miall and Kuiken, 1994b). But much research still remains, given that the new discipline of cognitive poetics emphasizes interpretive analysis to the neglect, once again, of feelings (Chapter 4). It seems probable that feelings are the most reliable processes of human psychology—which is not to say that feelings are always transparent and that we necessarily understand what our feelings mean. But the evolutionary context in which feelings evolved seems likely to have given us accurate readouts of our immediate relationships to ourselves (the self concept), the social environment of other people, and the natural environment around us. Given that their primary role is to enhance the survival and instrumental capacities of the self, feelings are neither arbitrary nor inaccurate in the meanings to which they conduct us. Studying literary reading is, beyond all other venues for feeling, the royal road to understanding the complexities of feeling, the interactions they have with other psychological processes, and what our feelings may mean for the fate of the self.

CHAPTER SEVEN

The Empirical Approach: A Survey and Analysis

7.1 Introduction: Literary Reading

7.1.1 Literature and Discourse

Literary reading has been a topic of inquiry among scholars of literature and educationalists for nearly three quarters of a century (Richards, 1929; Rosenblatt, 1937).* Among empirical researchers, on the other hand, attention to literature is quite recent, with most studies having been carried out only over the last twenty years. The literary field is fraught with controversy, however. Basic differences over the object of study militate against the emergence of a single paradigm for empirical research. Disagreement over the nature of literature itself centres on whether "literature" is a fundamental category of discourse with distinctive properties or a cultural formation produced during the last two or three hundred years (e.g., Terry, 1997) and sustained by specific conventions (possibly facing extinction in the face of new electronic media). In this chapter, therefore, while it will be possible to elaborate a number of specific components of literary reading that have been studied empirically, at the present stage of research a coherent account of literary discourse remains out of reach.

One notable feature of the research to be discussed is its limited attention to questions of interpretation, or literary meaning. In contrast, mainstream literary criticism has traditionally been dominated by a focus on interpretation, carried out within one of two main traditions: either a hermeneutic approach

* This chapter is based on "Literary Discourse," in Art Graesser, Morton Ann Gernsbacher, & Susan R. Goldman (Eds.), *Handbook of Discourse Processes*. Mahwah, NJ: Lawrence Erlbaum Associates, 2003. It is reprinted here by kind of permission of Lawrence Erlbaum Associates.

centered on the text itself, or a contexual approach that appeals to major cultural formations thought to impose certain requirements on literary production and reception (e.g., gender issues, or the economic and social concerns of the new historicism). When considering reading outside the academy, however, an emphasis on interpretation may be misleading, as Sontag (1964/1983) argued forcefully some years ago. Although readers are at times undoubtedly concerned to understand what they read, this should not overshadow another and perhaps more primary mode of engagement, which is to experience literature—whether to appreciate its formal qualities, be aroused by a suspense filled plot, or to suffer empathically the vicissitudes of its fictional characters. To be asked to generate an explanation of a literary work, as commonly occurs in the literature classroom or in many empirical studies, is perhaps atypical of most reading situations. Yet it is clear that the demand for techniques of explanation has tended to drive research on reading, which has been dominated by the prevailing cognitivist emphasis on the processes of comprehension (Kintsch, 1998). This will be considered further in the studies described below; but the limitations of this approach to literary discourse will also be suggested, preparatory to outlining a range of other approaches to literary reading.

The predominant questions of this chapter are: What is literary discourse? and does it result in a type of reading different from that studied in mainstream discourse processing research? Among a number of possible markers of the distinction between literary and non-literary processing to be discussed below, empirical research suggests that literary readers form specific anticipations while reading, that the interpretive frame may modify or transform while reading a literary text, and that markedly more personal memories are evoked during reading. There is evidence for a constructive role for feeling in the reading process, a process that may in part be driven by response to stylistic and other formal qualities. First, however, I sketch the relationship between empirical research and mainstream literary scholarship, since this continues to provide an important, if problematic, context for considering literary issues and framing empirical studies. While the gulf between literary scholarship and empirical research remains wide, three issues in particular will serve to illustrate the difficulties and prospects of this relatively new discipline: the history of reader response theory, the role of genre, and the question whether literature has distinctive qualities.

7.1.2 The Role of the Reader

Although reader response study had its inception with the work of I. A. Richards in his book *Practical Criticism* (1929), Richards's one foray into empirical study had the unfortunate effect of suggesting to the community of literary scholars that readers, as represented by the undergraduate students he studied at

Cambridge University, were poor at discriminating between poems, badly in need of the guidance of the experienced literary critic (cf. Martindale & Dailey, 1995). The experience of the ordinary reader, in contrast to the professional reader, thus fell under a cloud, a fate confirmed twenty years later by the influential essay "The affective fallacy" of Wimsatt and Beardsley (1954/1946). This effectively placed an interdiction on attention to actual readers, whose responses were deemed impressionistic and relative. The critic E. D. Hirsch (1967, p. 204), for example, referred to the ordinary reader's "whimsical lawlessness of guessing" at literary meaning, an initial first step subject to correction in the light of what could be determined about the author's intention.

When reader response criticism eventually emerged, with publications by Holland (1968), Fish (1970/1980b), Iser (1978), and Jauss (1982), Holland's work was confined to developing his own psychoanalytic approach which concentrated almost exclusively on the stories of individual readers. On the other hand, Fish, Iser, Jauss, and their followers remained at the level of theory. Fish proposed an "affective stylistics" of reader's hesitations and errors that he considered an integral part of literary meaning. Iser, drawing on the phenomenology of Ingarden, placed reading within the reader's "horizon of expectations," in which the text's gaps and indeterminacies called for constructive interpretive work. Jauss, who worked alongside Iser at the University of Constanz, developed a reception theory attentive to historical changes in literary reading. Although this work, offering new and suggestive theories of reading, has been influential in redirecting attention to questions about the reader, this generally consisted in postulated reader-based modes for interpreting literary texts. The study of actual readers was either neglected or actively discouraged. Culler (1981, p. 129), for example, suggested that study of actual readers would be fruitless, since the critic's focus of research should be on the conventions that he considered paramount in determining all reading, whether literary or nonliterary. These conventions could be examined in the numerous interpretations already available in the professional literature on a given text.

On the one hand, then, critics such as Fish or Iser hypothesized specific reading processes that were based on demonstrable features of literary texts and their purported effects. On the other hand, it turned out that attention to such features was constituted from the start by conventions of reading. Since readers were thought to acquire such conventions through a process of training, usually in the classroom, professional attention shifted away from considering what individual readers might actually be doing. Among the most influential formulations of this view, Fish's (1980a) forceful and widely accepted assertion that the "interpretive community" to which a reader belonged determined any possible reading, appeared to make reading a purely relativistic process. The comprehensiveness of this approach, which redirected attention away from the reader towards questions of culture and history, foreclosed attention to reading almost as soon as it had begun: the reader response project was described by one of its reviewers as "self-transcending" and "self-deconstructing," suggesting "that it has a past rather than a future" (Freund, 1987, p. 10).

Yet the issues raised by the reader response theorists were of considerable interest, and in various ways continue to be reflected in empirical studies of literary reading. Thus Schmidt (1982) and his colleagues, although motivated by a research tradition quite different from that of Fish, have placed the conventions of reading at the centre of their approach. They have hypothesised that literary reading depends on two conventions: (1) the *aesthetic* convention (opposed to the *fact* convention that is held to apply in regular discourse); and (2) the *polyvalence* convention (opposed to the *monovalence* convention), that is, the supposition that in a literary context readers will recognize the possibility of multiple interpretations of the same text. If reading is held to depend on the acquisition of the appropriate conventions, we might also consider the impact of literary training on reading. This issue has motivated several studies of literary expertise, where the range of interpretive strategies shown by novice and expert readers has been investigated through empirical study (e.g., Graves & Frederiksen, 1991; Hanauer, 1995a). If readers differ according to their local interpretive community, then cultural differences in reading the same text should also be discernible. This topic has been the focus of empirical studies by László and his colleagues (e.g., László & Larsen, 1991).

Other approaches that develop the suggestions of reader response theory will be considered in more detail below. Meanwhile, two other specific issues raised by literary scholarship should also be outlined.

7.1.3 Genres

Perhaps the most significant convention dominating contemporary literary scholarship is that of genre. While interpretation has tended to dissolve the distinctiveness of the text by relating it to underlying structures of power and desire, genre focuses attention again on the specific qualities and structures of the text. The features of a text are determined by its particular generic form. Genre, which used to be considered descriptive, is thus now considered explanatory: genre is held to embody certain social roles that govern the relation between text and reader. As Bawarshi (2000, pp. 346–7) puts it, "genres create a kind of literary culture or poetics in which textual activity becomes meaningful"; they "constitute the social reality in which the activities of all social participants are implicated." Genre is said to provide an essential framework for reading. As Derrida (1980, p. 65) insists, "a text cannot belong to no genre, it cannot be without or less a genre. Every text participates in one or several genres, there is no genreless text." In this respect, genre can be understood as the defining context for all textual behavior, literary and non-literary, constituting textual relations in such spheres as the university classroom (lectures, the production of assignments), the law court (speeches for the defence, instructions to the jury), as well as readers' engagments with plays, novels, or sonnets. Moreover, genre governs what Halliday (1978) referred to as the "register" apparent in any given text, that is, the semantic and syntactic features that create the communicative situation, including the stance of the participants (cf. Viehoff, 1995, p. 73).

While Bawarshi (2000) argues that the primary theoretical question is whether genre is regulative or constitutive, he gives little consideration to the possibility of variance or play within a given genre. Our response to a sonnet, for example, is a product both of our relation to its obligatory formal features as well as to the distinctive semantic or formal qualities that the writer has embodied within the constraints of the form. The rules of genre allow us to specify both what is conventional and unexpected (a view that would suggest that the laws of genre are regulative). As discourse structures, therefore, genres are characterized in part by the types of story grammars, or schemata they call for; they specify situation models that characterize a given literary text and enable us to make predictions about how the text is likely to unfold. In this respect, genre theory provides a potentially rich resource for more precise empirical studies of literary reading, enabling us to build on the research (which is so far not specific to literary reading) on how readers construct and monitor situation models (Zwaan & Radvansky, 1998).

While differences between discourse types have received some attention (e.g., Zwaan, 1993), the laws of genre have received little consideration in empirical research on literature. If they exist with the force that has been attributed to them, then we might expect to find traces of their presence everywhere in the data obtained from readers. For example, when the readers studied by Brewer and his colleagues (e.g., Brewer & Lichtenstein, 1981) reported suspense only in the case of stories with appropriately ordered components, this seems to reflect genre expectations: a story that arouses suspense must also satisfy it, otherwise it is considered ill-formed. My study of responses to a short story by Virginia Woolf (Chapter 5) can be seen as the hesitation of readers as they tried first one genre (a romantic story about a relationship) then another (a story about the impossibility of forming genuine relationships). In brief, empirical study which, so far, has tended to take genre for granted, stands to benefit from the more detailed specifications of genre knowledge available from literary scholarship.

7.1.4 Literariness

Empirical studies have also replicated, in foreshortened form, a debate that was central in literary theory until recently: whether literary texts enjoy some distinctive status or "literariness." Although the term "literariness" was first coined by Jakobson in 1921 (Erlich, 1981), conceptions of literature that imply its distinctiveness from other types of text are apparent in discussions from Plato (who wished to banish literature from his Republic) and Aristotle up to Coleridge and beyond. Recent theorists, on the other hand, in emphasizing the conventional nature of literary response, have dismissed the argument that literary texts are distinctive by virtue of specific features. In Eagleton's (1983, p. 10) view "Anything can be literature" or "can cease to be literature" depending upon the doctrine currently in force. More specifically, Fish (1989) has objected to the notion that literary texts contain distinctive formal features. Since formal aspects of language cannot guarantee stable meaning, as students of stylistics had tried to claim, there can be no formal aspects of language; these are an illusion.

Similar arguments have been made by prominent scholars in the empirical domain. Van Dijk (1979), for example, proposed that the cognitive processes shown to underlie text comprehension applied to all discourse including literature: "our cognitive mechanisms will simply not allow us to understand discourse or information in a fundamentally different way" (p. 151); "therefore, we strictly deny the completely 'specific' nature of so-called 'literary interpretation'" (p. 151). The differences, such as they are, are said to lie primarily in the pragmatic and social functions of literature. Similarly, the constructivist approach of Schmidt (1982, p. 90) led him to suggest that locating the attributes of literariness in the surface features of texts is an "ontological fallacy"; it is "the human processes performed on such features that define the attributes in question."

This controversy has been framed as a contrast between conventionalist and traditionalist approaches (Hanauer, 1996; cf. Zwaan, 1993, pp. 7–12). The argument is a problematic one, however, since the two positions focus on different aspects of the reading process. While the conventionalist examines reading for the effects of prior cognitive frames, whether prototypes, genres, or schemata (e.g., Schmidt, 1982, pp. 135–6; Viehoff, 1995), the traditionalist focuses on specific text features such as metre or personification, and attributes changes in readers' feelings or evaluative responses to this source (e.g., Hunt & Vipond, 1986; Van Peer, 1990). This might suggest that two different systems of response are at issue, one based on cognitive processes, the other on affective processes, and that the latter might be more appropriate for embodying what (if anything) is unique to literary processing. Perhaps the conventionalist has simply been looking in the wrong place. However, the question is not as simple as this might make it seem. Feelings are also subject to conditioning by convention, and readers' evaluations are clearly bound up with the norms imposed by a specific local culture. Thus convention may operate here too, although in a less apparent and measurable form.

On the other hand, some of the features said to be distinctive to literary texts may have been dismissed too readily. For example, while Gerrig (1993, p. 100–101) agrees with the conventionalist position in asserting that "The 'look' of the language . . . cannot differentiate factual and fictional assertions," he cites a short fictional extract in which a character is described surveying the people in a department store, "studying the crowd of people for signs of bad taste in dress" (p. 99). The limited omniscient narrative mode, of which this is an example, provides access to a character's mind in a way that is distinctive to fiction (one of its characteristic markers is free indirect discourse). In this respect, the feature cited by Gerrig is unmistakably "literary" and could only occur in another context in violation of that context's genre rules (for example, if a journalist were to impute thoughts to a person in a news article). Another example comes from the field of poetry, where sounds effects are often distinctive and measurable. As Bailey (1971) showed, compared with ordinary language, higher frequencies of a particular phoneme group can be shown to occur in poetry; it seems possible that this will influence a reader's response. While empirical studies in this area are sparse (e.g., Tsur, 1992, pp. 25–29), such phonetic features, like free indirect discourse, seem to be characteristic of literary discourse and deserve more careful examination. The principal issue will be, not their presence as such, but whether it can be shown that readers of literary texts are influenced by them in measurable ways.

7.1.5 Theoretical Issues

In comparison with the often divisive debates that have occurred in mainstream literary scholarship, empirical researchers have generally been preoccupied with other theoretical issues. Reviews of earlier empirical work in North America (e.g., Purves & Beach, 1972) show that workers in the field were primarily concerned with improving educational practices. In her review, Klemenz-Belgardt (1981) criticizes extant studies for offering poorly theorized views both of literary response and of the literary texts under examination. While the studies helped to inform classroom practice, the result was an under-theorization of the nature of literary response (cf. Galda, 1983). Over the last twenty years, however, researchers have drawn upon a much wider and better developed set of theoretical contexts, ranging across discourse processing theories, psycholinguistics, social psychology, personality theory, emotion theory, and psychobiology, in addition, of course, to several branches of literary theory. However, a consensus on theoretical issues has yet to emerge.

A new paradigm for research has been claimed by Schmidt and his colleagues, known as the Empirical Science of Literature, or ESL. ESL undertakes to widen the focus to the actions within the literary system as a whole, including producers, readers, publishers, and critics. In this way, it is argued (Hauptmeier & Viehoff, 1983; Schmidt, 1983), ESL will bring about a Kuhnian paradigm shift, establishing a scientific program of research on literature, one independent of hermeneutic assumptions. Among the theoretical bases of ESL, literary study is based on a theory of human action. It also gives up all ontological commitments, notably the view that there is an essential "literariness" that distinguishes literary texts. In this perspective, literature is an outcome of linguistic socialization carried out in the interests of social groups; thus "literariness cannot be regarded as a textual property but as a result of actions of analysis and evaluation performed by subjects within an action system" (Schmidt, 1983, p. 31). Perhaps the best known aspect of Schmidt's work has been to define literary response in terms of the aesthetic and polyvalence conventions, a claim that has prompted some empirical study (e.g., Meutsch & Schmidt, 1985).

Outside Germany, however, the theoretical claims of ESL have not been generally accepted by other empirical researchers. Viehoff and Andringa (1990) assert that the Empirical Science of Literature model "is nearly without any psychological relevance in literary reading processes" (p. 223). Within Germany, too, the principles of ESL have been disputed: Groeben (Schmidt & Groeben, 1989) argues that Schmidt's radical constructivism has no way of assessing the subjectivity of responses: without independent descriptions of a text, any response must be accepted. Groeben is concerned that appropriate and inappropriate responses should be distinguishable, implying a normative framework for understanding. As he went on to suggest (Groeben & Schreier, 1998), Schmidt's polyvalence convention itself implies a norm. If readers fail to follow the convention, "they are by definition not participating in the literary system," which is only one step from saying that literary readers "must strive for polyvalence" (p. 58).

In fact, normative conceptions of literary response seem inescapable, although they are rarely acknowledged in the studies to be discussed below. This is shown, firstly, by the choice of literary texts of acknowledged quality in most studies, sometimes in comparison with manifestly non-literary texts (such as extracts from newspaper articles). Studies of response with sub-literary genres, such as popular fiction, have been less common (e.g., Nell, 1988; Hansson, 1990). Secondly, certain qualities of literary response, such as polyvalence, personal relevance, or a sensitivity to poetic features, imply qualitatively different, and hence, desirable dimensions of reading. As Beach and Hynds (1991) put it in their review of the instructional research, researchers may try to avoid privileging particular styles of reading, but "an underlying assumption seems to be that developing a sophisticated *repertoire* of response options to use in a variety of reading situations should be a major goal of literature instruction" (p. 459). Thirdly, although Halász (1995) warns, "We may be inclined to evaluate [the] literary reading process itself as a superior kind of reading," investigating the phenomenon for its own sake in order to understand its processes is but one step from valuing such processes. This step, easily taken, also leads to examining the conditions under which literary reading takes place in education with a view to improving them (e.g., Miall, 1993).

In this respect, the argument over whether literary processes are driven by socially determined conventions or by innate proclivities takes on a new significance. To put it simply, is the literature teacher transmitting an agreed, socially sanctioned technique of reading, or facilitating an inborn facility for literary experience? Although an interaction of the two processes seems most likely, strong arguments have been advanced that only the first view can be valid (e.g., Schmidt, Fish). Since traditional literary scholarship has no way of assessing such an issue outside its own conflicting theoretical perspectives, the empirical study of literature, with its access to a range of powerful theories and methodologies is well placed to play a critical role in this debate.

In the sections that follow, studies of literary discourse and literary response are placed within several different frameworks. This will suggest a problem in theoretical contexts that can be said to exist on two levels. First, it will be suggested that the familiar paradigm of discourse processes is necessary but insufficient as a basis for understanding literary questions. The phenomena involved in experiencing and understanding literary texts such as novels and poems constitute a larger, but still little understood, system of psychological processes within which discourse processes play an essential, but possibly not the most important, role. This is not a new problem: limitations of discourse theory were suggested by Spiro (1982), who contrasted it with experiential understanding, by Hidi and Baird (1986), who called for the inclusion of motivation in reading studies, and most recently by Zwaan (1999), who outlined the limitations of amodal representations in discourse theory. Empirical literary studies provide a promising field for examining some of these alternative perspectives and working towards a better formulation of their role in discourse.

Second, an important theoretical problem is revealed by a difference inherent in two kinds of empirical method. This is evident, for example, when content analysis methods, such as those of Andringa (1990) and Kuiken and Miall (2001), are compared. While the first predetermines categories in which think-aloud data will be located, the second allows categories to emerge from the data itself. While the second method may allow for those categories (such as certain kinds of feeling, or personal memories) that participate in processes distinctive to literary response, its dependence on readers' verbal facility and its closeness to the text being read, may make theoretical generalizations about such evidence problematic. While the first method may inadvertently filter out precisely that which, from another perspective, makes the responses distinctively literary, the second method with its idiographic focus risks limiting its conclusions to the specific case being analysed. The larger problem this suggests is the difficulty of capturing empirically what is distinctive to literary response, given that a specific literary text may call for a mode of response that is more or less unique to that text. Perhaps responses to different literary texts are not entirely incommensurable, but it may be difficult to establish what (if anything) literary response has in common that distinguishes it from other experiences of discourse. The range of approaches to be described below is thus an important feature of the empirical study of literature, helping to maximize the opportunities for triangulating on the significant issues. But like the blind observers in the fable about the elephant, each empirical researcher has a somewhat different conception of the object of study, and certainly none of us has yet seen the whole animal, while others again deny that any such animal exists.

7.2 Discourse Processing

7.2.1 Discourse Structures

While theories of discourse processing in general will not be discussed here, several specific studies will be mentioned in which literary processing is at issue. Its emphasis on comprehension rather than affect gives discourse processes both theoretical power and methodological precision, but also limits its scope in capturing literary processes (Miall & Kuiken, 1994a), as Van Dijk's discussion (cited earlier) suggests. In brief, discourse processing, with its emphasis on comprehension, forestalls attention to those features of literary response that might signal the presence of a different class of response processes. As Spiro (1982) pointed out, referring to a story by James Joyce and the comments made in it by an enigmatic priest, what is central to our experience of the story is that we cannot know what its situation is about. It could be argued that it is just those aspects that resist ordinary comprehension that trigger the response modes specific to literature, such as the emotive, evaluative, and attitudinal. Even this way of putting the issue is, perhaps, misleading, if it implies that the alternative modes of response only come into play when the normal cognitive processes have broken down. It may be more plausible to postulate several systems operating in parallel, as a review of two typical discourse studies will suggest.

In one study Van den Broek, Rohleder, & Narváez (1996) examined the role of causal connections in a story, as revealed by a recall measure. Their model of story understanding proposes that at each statement the reader "attempts to establish *sufficient explanation* for each event or state that he or she encounters" (p. 187). While 50 per cent of the variance in recall could be explained by the causal connections they had modeled, several other factors also appeared to influence recall, such as statements describing setting, those with a strong impact due to emotion or imagery, or statements relating to the theme of the story. Thus causal relationships were found to be a major, but not the only component, of story structure influencing recall. Their model of literary comprehension, as the authors suggest, cannot tell the whole story. In fact, while it makes use of a literary text, the findings illuminate that component of response that may be least significant to *literary* texts.

Another study, Zwaan, Magliano, and Graesser (1995) focused on literary short stories. In order to examine how far the theoretical components of the situation model were reflected in readers' responses, the segments of the story (its successive sentences) were analysed for shifts in causal explanation, shifts in time and space, and for propositional complexity. Analysis showed that each of the factors of the situation model contributed to predicting the time taken to read a sentence. For example, there were longer reading times when the story shifted location, requiring readers to construct another spatial setting. Such situation model components appear to be a necessary dimension of response to any narrative. In a subsequent study, based on a subset of the reader response data of Zwaan, et al., we (Miall & Kuiken, 1999) showed that reading times were predicted as strongly by stylistic features in the sentences of a story (e.g., by alliterative patterns, syntactic deviations, or striking metaphors). It might be hypothesized that only literary texts are likely to influence readers through such effects. How response to stylistic features develops downstream from our encounter with then, however, remains a difficult issue to examine (Miall & Kuiken, 2001).

7.2.2 Expert-Novice Differences

To the extent that literary response is more fully developed in experienced readers, the difference between novices and experts may help to illuminate what is distinctive to literary discourse. Are experts merely more elaborate in their responses, or are there qualitative shifts in response as readers gain expertise? Graves and Frederiksen (1991) employed a form of semantic analysis of readers' comments; Zeitz (1994) measured expertise with comprehension and memory for gist. These can be compared with two other studies by Hanauer (1995a) and Andringa (1996) based on ratings for literariness and for degree of involvement.

In their study of think-aloud data from 8 students and 2 experts, Graves and Frederiksen (1991) asked readers to describe a passage from a novel while reading. The protocols were analysed with "discursive patterns grammar," a form of semantic analysis whose categories were decided *a priori*. Comparison showed that experts provided more complex, inferential descriptions, generating more than 2½ times the number of comments on linguistic structures than the students. Among these, experts' comments were focused more on syntax, whereas students focused on individual word forms. In general, students tended to remain at the level of paraphrase; experts made more inferential, derived descriptions. Zeitz (1994) distinguished between what she called the *basic* representation of a literary text (e.g., what happens) and the *derived* represention (e.g., theme), and proposed that while novices and experts may be alike at the basic level, they would differ at the derived level. She found superior performance of skilled readers on gist-level but not verbatim recall, better recognition of "multi-level sentences" (i.e., those rich in literary style, such as irony or metaphor), a greater facility in producing interpretive sentences, including references to language or themes, and more complex levels of argument in essay responses.

In the terms of Graves and Frederiksen (1991) the reading processes examined in both studies can be characterized as "goal-directed": in both cases readers were instructed to comprehend the texts and to describe them. It is not evident that the methods were appropriate for reflecting what, if anything, is distinctive to literary processing. In the first study it is perhaps significant that up to 10 per cent of readers' comments were discarded as fitting none of the categories, e.g., quotations from the text, comments on thought processes, and general evaluative statements. In contrast, a think-aloud study of Olson, Mack, and Duffy (1981) found that reader's comments about a story or about their own understanding were infrequent, but very diagnostic of those aspects of a story to which a reader was particularly attentive. While expertise, of the kind studied here, reflects in significant ways on how literary training enables readers to analyse texts and report on their features, it seems likely to differ significantly from the processes manifested by those reading for pleasure.

In two other studies, measures of appreciation and involvement by Andringa (1996), and measures of literariness by Hanauer (1995a) appear to indicate types of response in which little difference is found between expert and novice readers. Andringa manipulated story frames or narrator comments in two literary stories in order to vary hypothesized degree of reader involvement. She reports that although with greater literary expertise more complex aesthetic structures can be appreciated, emotional involvement seems to change little. Hanauer (1995a, 1995b), comparing undergraduate and gradate students of literature, presented 12 texts for rating, of which 9 were poems. While experienced readers gave higher ratings overall, suggesting that they were able to recognize more texts as literary, ratings for poeticity correlated rather highly across groups, while the ratings for literariness showed less correspondence. This suggests that training in literature has a greater influence on recognition of literariness than the ability to recognize poetry. Both studies thus suggest ways of discriminating expertise based on aesthetic and affective factors, but so far this line of inquiry has not been pursued further.

7.2.3 Beyond Discourse Processes

Other studies that go beyond the discourse processes model also suggest that affective factors may have a constructive role to play in literary response. For example, Long and Graesser (1991) found that memory for surface structure is stronger in the context of a literary story than theories of comprehension memory have suggested. In their study readers of two short stories, who were tested for recognition of two versions of conversational sentences from the stories, gave 68 per cent correct answers, well above chance level. Additional analyses of the sentences showed that memory was facilitated the closer the style of a sentence to oral discourse, or when a sentence was high in "expressive evaluation"; sentences showing both oral and expressive qualities were best remembered. An affective component consistent with this was proposed by Kintsch (1980), who described "cognitive interest" as a factor supervening on the processes described in the standard text comprehension model. The reader of a story, in contrast to an expository text, "sets up his own control schema" based on his interests, which may differ from the event-based model of the conventional story schema. Following this suggestion, Zwaan (1993, p. 31) proposed a "literary control system." Once a literary work, such as a novel, has been recognized the control system activates a distinctive form of processing that regulates the basic comprehension processes. Kintsch suggested that "stylistic variations . . . serve as cues for invited inferences" (p. 94), and that these and other semantic surprises in literary texts cause the reader to make inferences about matters not stated in the text. In particular, the appearance of interesting items in the story that fall outside existing schemata invite the reader to activate or to construct a schema to account for the story. Alternative processes that construct literary meaning may thus operate in conjunction with the standard comprehension processes (Miall & Kuiken, 1994a).

7.3 Alternative Frameworks of Literary Reading

7.3.1 The Literary Perspective

The reader's knowledge of the genre of a text, as noted above, is a control condition influencing the reading process. Readers' responses will be shaped quite differently according to whether a text is a poem, a newspaper story, or a joke. But the limits of genre as an explanatory factor are suggested by three studies in which genre was manipulated experimentally.

Zwaan (1991) compared the effects of placing reading in either a newspaper or literary perspective. With the help of a pilot study, six texts were chosen from newspapers and novels that could be read either as newspaper or as literary prose (texts were thus devoid of marked literary features). As expected, it was found that in the newspaper condition readers read faster, on average about 12 per cent faster than readers in the literary condition. In a recognition test, the literary condition readers were more accurate in identifying words that had occurred in the text just read. In a second study using the same paradigm (Zwaan, 1994), readers in the literary condition were found to have a poorer memory for the situational information in the texts than the newspaper condition readers. The study suggests that when readers believe themselves to be engaged in literary reading, they read more slowly and form a better representation of the surface structure of the text.

Zwaan's study argues for the regulative functions of genre. On the other hand, genre information is not invariably decisive. As Hoffstaedter (1987) showed, it cannot always take precedence over textual features. She presented 24 poems to readers in two conditions, a newspaper reading condition (modifying the layout of the poems appropriately) and a poetry reading condition. Readers were asked to make judgments of poeticity on a scale from non-poetic to poetic. She reports that for only 10 out of 24 poems were judgments significantly different across the two conditions. For 14 of the poems it was their poetic properties that appear to have determined the reading condition. This study shows how the text features encountered here, such as prominent metaphors, personifications, or unusual syntax, can override the supposed genre in a bottom-up fashion.

The reading framework manipulation is called into question by László (1988): a reader may be told a text is literary but not read it as such. Devising a different method, László implemented changes in the texture of an American and a Hungarian literary story in order to examine effects on both reading times and on reader's deployment of schema knowledge. Three different versions of each story were presented: the Original version, the Insert version (where two or three key passages based on an action sequence had been rewritten in summary form), and a Script version (where the whole story was rewritten in summary form, keeping the plot structure clear). Readers of the Original and Insert versions read the stories on paper, except for the critical passages (original or rewritten) which they read on a computer screen in order to collect reading times, after which they were asked to choose between three alternative plot continuations; they then continued reading on paper. Script readers read the whole story on computer. Both stories were about short-term romances that turned out to be unstable because of social differences, thus suggesting two "themes," a social and a romance theme. László suggests that readers' expectations regarding the "romance" theme might stem from "script-like" cognitive structures (cf. Chapter 5).

László reports that reading times were longest for the Original story, but shorter for the Script than for the Insert version in the case of the American story, while reading times for the Script and Insert versions were the same for the Hungarian. Although these results are equivocal in part, they show that the literary texture of the original stories prompted the longest reading times. On the other hand, the manipulation of the stories had no consistent influence on the plot continuation choices, a finding that seems to show construal of the "romance" plot to be a feature of the discourse level, not the literary level of processing. In this respect, the longer reading times found in both Zwaan's and László's studies can be attributed to the distinctive components of literary processing, at least part of which springs from closer attention to the surface features of texts. One wonders what processes are occurring in literary readers during that extra time. This question is addressed below.

7.3.2 Polyvalence

One answer is suggested by Meutsch and Schmidt (1985). In their conception, literary reading centres on problem-based understanding. Polyvalent constructions are said to reflect the reader's response to reading problems. In their study, readers' think-aloud data was collected in response to either a poem or a short literary narrative and analysed in terms of four classes of response: (1) descriptions of, or (2) comments on the reading process, (3) references to literary conventions, and (4) anticipatory or retrospective comments on text meaning. Among other findings, Meutsch and Schmidt report that a mean of 2.7 changes of frames of reference was found per reader (more in the case of the poem than the narrative), and changes of frames of reference were in general evaluated positively more strongly than they were negatively.

The conception of literary reading as problem-based is questionable, however, especially the assumption of Meutsch and Schmidt that think-aloud responses are only elicited by problems during reading. Readers may be prompted to comment by interest, surprise, pleasure, and other immediate impulses while reading. In a number of instances, however, the presence of more than one meaning, or a transition from one meaning to another, is signalled by such comments. Thus polyvalence appears to be a characteristic of literary reading, although not necessarily in a form that requires readers to entertain several meanings at the same time. However, the study only shows that readers deploy polyvalence during reading, not whether the polyvalence convention is a governing condition of literary reading, as Schmidt and his colleagues have proposed.

Other examples of empirical findings that tend to support the polyvalence conception are provided by Graesser, et al. (1998) and Miall & Kuiken (2001), where evidence for changes in meaning was obtained, although under rather different conditions. Graesser, Kassler, Kreuz, and McLain-Allen (1998) studied changes from the normal schema for time prompted by reading Alan Lightman's novel, *Einstein's Dreams* (1993), where each chapter offers a different deformation of time (e.g., time running backwards, or repeating each day). The findings showed that readers were able to develop conceptions of time inconsistent with their normal conception, not only polyvalently developing conceptions of time across several chapters, but also being able to assess deviation in the time schema in each chapter in relation to the normal model of time.

In one of our studies (Miall & Kuiken, 1995) we asked readers of a literary short story to register shifts in story understanding explicitly while reading, using a modified version of the Remindings paradigm (the paradigm is discussed in more detail below). This instructed readers to mark those segments of the story that they found striking or evocative, then later to describe what memories or shifts in story understanding might have occurred. The story had also been analysed for stylistic effects. We found that the mean number of story shifts per segment reached a peak systematically at around 12 segments following a marked cluster of stylistic features. This sequence of events appeared to occur three times. This finding suggests that readers are likely to experience stylistically-prompted changes in understanding several times during the course of reading, depending on the style and structure of the story in question. Theoretical conceptions of shifts in understanding have also been proposed by Harker (1996) and Cook (1994, p. 10). Harker portrays literary meaning as emergent, appearing in repeated cycles of familiarization and disruption that require the reader to engage in what Harker calls "reattentional" activity. Cook argues that literary texts are "a type of text which may perform the important function of breaking down existing schemata, reorganizing them, and building up new ones." The studies of Graesser, et al. (1998) and Miall and Kuiken (2001) not only provide empirical support for this process, but also indicate some of the initiating causes for schema change.

7.3.3 Anticipation

The emergent nature of literary meaning suggests that readers' understandings during reading may be provisional. At the point when a shift in meaning occurs, or a reader polyvalently entertains two or more possible meanings, such meanings may be held somewhat like hypotheses, provisional interpretations to be tested against incoming evidence while reading continues. The polyvalence of literature thus may predispose readers to experience a greater degree of anticipation during reading. This phenomenon was demonstrated in two studies by Olson, Mack, and Duffy (1981) and Langer (1990).

In Langer's (1990) study, think-aloud data were obtained from 7th and 11th grade students in response to literary and expository texts. She reports that literary reading was characterized by a forward looking and shifting context of understanding, whereas expository reading was characterized by successive and cumulative relationships to a fixed point of reference established early in reading. A similar finding was reported by Olson, at el. (1981), who also studied think-aloud responses elicited by two texts, expository and narrative. In comparison with readers of the expository text, the story readers produced a number of anticipatory comments while the expository text readers generated almost none. Olson, et al. also collected reading time data from other readers, and were able to show through multiple regression analysis that at the points where reading was longer per syllable, the think-aloud readers were generating more inferences and predictions. Along with polyvalence, anticipation may thus be one of the distinctive markers of literary response. Elsewhere I have developed a neuropsychological model of anticipation in reading, based on feeling (Miall, 1995).

7.3.4 Rereading Effects

Another method for examining emergent effects during literary reading is rereading. Measures of reading, such as evaluative judgments, ratings of feeling, or interpretive statements, are taken during two or more readings and then compared. Dixon, Bortolussi, Twilley, and Leung (1993), for example, argued that the literariness of reading is more likely to appear during a second reading, and developed a simple measure of literary appreciation to evaluate it. Using a literary story by Borges, and a sub-literary detective story, they found a marked upward shift in appreciation following the second reading of Borges but not the detective story. In a second study, postulating that the literariness of Borges was due in particular to passages that suggest the unreliability of communication, they prepared a second version of the story in which these passages were regularized and made unproblematic in relation to the issue of communication. The same test for appreciation showed that little or no shift occurred when the manipulated version of the Borges story was read a second time.

In a more complex experimental design, Cupchik, Leonard, Axelrad, and Kalin (1998) were also able to show systematic changes during a second reading. Cupchik, et al. prepared passages from four stories by James Joyce, chosen to be either "emotional" (showing character's actions and emotional responses) or "descriptive" (stylistically complex descriptions of settings and characters). After reading each passage readers gave ratings on several text-focused judgments and several reader response qualities; they then either generated an interpretation or received one, after which they read the passages again and re-rated them. While readers' evaluative ratings showed that the two "emotional" passages were preferred and were read more quickly than the descriptive passages, this effect somewhat diminished during the second reading. The ratings for complexity and expressivity of the emotion episodes diminished at the second reading. Overall, there was some evidence that the descriptive passages, at first seen as less complex and interesting, increased in significance for readers at a second reading. The authors suggest that "the language which has passed by takes on new potency, finding a meaningful role that goes beyond mere description to serve as rich allusion" (pp. 843–844). In other words, readers tend to move beyond a story-based understanding towards one focused on stylistic and evaluative components, a finding that can be compared to the pattern of responses to a Woolf short story I described earlier (Chapter 5).

In contrast, Halász, Carlsson, and Marton (1991) found no reliable differences in a rereading study. Halász et al. report that little improvement in recall occurred across four trials, and in addition readers appear not to have changed their understanding of the stories during the rereadings. They suggest that readers "form a frame" based on their initial impressions which then determines subsequent readings. Unlike the first two rereading studies, however, in which affective and evaluative measures were employed, the recall task in this study may have served to concretize readers' understandings early in the process. The "recall" question they used, it should be noted, was "Could you tell us what the text is about?" It seems possible that directing readers' efforts to a verbal report on comprehension forestalled attention to the literary qualities of the texts.

7.3.5 Literary Meaning

Ensuring that readers in an empirical study are engaged in a *literary* reading may not be entirely straightforward. In the first of a sequence of reports on studies of reading, Vipond and Hunt (1984) outlined three different strategies for reading: information-driven, story-driven, and point-driven. They proposed that the reading of literary narratives is best characterized as point-driven, a process in which the reader considers what the narrator is "getting at." Among other components, they suggest that point-driven reading involves a sense of an author seeking to make a point. At the same time, construction of a point will be culturally relative, and in part based on expectations derived from genre, that is, what kind of story is being told. Yet they found it surprisingly difficult to locate point-driven reading, at least among the student readers they studied. A questionnaire survey of over 150 readers of Updike's short story "A & P" showed that only about 5 per cent were engaged in a point-driven form of reading; most students found the story incomplete and without a point. Only after adopting different methods, including a non-experimental method based on classroom discussion, did point-driven reading clearly emerge (Hunt & Vipond, 1991).

Reading for point may be an effective strategy for approaching literature, but it is not evident that literary meaning is necessarily to be captured by points. Vipond and Hunt (1984) hypothesized that the components of point-driven reading included (1) *coherence*, the attempt to connect apparently unrelated or unnecessary parts of a story; (2) greater attention to *surface* features, such as syntax or style, on the assumption that these features are motivated and contribute to meaning; and (3) the *transactional* stance, an awareness of an author in control of a narrative who has a point to make. Each of these strategies could be tested empirically, as they suggest, yet responsiveness to any of these components does not oblige the construction of an overall point. Authors may be understood to have succeeded in producing a compelling and thought-provoking narrative, such as Coleridge with "The Rime of the Ancient Mariner," or Beckett in his play *Waiting for Godot*, without readers being in a position to know what the point of either of these texts may be. Readers may engage with texts in other ways yet still be reading in a literary mode: some of these modes of reading are examined in the next sections in discussions of personal readings and of the several roles of feeling.

7.4 Personal Readings and Feeling

7.4.1 Implicating the Self

Literary reading may in part be distinctive for interacting with a reader's self-concept and personal goals. Klinger (1978), for example, reported a series of studies in which he found readers' "current concerns" (their personal and unconsummated goals at the time of reading) were reliably evoked by a literary text. In one study readers heard excerpts from two texts played simultaneously in the reader's ears, where one of the texts was modified at specific locations to embody words and phrases known to be relevant to the individual's concerns. When readers were interrupted with a tone during one of the locations and asked to report their thoughts, readers responded with concern-related thoughts in relation to the modified passages about twice as often as to the unrelated passages. What is not evident from this study is the nature of the relationship between the process of reading and the reader's concerns. While we might suppose that literary reading assists readers to conceptualize and evaluate their concerns, gaining evidence of this within the confines of an experimental situation is a difficult task. The systematic influence of literary texts in calling up personal meanings, however, has been suggested by findings within several experimental conditions.

Halász (1996) examined the frequency with which personal meanings were invoked by a literary in comparison with a non-literary text. After reading each of three short sections participants were asked to generate its "accepted" meaning and its personal meaning. In counting the frequency of accepted and personal meaning units, Halász found that while the expository text produced three times as many general to personal meaning units, the literary text produced almost the same number in both categories, showing that the literary text enabled readers to generate a markedly higher proportion of personal meanings. Among the personal meanings, the predominant types were actions, feelings, evaluations, and "cognitive qualities" (images, daydreams, intuitions, etc.).

Several studies that have examined the role of personal meaning have made use of the Remindings method, or "self-probed retrospection." Developed by

Larsen and Seilman (1988) as a less disruptive procedure than think-aloud method, readers are asked to note with a marginal mark when a reminding occurs (that is, when they think of something they have experienced). After reading, readers are asked to describe what they were reminded of at each marked passage. In a study by Sielman and Larsen (1989), the authors proposed that when comparing responses to a literary and an expository text, the literary text would involve more memories of the reader as an actor than as an observer. Using two texts, a short story and a text about population growth (each of about 3000 words), they found that while a similar quantity of remindings was elicited by both texts, twice as many actor-perspective remindings were elicited by the literary text, while the expository text elicited more receiver remindings (memories of things read or heard about). Thus, they suggest, literary reading "seems to connect particularly with knowledge that is personal in the sense that one is an agent, a responsible subject interacting with one's environment" (p. 174). Remindings were also found to occur more frequently in the opening section of each text, but more markedly so in the case of the literary text. This suggests that readers call on specific, personal information in order to contextualize the world of the text.

Halász (1991), using the remindings method with a literary and a non-literary text, also found actor role memories were more frequent in response to the literary text than either observer memories or memories of events heard about. Halász suggests that the inappropriateness of readers' existing schemata for a literary text impels the reconstrual of readers' knowledge to overcome the obstruction: personal remindings may be a source for this reconstrual, and in turn readers' self knowledge may be enriched as a result. A preliminary study of our own (Miall and Kuiken, 1999) points to this possibility. Readers in a remindings study responded to Coleridge's "The Rime of the Ancient Mariner." Think-aloud material from one reader is analysed. Her comments show an evolving pattern of existential concerns about death, in which the world of the Mariner in the poem and that of the reader appear to merge in the final set of comments. This convergence of the situation of the (fictional) protagonist with the concerns of the reader suggests how the encounter with a literary text can significantly alter the reader's self-understanding.

Another way of conceptualizing variance in reading due to personal meaning is to consider readers' proximity to the setting and themes of a particular literary text. This may be mediated by formal features in the text such as free indirect discourse, where a third person narrator indirectly represents a character's thoughts and feelings, bringing the reader close to the character. Dixon and Bortolussi (1996) found that by manipulating free indirect discourse they were able to bias readers towards favoring one or the other of two characters in a story. Or the degree of personal meaning may depend on the extent of the reader's familiarity with the culture shown in the text. In several studies by

László and his colleagues (e.g., Larsen, László, & Seilman, 1991), culture was the variable manipulated. It was found that readers presented with a story from their own culture generated more personal experiences. When point of view was manipulated, however (László and Larsen, 1991), inside point of view elicited more personal experiences (sensations, affects, and images) regardless of culture of reader, suggesting that point of view has universal effects on readers.

Another form of proximity has been proposed by Dixon and Bortolussi (2003, Chapter 3). They suggest that readers of a literary text are likely to process it as though it were a communication of the narrator; thus readers form a model of the narrator and his or her stance towards the narrative. They point out that some aspects of the narrator's stance will be computed automatically, as they are with a partner in a conversation. Other aspects, such as the narrator's view of the characters or of the theme of the story may require more deliberate processing. The reader's relation to the narrator may thus form an important component of literary reading.

7.4.2 Two Types of Feeling

The feelings mentioned in the previous section have been invoked by fictional representations. The feelings of readers resonate in various ways in response to characters and their settings, prompted by free indirect discourse or by remindings that arouse personal action memories. But as Kneepkens and Zwaan (1994) point out, building on a suggestion by Frijda (1986, p. 356), readers also experience feelings about the form of the texts they read, such as appreciation for stylistic, or structural features. Thus they refer to two types of feelings: feelings aroused by fictional events, i.e., narrative emotions, and feelings in response to the artefact, i.e., aesthetic emotions.

One class of narrative feelings can be related to the textbase, linked to characters and events. Thus readers of a narrative may experience suspense or curiosity (Brewer & Lichtenstein, 1982; Brewer & Ohtsuka, 1988), feelings of empathy for a character (Bourg, 1996), or the feelings aroused by major thematic concerns such as death, danger, power, or sex. However, narrative feelings can be divided into two subclasses: those directed to others in the story (altercentric), and those directed at the self (egocentric). I may, for example, re-experience a feeling on behalf of a character; or the events in a story may cause me to experience a feeling about myself.

Kneepkens and Zwaan (1994) also postulate a phasic model of response. They suggest that egocentric feelings will be called into play when a particular literary passage seems unusual, abstract, or vague. As the story becomes clearer, however, the egocentric feelings will fall away, until a new episode begins. Although this proposal has so far received only one confirmatory empirical study (see Chapter 8), we (Miall, 1988; Miall and Kuiken, 2001) have reported an initial positive correlation between reading times and affect ratings at the beginning of story episodes, where the coincidence of longer reading times and higher affect suggested that readers' feelings were implicated in helping to contextualize the new episode. In one of the stories we studied (Miall and Kuiken, 2001) a cluster of striking stylistic features appeared to signal the onset of a new episode (an example of the role played by aesthetic feeling).

This last finding calls into question the suggestion of Kneepkens and Zwaan (1994) that the prevailing cognitive model of text understanding provides an appropriate framework for situating effects due to feeling (cf. Miall, 1995). This approach is taken in a study reported by Dijkstra, Zwaan, Graesser, & Magliano (1994). When reading times were collected from readers of short stories, it was found that text difficulty was a significant variable in the case of narrative emotions. For passages portraying character emotions the more difficult stories elicited slower reading times; for less difficult stories reading times for such passages were faster. This may not only have been because the characters' emotions were more difficult to understand, as the authors suggest (p. 155). It may have been that emotion felt by the reader was being used as a prompt for emergent story interpretations based on analogies in the reader's experience. This possibility is examined more closely in the next section.

7.4.3 Feeling-Based Understanding

An initiating role for feeling in readers' developing understanding is shown by a study of Andringa (1990), who collected think-aloud protocols. Her primary intention was to develop a systematic method for classifying think-aloud comments. Thus two levels of analysis were elaborated, consisting of a range of speech acts and reception acts. The method was applied to analysing readers' comments on a Schiller short story. The most notable finding was that for the less experienced readers the most common sequence consisted of emotion references, followed by evaluation, then argument. Andringa comments that in most of the protocols this "seems to be a regular sequence," suggesting that emotion "initiates, selects, and steers the way of arguing." An example of such a sequence is provided by Andringa (slightly modified here): "[Emotion] Oh (smiles, laughs), [Evaluation] yeah, that's a little bit theatrical . . . [Argument] I can only say she was very stupid, that woman, because . . ." (p. 247). Among her more skilled readers the more regular sequence was a reference to the text followed by a metacomment elaborating the meaning of the reference, then interpretive comments.

In the study of responses to a Virginia Woolf short story that I described earlier (Chapter 5) I also found evidence for the constructive role of feeling. While readers' responses to the relationship schema can be seen as the application of familiar feelings, the feeling for setting appears to have prompted new feelings for most of the readers, feelings that became more appropriate later as a context for understanding the story. A similar contrast is made in a study by Cupchik, Oatley, and Vorderer (1998), who compared emotion memories and what they termed "fresh" emotions in a study of responses to short stories by Joyce. Passages in the stories were identified as either descriptive or focused on characters' emotions. After reading each of four segments from a story, classified as either emotional or descriptive, readers answered questions about the emotions they experienced, and whether they were fresh or remembered. Results showed that in general fresh emotions were elicited more often than emotional memories, and were less pleasant, whereas emotional memories were more powerful. As expected, descriptive passages tended to evoke fewer emotion memories than fresh emotions. Over the four segments of a given story, however, emotion memories were more frequent early in the story, whereas fresh emotions became more frequent later. As in my study with Woolf, this seems to imply a schema-setting role for emotion memories, but an interpretive role for fresh emotions.

7.5 Literary Components

7.5.1 Imagery

Denis (1984) pointed to several effects of imagery in a review of the role of imagery in prose. In general images appear to facilitate recall of texts, although individuals with a tendency to form imagery spontaneously showed better recall than those without. It has also been found that high-imagery subjects have longer reading times than low-imagery subjects. Denis suggests that imagery enhances recall because it facilitates encoding of information in a structured form where items interact rather than remain separate. In normal reading, however, it is questionable whether readers form detailed imagery except under special circumstances. Spatial imagery was studied by Zwaan and van Oostendorp (1993), and found to be quite poor when readers were asked to report the position of items in a setting.

On the other hand, the occurrence of imagery in response to narrative appears to be consistent and to correlate significantly with other features of response. Goetz and Sadoski (1996), for example, asked readers to rate the strength of imagery at the different sections of a literary story. They found that readers showed a surprisingly high level of agreement, with alpha reliability coefficients of above .90; imagery ratings also correlated consistently with ratings for affect. As the authors point out, their studies suggest that "visual imagery and affective, or emotional imagery" play a key role in the reading experience. Visual imagery may thus provide one, concrete matrix for registering emotional responses during reading. Other image modalities that may function in this way, such as olfactory or kinaesthetic, remain to be studied.

7.5.2 Foregrounding

As mentioned in the earlier, stylistic features have been considered a hallmark of literary language until recently. Evidence for their influence on reading is available in several studies, suggesting that contemporary critical disregard for this aspect of literariness may be premature.

Hunt and Vipond's (1986) study of the effect of local features of a narrative, what they termed evaluations, provides such evidence. Evaluations were of three kinds: discourse (unusual style), story (unusual plot elements), and telling (unusual comments by a narrator). It will be recalled that Hunt and Vipond prepared a second version of a story in which evaluations in the original version were replaced by semantically equivalent neutral statements (e.g., "they camped around the room" was replaced by "they sat around the room"). Asked to note what they found striking in the text, readers of the original version, as expected, noticed discourse evaluations more frequently than the equivalent normalized passages in the revised version.

Comparable studies by Van Peer (1986) and Miall and Kuiken (1994a) focused more closely on linguistic and phonetic features of style, termed foregrounding after Mukařovský (1964/1932). Van Peer (1986) examined phonetic, grammatical, and semantic features in six short poems, and ranked the lines of each poem for the presence of foregrounding. For example, this opening line from a poem by Roethke, ranked high: "I have known the inexorable sadness of pencils." The pencils are personified; it contains an unusual word, "inexorable"; it contains repeated phonemes such as /n/ and /e/. Foregrounded features can be classed either as deviations from normal language use (e.g., a metaphor), or they constitute an unusual parallelism (e.g., the use of rhyme, or a repeated stress pattern). Among other tasks, readers were asked to rate the lines for strikingness. Van Peer found that the mean ratings for strikingness were strongly predicted by the presence of foregrounding. This effect was obtained whether experienced or novice readers were involved.

We carried out a similar study with three modernist short stories (Miall and Kuiken, 1994a). We scored each segment of the stories (roughly one sentence) for foregrounding. Readers read the stories on computer while reading times per segment were recorded. In a second reading they then rated the segments on one of four judgments: feeling, strikingness, importance, or discussion value. For each of the stories, foregrounding was found to strongly predict reading times and ratings for feeling and strikingness. This effect was also found whether readers were experienced, senior students of literature, or whether they were relatively unskilled readers. Ratings for discussion-value and importance, on the other hand, were not reliably associated with foregrounding, possibly because segments high in foregrounding did not always coincide with the most important sections for narrative events. We argued that structures of foregrounding, in contrast to the semantic and narrative features usually at the center of discourse processing studies, offer readers an alternative, feeling-based mode of response. Temporally speaking, as readers encounter foregrounding, they first find the passage striking. It defamiliarizes customary or accepted meanings, arousing feeling in the process. This then leads readers to engage in a search, led by feeling, for a context in which to locate the unusual meanings suggested by foregrounding. This phasic sequence of response has as its outcome the registering of a shift in understanding downstream from the moment of foregrounding (Miall & Kuiken, 2001).

Evidence for the moment of defamiliarization is provided by Hoorn (1996), who studied the electrophysiological response of readers. Hoorn proposed that event-related potentials (ERPs) would mirror the response to deviations in semantic or phonological expectations in the last word of a four-line verse. In his study, the final word was made either consistent or inconsistent with the semantic content of the verse, or an expected rhyme word occurred or did not occur, or both inconsistencies occurred together. Hoorn found reliable differences in ERPs: phonetic deviation produced a response with significant negative shifts, N200, N400, and N700; semantic deviation produced a N400 shift (that is, a shift at 400 msecs. following the appearance of the anomalous word). While the experimental feature studied here violates poetic form (at the level of sound or meaning), it can be considered a test of stylistic deviation (Van Peer, 1986).

7.5.3 Phonetic Variation

The sound of poetry is perhaps one of the most distinctive features of "literariness," offering unusual rhythmic features, or striking clusters of phonemes such as alliteration or assonance. Van Peer (1990) argues that literary language thus does more than refer to a state of affairs; it also creates a sense of significance beyond the ordinary meanings of the sentences. This forms a part of that extra level of meaning that has usually been considered "aesthetic." Meter is one such device, which appears to have a double function, aesthetic and mnemonic. It enables a text to be better remembered, and it helps create the significance of the text.

In his study a modern humorous Dutch poem with a marked metrical structure was varied by creating a second version where the metrical features were largely removed while keeping other literary features intact as far as possible (e.g., alliteration, rhyme). Readers read either the original or the altered version silently, then completed two tasks. First, they made judgments on a set of 16 semantic differential ratings designed to elicit aesthetic judgments. Second, they completed a questionnaire that tested recognition and recall. The overall ratings on the semantic differential showed a significant aesthetic advantage for the original poem; readers of the original poem were also more accurate in identifying lines from the poem. However, both groups of readers performed at the same level in recalling content from the poem. The results "show the *form* of literary texts to carry specific informational possibilities in its own right"; thus responding to a literary text is not confined to understanding meaning (p. 270).

Another form of phonetic variation was examined in one of my studies (Chapter 11). It has been a common intuition that the sound of language supports its meaning, e.g., a narrow, front vowel such as /i/ will be used to signify something small or high. I found that rank orderings of vowels and phonemes according to their position of pronunciation in the oral tract (e.g., from high to low, or front to back) were related to several features in non-literary texts, such as differences between groups of male and female names. They also reliably distinguished different parts of literary texts, such as Milton's descriptions of Hell and Eden in *Paradise Lost.* In a study of readers of a short story, phonemic contrasts were found to contribute to variations in reading speed and readers' ratings of story segments, suggesting that readers were sensitive to variations in tonal patterns while reading the story.

Another approach was introduced by Bailey (1971). He developed a "prominence index" for phonemes, where frequency in a given poem was used to place phonemes in rank order; these ranks were compared with the ranks in a sample of standard English. He argued that higher frequency of a given phoneme was more likely to be noticed by a reader, especially when a phoneme was relatively rare in standard English. This test revealed several systematic effects in the poems selected for study. In Dylan Thomas's poem "Fern Hill," for example, he found a prevalence of voiced over unvoiced phonemes. While this approach has not been verified with studies of readers, a sensitivity to phonetic effects has been shown in a non-literary context by Zajonc, Murphy, and McIntosh (1993). Other accounts of phonetic patterns in poetry are offered by Tsur (1992). These results challenge the claim of Meutsch (1989, p. 69), that "we can state the irrelevance of textual qualities for the management of problems during the cognitive process of comprehension." It seems probable, on the contrary, that literary readers will be influenced by the sounds structures of a text in their effort after meaning.

7.6 Prospects

The components of a future theory of literary processing may emerge from the studies discussed above. In most of the studies the focus is confined to one or two features of the response process, thus the findings cannot be related to a larger theory of processing except in a preliminary way. Studies that triangulate on a postulated phenomenon from a number of positions will clearly be required, given the complexity and considerable variance apparent in all the dimensions of the literary process—the range of texts of different genres, the wide variety of responses exhibited by readers (although focusing on differences in interpretation may not be a priority), and the range of response processes from inferences to feeling. Magliano and Graesser (1991) are undoubtedly correct in advocating a "three-pronged" approach to literary understanding. This requires us to (1) make predictions based on medium-level theories about literary response, (2) analyse think-aloud data from readers, and (3) use behavioral measures such as reading times. The studies reviewed here, however, suggest that the addition of several more "prongs" might be required before an appropriately complex and powerful methodology is available, prongs that would be applied and coordinated within a single research program.

As the discussion has already shown, methodological questions are decided within the perspective of the researcher. Broadly speaking, literary processing has often been approached as a branch of discourse processing, with preset categories for analysing response. However, this may deselect those features that are most characteristic of literary reading. A specific example of this problem lies in the type of instruction sometimes given to readers. For example, in the study of Graves and Frederiksen (1991) readers were asked "to provide a verbal description of the passage while reading it, commenting on its content and style," an instruction that appears directed to comprehending rather than experiencing the text. Similarly, the readers studied by Olson, Mack, and Duffy (1981) were told before reading that "later we would explore how well they understood each story." An informal study of my own (Miall, 1986a) suggested that when asked to write freely about their responses to a poem, the first responses of readers are predominantly affective. Only later, as readers comes to define their experience of the poem do more conceptual, analytic comments appear. Finding appropriate ways to elicit information about their response processes from literary readers, devising methods sensitive to the complex and fugitive aspects of the response, will continue to present a major challenge to future researchers.

Several key questions about the reading of literature remain. First, while the limitations of the cognitivist basis of research on reading has been pointed out (e.g., Miall & Kuiken, 1994b), a number of effective studies situated in alternative frameworks are now extant, ranging from studies of personal meaning (Halász, 1996) to electrophysiological measurement (Hoorn, 1995). Thus it is evident that a rapprochment of cognitive and alternative approaches that examine affective, self-referential, and cultural issues, must be sought. This may help to distinguish the boundary (no doubt a blurred one) between literary and nonliterary processes. For example, do the situation model processes demonstrated in Zwaan, Magliano, and Graesser (1995) operate in parallel to foregrounding processes (Miall & Kuiken, 1999)? Do features distinctive to literary processing displace cognitive forms of processing in some instances?

Second, the problem of understanding what may be innate in literary experience calls for careful and innovative kinds of study. While it is clear that in major respects literary reading is premised upon the cultural and educational context in which a reader learns to experience literary texts, it remains to be examined how far "literariness" is based on features of response that are a part of the evolutionary acquirement of human beings. Given that artistic production in the visual mode is known to date from at least 30,000 years before the present, it seems probable that literary experience (first oral, then in written form) has an equally long history, which may be embedded in the human genotype (see chapter 12).

Finally, while literary reading has a prestigious past, its future has been called into question, given the advent and rapid spread of digital media. While advocates for electronic forms of literature, including proponents of innovative hypertext literature, have cast doubt on the validity of literature in the printed book, it is far from clear whether the repurposing of literature for the electronic medium will continue to offer the same experience (Miall, 1998). It thus becomes the more urgent to understand what literary reading is, what role it plays in the ecology of human culture and the health of individuals, before it is reconfigured or disappears in the face of new forms of electronic literacy.

•PART TWO•

Contexts of Reading

• CHAPTER EIGHT •

Episode Structures in Literary Narratives

8.1 Linear Reading

Investigation of the structure of literary texts is as old as literary theory itself: Aristotle's *Poetics*, for examples, provides a foundational set of perspectives on the most effective organization of tragic drama—the coherence of the plot that unfolds over a day, the place of peripeteia (a sudden change in fortune), or the effect of catharsis.* Yet most discussions of structure have tended to focus on imbricated rather than linear components, that is, elements that recur and are interwoven at various levels, such as perspective effects (e.g., shifts in point of view), the recurrence of thematic elements, or an organizing metaphor. Less attention has been given to the moment-by-moment unfolding of the text itself as we might suppose the reader to experience it. The authors of standard treatments of narrative, such as Rimmon-Kenan (1983) or Seymour Chatman (1978), focus attention on other structural features and largely overlook the sequential experience of reading. The primary source of insight into this linear aspect is found, as might be expected, in the writings of the phenomenological theorists, notably Roman Ingarden and Wolfgang Iser, as I will note later, while some attention to sequence in narrative was offered in Roland Barthes's earlier structuralist work. Among the few other theorists who have discussed it I will mention Roland Barthes, Umberto Eco, Jim Rosenberg, and Ed Tan; but perhaps the most useful discussion is found in an essay on narrative structure dating from 1922 by the Russian Formalist critic A. A. Reformat-

* An earlier version of this chapter appeared as "Episode Structures in Literary Narratives." *Journal of Literary Semantics* 33 (2004): 111–129. It is reprinted here by kind permission of the publisher, Mouton de Gruyter.

sky, who analyzes a short story by Maupassant (an example that I examine in some detail).

In considering the structure of a literary text as it unfolds in the reader's experience, the distance at which we make our observations can be varied. Close to the surface of the text we find the type of effect described by Stanley Fish (1980b) under the rubric of "affective stylistics" in which a given sentence arouses expectations that it then subverts; or we see clusters of phonetic effects, an ellipsis, or a figurative expression—stylistic features that have been termed foregrounding (van Peer, 1986; Miall & Kuiken, 1994a). Moving further back from the text, larger-scale features come into view, such as the articulation of plot into its sections (induction, rising action, etc.), or the scenarios of successive chapters. In this chapter, however, I consider a structure that is in between: a mid-level focus on what I will term the *episode*. In prose this is likely to consist of a number of sentences taking up half a page or a page, usually demarcated by a coherence in the temporal or spatial setting or both. The most signal feature of the episode, however, is that it offers a thematically distinctive topic requiring a shift in the reader's understanding. As I will suggest, episodes often function by introducing and establishing a certain setting or concern, then offering a special twist, or insight, in the final sentence or two. Such a twist has the effect of motivating reader interest in the next episode, which it thus helps to launch.

A conception analogous to this can be found in Eco's (1984) work on the reader. He distinguishes three levels of topic: sentence, discursive, and narrative topics. Discursive topics, which "at the level of short sequences can rule the understanding of microstructural elements" (p. 26) seem the closest to my sense of the episode as consisting of a series of sentences. While Eco's "topic" organizes lower-level semantic elements, hence the unity of elements in terms of time and space and their relevance to the actions of the characters, it also appears to participate in elaborating the larger meanings of the text, its macropropositions. These emerge for the reader, in Eco's words, from the "changes of state" undergone by characters in the text (the macroproposition, a statement about the larger meaning of the text, usually inferred by the reader from the details of the text):

> Since every step usually involves a change of state and a lapse of time, the reader is led to make an intermediate extensional operation: he considers the various macropropositions as statements about events taking place in a still-bracketed possible world. Each of these statements concerns the way in which a given individual determines or undergoes a certain change of state, and the reader is induced to wonder what could happen at the next step of the story. (p. 31)

While Eco's formula suggests how the reader is motivated to read, progressing from one topic to the next, it is less clear how Eco defines a topic or a change of state. The conception of the episode I offer here provides working definitions of both these aspects.

The homogeneity of such topics is developed by Barthes (1977), who considers the logical relationships that help tie the sequences of narrative together. Thus, "A sequence is a logical succession of nuclei bound together by a relation of solidarity: the sequence opens when one of its terms has no solidary antecedent and closes when another of its terms has no consequent" (p. 101). As I argue in more detail below, one implication of this view is that the coherence of a sequence lies not only in terms of time and space, since we usually recognize the event that motivates a sequence as delimited by where it occurs and how long it requires, but also in representing an advance in the narrative action. What occurs in the sequence unfolds a new phase that is in part unprecedented, but also constitutes the completion of an action on which subsequent sequences will build—eventualities that the current sequence, indeed, appears to invite. As Barthes goes on to say, a sequence "always involves moments of risk" (p. 102): since the action involved is not predetermined, what a character says or does in it represents a choice, and this will have consequences that the reader may partly anticipate, but that invite attention to the ensuing narrative.

Similarly, Roman Ingarden (1973a) has provided an account of the experience of sequential reading. Having considered at length the different "strata" of the literary work (which interweave and co-exist), Ingarden goes on to look at it in "longitudinal section" (304); this is realized in temporal terms when the work is "concretized" during reading. In this perspective "every literary work of art contains an order of sequence, a determinate system of phase positions, in which every phase consists of corresponding phases of all the interconnected strata of the work" (p. 309). Each phase of the work, says Ingarden, contains elements from earlier phases, elements that are new, and elements that provide the foundation of later phases (p. 310). Thus we might see a given episode developing a character or a plot motif that is also manifested in previous or following episodes. "The presence of a 'sequence' of phases of a work has the consequence that every work has a determinate line of development and thus an *internal dynamics*" (p. 312).

While Ingarden's "phase" would seem to correspond to the term "episode," in fact elsewhere he shows that the unit he has in mind is smaller. While the "phase," defined as the present moment of reading, can vary considerably, encompassing a single sentence, several sentences, or a part of a sentence, "Usually the scope of the vividly present phase is identical with the semantic unit, the sentence" (1973b, p. 98). The sentences then flow into the past, appearing "as complete units of meaning" and "retained in active memory . . . condensed into a relatively simple meaning" (p. 99). For Ingarden the active memory is "a kind of peripheral feeling, which has no more precise content than that something has happened which is closely connected with our present moment" and has "a certain continuation in the present" (p. 101)—in other words, it will influence and help shape response to subsequent phases. It seems unlikely, however, that each sentence of a text will be so remembered. I suggest that it is the episode that leaves readers with a "peripheral feeling," first for the implications of the "twist" that impels a reader's interest in the action or the situation of the characters, and second for the ambience (overall setting in time and place) to the extent that this prepares for or enables the "twist," making it possible. For example, in the Maupassant story discussed below, "Un Coq Chanta," we are unlikely to remember that it was during a party that Madame d'Avancelles said she would probably yield to the Baron in the Autumn, since this is incidental to her statement; however, we are likely to remember that it is at night in the park that the couple first kiss passionately, since the natural setting seems an incentive to the characters' erotic potential.

In building on Ingarden's work, Wolfgang Iser (1978) points to the shifting and constructive nature of the reader's response, coining the term "wandering viewpoint" to characterize it. At any given moment the reader is occupied with one perspective or theme, but the others remain present as the horizon of his current view, while the previous perspectives condition his current understanding; thus a continual shifting of theme and horizon occurs in which "each position is set in a fresh context, with the result that the reader's attention is drawn to aspects hitherto not apparent" (p. 97). Thus arises the "wandering viewpoint" of the reader, which "constantly switches between the textual perspectives, each of the switches representing an articulate reading moment" (p. 114). As the viewpoint changes, what was foreground becomes background, "which is now to exert its influence on yet another new foreground" (p. 116).

> Here we have one of the basic elements of the reading process: the wandering viewpoint divides the text up into interacting structures, and these give rise to a grouping activity that is fundamental to the grasping of the text. (p. 119)

Iser goes on to apply the term *gestalt* to the grouping process, in the sense that the coherent sections constructed by the reader constitute a series of *gestalten* (p. 120). Bal (1985) offers some concrete suggestions for identifying the discrete narrative structures that would constitute a *gestalt* (chronology, the role of the actors, the nature of their confrontation, the location), although she leaves them undeveloped (pp. 23–24). However, when Iser turns to examples of *gestalten* his conception appears to relate more to vertical components of the text than to linear ones, and the extent to which the perspectives constitute episodes in my sense of the term remains unclear. The concept of the wandering viewpoint, however, is undoubtedly appropriate to understanding the function of episodes, since each successive episode tends to promote attention to a different and, in part, unprecedented aspect of the narrative's thematics—a phenomenon that will be particularly evident in explaining the role of the narrative twist that often closes an episode.

The clearest example of episodic analysis is provided by Reformatsky (1973), the Russian Formalist critic, in an essay first published in Russian in 1922 in which he develops the structural approach to narrative of his teacher A. M. Petrovsky. Complaining of the inadequate state of the field, Reformatsky begins by listing the components that he feels should be considered in the morphological analysis of narrative. These include the distinction between descriptive and action-oriented aspects of narrative; the role of place and time (whether time is treated chronogically or not, for example); how characters are characterized (whether overall or for a specific scene); the themes or motifs that underlie plot construction, and the different plot types that result. While Reformatsky outlines these and related aspects, providing briefly and schematically various examples of their functioning, as Doložel (1973) points out he "fails to establish relationships and hierarchies of the particular components of his 'model'" (p. 82). This limitation is partly overcome in the second half of his paper, which is devoted to a detailed analysis of "Un Coq Chanta" by Maupassant. I will first describe the salient features of Reformatsky's analysis, then show how the conception of the episode I outlined above can be built on his work.

8.2 Episodes in Maupassant's "Un Coq Chanta": a Formalist Analysis

In Maupassant's story,† Madame Berthe d'Avencelles is being pursued by Baron Joseph Croissard, a liberty that she is able to encourage without satisfying, as her own husband, who is said to be weak and small, takes no notice. In her honour the Baron lays on hunting parties at his estate. The main part of the story focuses on one particular boar hunt, during which Berthe plays the coquette with the Baron. She delays his participation in the hunt while seeming to promise herself to him if he will kill the boar in her presence. Although this fails to occur, the Baron is nevertheless able to find his way to her bedroom that night. But Berthe delays joining him in bed and, exhausted by his efforts during the day, the Baron falls asleep and wakes the next morning to satirical comment by Berthe.

In Reformatsky's analysis, there are two main "themes," that of the Baron (a_1) and Berthe (b), with the husband as a secondary theme (a_2). By "theme" here, Reformatsky appears to mean the disposition of the characters and what

† The text of Maupassant's story is available in French at: http://maupassant.free.fr/textes/coq.html (site visited June 30th 2004). The English translation is cited with minor changes from "A Cock Crowed," in Guy Maupassant, *The Complete Short Stories*, Vol. 1 (pp. 448–452). London: Cassell, 1970.

this implies for their actions: Berthe is "tall, dark and determined"; the Baron has "broad shoulders, strong build and fair moustaches," while the husband has "short arms, legs, neck, nose and everything else." Thus the outset of the story, where the characters are described, disposes the reader to see Berthe and the Baron as appropriate sexual partners. Reformatsky goes on to state that the main motif (A) is the courting of Berthe by the Baron, while the hunt provides the second motif (B); the second motif both complements the first, while also being in opposition to it (the Baron expresses his desire for Berthe by pursuing boar, while the specific hunt that is narrated serves only to thwart the consummation of his desire). Reformatsky divides the story into a prologue (*Vorgeschichte*) and story proper (*Geschichte*); the latter begins with the account of the particular hunt in which the Baron will pursue and forfeit access to Berthe. Chronologically the story is told in natural sequence ("dispositional order") except for two analepses (flashbacks) in the *Vorgeschichte*. While the main setting is Autumn, two brief references allude to the preceding winter and the spring. Reformatsky also draws our attention to two treatments of nature, what he refers to as the *paysage de la culture* (e.g., the hounds, the lawns) and the *paysage de la nature* (e.g., the Autumn season, the falling leaves). These become associated with developments in the story, e.g., Berthe's announcement to the Baron: "If I do succumb to you, my friend, it will not be before the fall of the leaf."

Reformatsky goes on to trace the introduction and development of the motifs of the story in the prologue and the story, but more important for our purpose is his division of the narrative into scenes. In his analysis the prologue appears to be made up of three sections (although this is not quite clear from Reformatsky's account), while the story itself consists, in Reformatsky's terms, of the "onset" and five scenes. Reformatsky also specifies "connective" passages of description occurring between scenes 1 and 2, and scenes 2 and 3, in keeping with his distinction between descriptive and action-oriented aspects, but I incorporate these passages into my account of episodes. Scenes are characterized primarily by the development of the motifs. Thus in scene 1, the Baron is described as "Frémissant d'amour et d'inquiétude" ("trembling with love and anxiety"), listening to both Berthe's banter and the sounds of the hunt in the distance. This develops respectively motifs A (the courtship) and B (the hunt), and signifies "the first appearance of the Spannung" (the narrative tension). But already Reformatsky divides this scene into two episodes, since he refers to the ensuing kiss as a further development of the Spannung. It is not clear what characteristics impel Reformatsky to see one scene with two episodes here, since several occurrences in this scene serve to develop the story. I will argue for merging the Onset with the opening of Scene 1, and dividing this part of the story into three episodes.

Reformatsky goes on to point out a number of felicitous features of the narrative construction in the scenes that follow: in particular, for each scene

Table 8.1 Episode Analysis of Maupassant's "Un Coq Chanta"

Scene	Opening words	Reformatsky themes, motifs	Episodes and twists
Vorgeschichte			
i	Madame Berthe d'Avancelles	A1 she had resisted B1 he was giving hunting parties A2 she had not granted B2 there was a constant round of hunting parties	Le baron se ruinait pour elle. [The Baron was ruining himself for her]
ii	Tout le jour, les chiens [All day long, the hounds]	paysage de la culture, pc1 paysage de la nature, pn1	une odeur de chair nue [the odour of naked flesh]
iii	Un soir, dans une fête, au dernier prin-temps [One evening, during a party, the pre-vious spring]	Complication: A3 'If I do succumb' B3 A great hunt was going to take place	"Baron, si vous tuez la bête" [Baron, if you kill the brute]
Geschichte			
Onset	Dès l'aurore, il fut debout [At dawn he was up and out]	B hero/hunt paysage: Les chasseurs par-tirent [The hunters left]: pc2	(1a. Dès l'aurore) Frémissant d'amour et d'inquiétude [trembling with love

1	a) Mme d'Avancelles, par malice [Mme d'Avancelles, out of mischief] b) Puis ils tournèrent à droite [Just then they turned to the right]	a) tension: A4. listening to her chatter and the hounds, + B4: his anxiety [d'inquiétude]; b) tension: A5. parallelism: soit hasard, soit volonté [either by chance or by design]; soit confusion, soit remords [either from confusion, or remorse] paysage: Le tumulte de la chasse, pc3 refrain: "Qui m'aime me suive!", rB	and anxiety] ---------------------- (1b. "Vous ne m'aimez donc plus?" [you do not love me any longer?]) "tant pis pour vous" [so much the worse for you] ---------------------- (1c. Puis ils tournèrent à droite) "Qui m'aime me suive!" [Let him who loves me follow me]
2	Quand elle arriva, quelques minutes plus tard [When she arrived a few minutes later]	B5: motif completed, with killing of boar	dans l'épaule le couteau de chasse [in the shoulder the hunting knife]
3	La curée se fit aux flambeaux par une nuit douce [The quarry was cut by torchlight on a soft night]	paysage: pn2, then pc4 A6: amorous couple refrain: "Qui m'aime me suive!", rA. Expect satisfactory culmination of A	(3a. La curée) leur besoin d'étreinte étaient devenus si véhéments [their longing for a closer embrace became so vehement]. ---------------------- (3b. Les cors ne sonnaient plus.) "Qui m'aime me suive!"
4	Une heure plus tard [An hour later]	tension: A7. "Je vais revenir" . . . du lit. [I will return]: anticipate final dénoument	sommeil des chasseurs exténués [sleep of the worn-out hunter]

5	Tout à coup, la fenêtre étant restée entrouverte [Suddenly, the window having remained half open]	Unexpected dénoument, A8. un coq, perché dans un arbre voisin, chanta [a cock, perched in a nearby tree, sang]	elle parlait à son mari [as she spoke to her husband]

described he cites one or more key phrases that occur at or close to the end of the scene. In each case the phrase signals a point at which the Spannung increases, until it is said to reach its culminating point in the penultimate fourth scene with its climactic promise, Berthe's "Je vais revenir. Attendez-moi," spoken as she points to the bed, a promise that seems set to fulfil the principle motivation of the story. Yet it is followed by the unexpected and anticlimactic failure of the Baron: he falls into "the unconquerable, heavy sleep of the worn-out hunter." Considered as part of the episodes, such key phrases as this last signal the closing move of an episode, and have the specific function of surprising us as readers and engaging our interest in the ensuing portion of the narrative. Such phrases are striking particularly because they include the "moments of risk" of which Barthes writes (1977, p. 102). The last example cited provides a clear example: as the Baron stretched out luxuriously in bed, he risked the eventuality that has now overtaken him—that of falling asleep. More poignantly, he has risked losing thereby the interest of Berthe, who will scorn him the next morning when he awakens. It is, in part, our sense of such contingencies that shapes our preoccupation with a narrative of this kind: events might have turned out otherwise.

The "Pointe" of the story, as Reformatsky puts it, lies in the way the hunt motif, apparently auxiliary to the motif of the Baron's courtship, turns out to be in opposition to it. While this is well observed, perhaps the more important development is contained in its succession of episodes. In the Table below I summarize the main divisions of the story made by Reformatsky, alongside my own division into episodes and the key phrases that signal the narrative twists that occur at the end of each episode. The right-hand column also indicates episode divisions where these differ from or subdivide Reformatsky's Onset and scenes 1 and 3 (e.g., 1a, 1b, etc.), but I retain Reformatsky's numbering in identifying episodes.

In general, it is evident that Reformatsky's scene divisions are based not only on development of motifs but also on unity of space or time, or both, although his account nowhere mentions this. Exceptions occur in scene i, which offers a general introduction to the characters and alludes only generally to the present time of the narrative, which turns out to be autumn, and to the main locations of the Baron's pursuits, Paris and Normandy; and scene iii, which refers analeptically to Berthe's anticipation in the spring that she might succumb to the Baron, then returns to the present. While Reformatsky divides the first part of the story into Onset and scene 1, characterizing the primary feature of the Onset as description, a consideration of time and place suggests that the Onset and the opening of scene 1 belong together in one episode: in both the hunt has been initiated, the Baron and Berthe proceed together (to the frustration of the Baron), while the setting specifies the park in which the hunt is taking place and its distance from the long alley in which Berthe keeps the Baron away from the hunt. The contrast of park where the hunt unfolds at a distance and alley is key to the position of the Baron, who we learn, far from being pleased with Berthe's company, is "trembling with love and anxiety" as the two major pursuits in his life become increasingly separated.

The intermediate level of focalization apparent in 1a then gives way to the closer focus of 1b in which we overhear the conversation between the couple and see the Baron's frustration intensify. In this conversation the absurd conditions that Berthe imposes on the Baron are presented: he must *both* continue by her side *and* kill the boar in her presence. If he doesn't, Berthe tells him, "so much the worse for you." The time and place in which this occurs is closely circumscribed. It is followed by an explicit change of place, "Just then they turned to the right," which initiates episode 1c. Here the couple first traverse a narrow path then the thickets of the forest where the boar suddenly appears. Having accidentally (or not) obtained a kiss on the lips from Berthe, the Baron is motivated to leave Berthe with the cry "Let him who loves me follow me!" (which, as we eventually learn, is the beginning of his undoing: the phrase will be repeated by Berthe at another critical moment at the end of scene 3).

The treatment of time and space constitutes a coherence-making strategy for staging episodes, one that has been reaffirmed in recent discourse processing models that point to the role of time, place, and other features in evoking the situation models of narrative (Zwaan & Radvansky, 1998). As studies with readers have shown (e.g., Zwaan, Magliano, and Graesser, 1995), shifts in time, place, or causality during a story require readers to reorientate; the extra processing that results is reflected in longer reading times. The validity of the episode structure emerged as a key outcome of studies of episodes in the earlier story-grammar tradition. For example, Haberlandt and his colleagues (Haberlandt, 1980; Haberlandt, et al., 1980) showed that readers of narrative take longer at episode boundaries: they must both assimilate the meaning of a completed episode and shift the current mental model to accommodate the new information presented at the beginning of the ensuing episode. In studies involving simple two-episode stories focused on elementary protagonists with basic goals and behaviours, readers were found to take longer to read sentences at episode boundaries, that is, the first and last sentences. At the close of an episode it was suggested that readers then organize the information they have assimilated into a higher-level "macroproposition," and this is likely to be among those aspects of the story transferred to long-term memory (Haberlandt, 1980, p. 115).

While it seems unlikely that readers of more complex stories of literary quality would show a comparable pattern of responses, the episodes of such narratives are still characterized by a range of internal features that endow them with a specific identity: not only unity of time or space, or the presence of certain characters, but also possibly stylistic resources, point of view, or thematic concerns. In literary narratives, in addition, as suggested in the Table above, each episode also presents an extra challenge to the reader's understanding at or near its end. This serves to develop the themes or motifs of the narrative in a specific direction, often unexpected by the reader; such narrative "twists," as I have called them, represent a focusing of issues for the characters involved, beyond which events may unfold in more than one way.

Thus the conversation of episode 1b elaborates the conditions that Berthe announces she is imposing on the Baron, which the Baron (not unnaturally) objects to as impossible. Yet Berthe seems to turn the screw on the Baron quite specifically at the end of this conversation by saying "laughingly" ("en riant") that he must comply, or "so much the worse for you," while then going on to speak "tenderly" to the Baron. Are we (and the Baron) to take her seriously or not? And how is the Baron to respond to such an impossible demand, which, now it has been placed in his path, threatens to disable his ardent pursuit of Berthe? This "twist" serves to cast Berthe in a new light, a coquet who only offers herself under impossible conditions. The structure of such episodes has some similarity to the "given-new" structure of the sentence shown by Clark and Haviland (1977)—and in various other forms, such as topic-comment. A situation is described for which readers can readily construct a situation model (the "given"), since the events shown are based either on structures already set up in the narrative (here, the hunt co-occurring with Berthe's response to the Baron's pursuit) or on situations that may be typical (Berthe's character as a flirt, toying with the man). This provides the background to the new element introduced at or near the end of the episode, which is calculated to catch the reader's attention in specific ways. In episode 1b Berthe's remark "so much the worse for you" strikes a new note, introducing a threat into the relationship whose consequences are unpredictable. We notice that in Berthe's previous statements to the Baron in episode iii, which seemed to promise eventual submission, nothing prepared us for this threat: her love was likely to be given on certain conditions only, which the Baron was well placed to meet.

In subsequent episodes the narrative twists seem new in the following ways. In the next episode, 1c, the cry of the Baron with its aphoristic structure, "Qui m'aime me suive!" ("Let him who loves me follow me"), introduces a ritualistic tone to the Baron's behaviour—it seems that now the boar is in sight, he is following some old, atavistic script, or perhaps citing some family motto, as he suddenly disappears from view. Evidently he expects Berthe to follow him, but the motto alerts us to another condition: does she indeed love him? The rest of the story will show one way or another.

The following episode, the shortest in our analysis consisting of only one sentence, ending in the phrase, "the Baron's hunting knife driven into [the boar's] shoulder up to the hilt." The detail provided here is isomorphic in relation to the two motifs analysed by Reformatsky; the violence and energy it derives from the hunt offers a parallel to the Baron's desire for Berthe. It is an anticipation of that gratification, but also a symbol for Berthe who perhaps witnesses it as a representation of her fate if she were to yield. The end of episode 3, nevertheless, seems to promise just this outcome, since for the first time Berthe is given a desire that appears to match that of the Baron: "their longing for a closer embrace." The "twist" at the end of episode 4 similarly seems to suggest that Berthe is now open to the Baron's wishes, as she repeats the motto, "Let him who loves me follow me." Since we already know that the previous utterance of this phrase by the Baron was followed by the violation of Berthe's condition (she did not witness the Baron actually killing the boar), the suspicious reader might anticipate that another miscarriage is in store here.

In episode 4 the Baron's enterprise takes him into Berthe's bedroom at last, where he is at least able to embrace her knees. But his own activity of the day has been too much, and the anticlimactic twist that closes this episode shows the Baron falling into "the sleep of the worn-out hunter." The activity by which the Baron had hoped to win Berthe ends by defeating him. In Reformatsky's words, "The Pointe and the actual dénoument of the novella confirm the fact that the auxiliary motif B is constructed in a seemingly concomitant, but actually contrasting manner with respect to motif A. It has the auxiliary function of creating the conflict" (p. 100). In the final episode the next morning, the magnificent figure of the Baron is unexpectedly reduced to the derided, weak figure of the husband when Berthe speaks to him as "she spoke to her husband." The passage (and the story) also ends with the crow of the cock, an ironic reversal given the failure of Baron's sexual role: "cela ne vous regarde pas"—that is nothing for you to consider.

From the reader's perspective, the "wandering viewpoint"of Iser seems an apt description for the succession of episodes in this story each with its narrative twist. From the first ("The baron was ruining himself for her") to the penultimate (the Baron's "sleep of the worn-out hunter"), each twist switches our attention to a further series of possibilities or indeterminacies, launching the issues for the next episode. Thus what was foreground at the end of one episode becomes background to the next, "which is now to exert its influence on yet another new foreground" (Iser, 1978, p. 116). In this process, Iser argues, the reader's viewpoint "switches between the textual perspectives" (p. 114). Reformatsky's account demonstrates this feature in pointing to the alternating roles of motifs A and B (the courtship, the hunt), with the subsidiary descriptive feature of the *paysage de la culture* and the *paysage de la nature*. These perspectives undoubtedly provide the most significant structuring components of the story, but the twists also allow us to refine them and glimpse additional perspectives (e.g., the cruelty implicit in Berthe's taunt, "so much the worse for you"), and to rectify the gap in Reformatsky's account noted by Doložel (1973), that the relationships and hierarchies between components are not specified (p. 82). We can consider each episode in this respect as being motivated by its twists. Just as each story we hear must confront and overcome the rejoinder "So what?", as Vipond and Hunt (1984) remind us in their account of point-driven reading, each episode also faces and answers that rejoinder in offering its concluding narrative twist. If, in episode 1b, we are led to ask what Berthe's behaviour to the Baron seems to mean and why we are being shown this particular conversation, the twist, with its unexpected insight into Berthe's attitude, provides a provisional answer: "so much the worse for you," she says "laughingly." The shift in viewpoint this offers opens another perspective on Berthe, whom we had earlier thought ready to accommodate the Baron's desires (she would succumb in the Autumn); this perspective then provides in turn a part of the background against which we read subsequent episodes (i.e., we ask what she will make of the Baron killing the boar before she arrives, or why she runs off to bed without the Baron).

The recognition of episodes and their points remains, of course, the responsibility of readers. For certain literary narratives episode boundaries, rather than being objectively determinable, may depend in part on the interpretive attitude of the reader (just as our perspective on the Maupassant story varies in certain respects from that of Reformatsky). The process of locating episodes is dramatized in recent interactive fictions or hypertext novels, where readers are rarely presented with a complete episode in one section (or "lexia"), but must activate links embedded within the text to move to additional lexia. Assuming the reader is actively constructing the narrative in so doing, the process of reading across links can be described in Jim Rosenberg's (1996) helpful term as "episode foraging." While, unlike hypertext narrative, the sequence of sentences in an ordinary narrative is not open to question, yet the concept of foraging is still relevant in that the reader is faced with the task of constructing episodes from sentences encountered one after another on the page. As we saw in the case of Maupassant's story, the division into episodes is not given by the author's paragraphing (and it is notable that the larger paragraphs of the English translator's version violate several of the episode boundaries identified here or by Reformatsky).

In addition to foraging on grounds of unity of action, time, or place, the narrative twist, as I have suggested, provides a compelling moment for reassembling the meaning of the current episode and inferring its point. In this respect, episodes also present an affective structure, as Tan (1994) has argued. Building both on discourse processing models and on emotion theory, in which an emotion felt during reading represents a particular "concern" of the reader (Frijda, 1986), Tan sees a story as a superepisode divided into a series of episodes. In his model, episodes are defined in terms of protagonist goals, as in the simple stories studied by Haberlandt and his colleagues (1980): i.e., problem, attempt, resolution, each with its accompanying emotion; and once emotion is instated, "emotion controls further cognitive processing to a considerable degree, feeding back onto its meaning determinants" (p. 184). Beyond the episode, Tan also notes that longer term emotions can be created, i.e., desires, hopes, or fears, which may be subject to alteration during the story (p. 183). In the Maupassant story it is clear that desire, to the extent that a reader feels empathy for the Baron, evolves and intensifies during the course of the story until the final episode. More specific emotions occur during particular episodes: in 1b, feelings of frustration (whether amused or irritated) at Berthe's provocations; in 1c, the erotic violence of the Baron's kiss and Berthe's answering gesture. In this way each episode can be characterized in terms of a specific feeling—although readers may vary in how they realize the feelings prompted in them by the story. In this perspective, the narrative twist becomes apparent either by intensifying the current feeling (as in 1c, when the Baron cries "Let him who loves me follow me!"), or by situating it unexpectedly (as in the opening episode, when we learn that the ardent and determined Baron "was ruining himself for her"). As Tan suggests, emotion may be the guiding feature of readers' responses, with predictive inferences primarily arising from them, while "spatial and temporal relations are only inferred in as far as they contribute to emotional appraisal" (184; cf. Miall, 1995).

8.3 Reader's Representation of Episodes in a Short Story

In the last part of this chapter I review responses to a short story and consider the evidence for episodes in readers' responses. The studies to be described were based on "The Story of an Hour" by Kate Chopin. The first study tests the proposition that each episode is characterized and distinguished from its neighbours by a particular feeling. In the second study we collected readers' think-aloud responses to the successive episodes of the same story.‡

‡ I am grateful to Don Kuiken who was my collaborator in designing and supervising this second study. The study was supported by a program grant from the Social Sciences and Humanities Research Council of Canada.

The story was divided as follows (see Appendix). In the first episode the young Mrs Louise Mallard is told of the death of her husband in a railway accident, and after weeping at once in response she decides to be alone. In the second episode she sits in her room facing a window through which she can see trees and patches of blue sky. In the third, a strange sensation gradually overcomes her—she realizes that she is free, and rejoices in the life ahead of her. In the last episode she is persuaded to emerge from her room, but as she comes down the stairs her husband unexpectedly appears through the front door, and at the sight of him she has a heart attack and dies. Each episode has a certain unity given by its location; while episodes 2 and 3 are both placed in Louise's room, the waiting that first occurs, the "suspension of intelligent thought," is followed by a marked shift in the next episode, where we are told that "There was something coming to her and she was waiting for it, fearfully." Following her response to her sudden sense of freedom, the fourth episode begins by returning us to the immediate situation: her sister "Josephine was kneeling before the closed door" and persuades her to come downstairs. Each episode also seems to arouse a characteristic feeling: grief, suspense, liberation, then triumph followed by shock. At or near the end of each episode, as in the Maupassant story, we find an important narrative twist. In each case it serves to advance our understanding of the main character and her predicament. At the end of episode 1 the narrator mentions Louise's decision to be alone (foreshadowing the recognition of her new status). The last paragraph of 2 notes that the lines of her face "bespoke repression" and her stare the "suspension of intelligent thought." In 3 the recognition of freedom that sweeps over her obliges her to realize that she had only loved her husband "sometimes" and culminates in the "self-assertion which she suddenly recognized as the strongest impulse of her being." The last episode ends with the tragic and ironic comment (now from a point of view external to Louise) that "she had died of heart disease—of joy that kills."

The first study I will describe was focused on readers' feelings, and investigated how far readers discriminated episodes on the grounds of feeling. If episodes 2 and 3 in the story, for example, are distinguished by a feeling of suspense followed by the feeling of liberation, then the reader's feelings can be expected to shift between episodes. If the reader approves of the liberation (and some of our readers didn't!), then the episode in which it occurs should be marked by a shift upward in the reader's positive feelings. By the same token, the coherence of a given episode seems likely to ensure that the reader's overall feeling remains more or less stable for the duration of an episode as its particular implications are unfolded. In other words, we can postulate that in response to the episodes of a narrative, between-episode shifts in feeling will be significantly greater that within-episode shifts. This proposal was tested by gathering responses to the four episodes of the Chopin story.

The story was subdivided into ten sections, such that the first two episodes comprised two sections each, while the last two episodes comprised three sections each. 36 readers participated in the study (they were recruited from an Introductory Psychology class, and participated for course credit). Readers were asked to read the whole story through once, then go back and rate each section (except the first) for shifts in positive and negative feeling on a 7-point scale, where 4 represented no shift. That is, comparing the current with the previous section, were their present feelings (either positive or negative) greater or lesser when compared with their feelings for the previous section. If greater, they gave a rating above 4; if less, a rating below 4. They also rated each section on a 7-point scale for how different the current section was from what they expected, where 1 meant no different (the present section is just what you expected) and 7 meant very different (the present section really surprised you); and they provided an optional rating on a 3-point scale for strikingness (but only if they found a particular phrase or sentence in the current section striking, which they were asked to identify by underlining it in the text of the story).

The findings from this study provide strong support for the proposal. To gain an overall measure of feeling, shifts in feeling were counted, regardless of direction of shift, for both negative and positive feelings. It was found that overall between-episode feeling shifted a mean of 1.87 points on the rating scale, whereas within-episode feeling shifted only 1.04 points—a significant difference, $t(35) = 3.478, p < .001$.

The direction of the feeling shifts were also measured separately. As shown below in Table 8.2., it is apparent that negative feelings remained largely static within episodes while declining between episodes, and that positive feelings increased markedly between episodes, as though at the end of an episode readers became more optimistic about the prospects in the new episode (as would be expected if readers did appreciate, for example, the move from suspension to liberation). The differences of within-episode and between-episode mean shifts are both significant.

Table 8.2 Means of Negative and Positive Shifts of Readers' Feelings Across Story Episodes (4 = no shift):

	Within	Between	*t*-test (df 35)
Negative shift	4.09	3.35	4.936**
Positive shift	3.69	4.23	-3.127*

$*p < .005$ $**p < .001$

The results of the third rating task, the difference of a section from what was expected, provide some support for this picture. The ratings capture the rising action of the first three episodes with a succession of upward moves followed by a decline. In the fourth episode, however, the climax of the story occurs near the end as Mr Mallard unexpectedly arrives home, and this provides the point of maximum difference from expectation. This progression can be seen clearly in a graph of the mean ratings, shown in Figure 8.1. The difference of between-episode from within-episode ratings on this measure is significant if the last episode is not included: mean between-episode ratings are 3.89, while within-episode ratings are 3.48, $t(35) = 2.227, p > .05$.

Figure 8.1 Graph of Mean Difference Ratings for Story Sections (between-episode sections: C11, E19, H31)

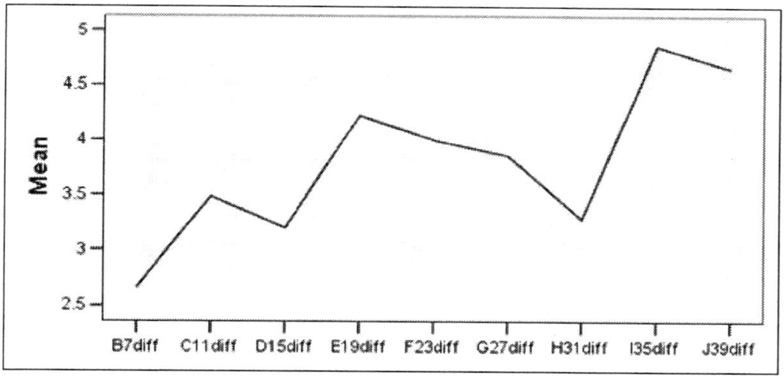

Readers were also asked to underline phrases or sentences that they found striking. 7 out of 36 readers did not mark any passages as striking, and some who marked passages did not provide strikingness ratings. But the underlinings themselves point to the episode structure of the story, since the passages marked most frequently point either to the narrative turning points of the story or to the "twists" at or near the end of episodes. For the purpose of this analysis the story was divided into its sentences (65 sentences overall). The frequencywith which each sentence or part sentence was underlined was counted. Where a reader's underlinings crossed more than one sentence, this was treated as one occurrence and the frequency of 1 was split across all the sentences underlined. In citing sentences in what follows, I give the paragraph number containing the sentence (see Appendix).

In Episode 1 the two sentences most frequently underlined (5 occurrences for both) were:

> 2. It was he who had been in the newspaper office when intelligence of the railroad disaster was received, with Brently Mallard's name leading the list of "killed."

> 3. She wept at once, with sudden, wild abandonment, in her sister's arms.

Here the initiating plot event, Mallard's supposed death, is selected, but not the first sentence which already announces the event, rather the occurrence of his name on a list. Readers had already read the story, so that they knew this report of the death to be incorrect, thus the sentence effectively represents the development of the story as a whole. The second sentence underlined demonstrates Louise's immediate acceptance of the death, thus it lays the ground for the assertion of independence that is to come.

In Episode 2 the last sentence was underlined most often (by 6 readers):

> 8. It was not a glance of reflection, but rather indicated a suspension of intelligent thought.

This is the last sentence of the episode, in which we have been shown Louise passively waiting. It is a typical "twist" statement, preparing us to find something new in the next episode. No mention of "reflection"or "thought" has occurred yet, and their introduction here signals the problem of knowing where Louise will find the resources to go on with life.

In the third episode 13.75 underlinings are given to the first mention of "free":

> 11. She said it over and over under her breath: "free, free, free!"

while the second most frequently underlined sentence (5 readers) is the reiterated assertion at the end of the episode:

> 16. "Free! Body and soul free!" she kept whispering.

This episode is dominated most obviously by Louise's discovery of her supposed freedom: her realization occurs early in the episode (paragraph 11 among paragraphs 9 to 16); the episode then plateaus, as it were, while Louise considers retrospectively and prospectively what her new-found sense of freedom means. That the second most frequently underlined sentence, 16, is the last in the episode may indicate a "twist" effect, with readers alert to the ironic implications of Louise's repeated assertion.

In the last episode the twist in the plot attracts the most attention, with 10 readers underlining the reappearance of Brently Mallard:

> 21. It was Brently Mallard who entered, a little travel-stained, composedly carrying his grip-sack and umbrella.

while 18 readers (the most for any sentence) underlined the last sentence (usually only the last phrase):

> 23. When the doctors came they said she had died of heart disease—of joy that kills.

The ironic last phrase, not surprisingly, attracts the most attention from readers—half of all readers underlined this sentence.

Overall, then, this first empirical study supports the conception of episodes as marked by distinctive shifts in feeling. Feeling overcomes the limitations of working memory by providing a platform for registering the significance of the events as they unfold within an episode. Feeling can also be seen to mark out the shifts from one episode to the next as tension rises, or as changes occur in the meaning of the narrative situation. Since feeling, as I discussed earlier, relates what is being read to a reader's self-concept, the feeling operative during episodes provides a vehicle for empathy, sympathy, rejection, and other potentially self-defining processes that position the reader, defining and perhaps serving to change her attitudes towards the subject matter of the narrative. In this respect the occurrence of episode feeling and its shifts can be seen as the most powerful and most binding of the literary experiences available from narrative, exceeding developments in plot, the invitation of point of view, and the potential intimacy of empathy, since episode feeling incorporates and relates all of these components. Above all, it is worth reiterating that episodes provide the frames within which shifts in meaning are negotiated by the reader (such as the shift in Chopin's story from repression to liberation across episodes 2 and 3), since episodes move the horizons within which meaning emerges; thus, a meaning apparent in one episode can be radically modified when it reappears in the next.

More evidence for the importance of episodes was gained from the second study that I will now describe. This study was also based on Chopin's story. For this study we presented the story on computer, sentence by sentence, but pausing after each episode, that is, four times: here readers were asked to make comments about their experience of the story so far by talking to a tape recorder; they then answered nine specific questions by entering ratings. After this their reading of the next section continued. The comments were later transcribed for analysis. We collected responses from 45 readers.

In examining the responses I discuss the extent to which readers characterize their overall sense of an episode, and whether the twist at or near the end of each episode is noticed. But, given that these were first readings, my concern is less with how often readers made such comments than with the light such comments would cast on readers' developing understanding of the story. For readers who were able to describe the point of the story (i.e., offer a plausible and coherent account of what it meant to them), how dependent was this on the episodic structure as I have described it? In the following paragraphs, I first describe the responses of several readers who appear to have developed a good understanding of the story; then examples of those who appear to have found it difficult.

Reader A231 offers a brief and largely impersonal reading of the story, yet manages to characterize central aspects of each episode while also mentioning its narrative twist. She interprets the first episode in the light of Louise's wish to be alone: while "people are trying to be gentle to her, the heartbreak of this situation is more than she can bear. She just flees. She runs away." In her comment on the second episode she suggests perceptively (having only read this far in the story) that while Louise appears to wish to forget, "She just begins to experience those feelings that she's trying to repress." In the third, the reader interprets the sense of freedom as a manoeuvre: "She only loved him sometimes. And she's trying to make it okay with herself." In the last episode the reader clearly grasps the ironic reversal in the final sentence: to see her husband after all "was almost a heartbreak"; "it wasn't a joy that killed her; it was the lack of the joy." The reader remains focused on Louise's point of view, seeking to understand it; and in attending to the twists at the end of each episode the reader is able to infer a coherent meaning for the story overall, as the final comment shows. The reader can be described as "point-driven," in the terms of Vipond and Hunt (1984), having noticed and responded to the "nonstandard elements" in the narrative, in particular the twists that open up new perspectives and call for interpretive effort.

Another reader, A240, applies the story more particularly to her own condition, both past and in the present. Commenting on the first episode, she recalls that when she read the story before in an English class her grandmother had just died: reading it now brings back the memory of her emotions then. While she did resist the significance of the death, unlike Louise, she says "I wanted to be alone, myself, but not for the same reasons as she." This difference may lie behind her lack of comment on the story in response to the second episode (she refers to the process of reading on the computer), but by the third episode she is strongly re-engaged with the story. She is impelled to reflect on her own sense of independence, and how when hiking across a high mountain pass her bodily sense of freedom was like that of Louise. But she also notes that love can compromise this: "I also was thinking about . . . how she had loved sometimes, often she had not. Didn't not. I was thinking about past boyfriends, actually," whether she had been in love. But then, "I was living for me now, as she was." In response to the last episode she recalls her earlier sense of shock on first reading the story, and how the story still compels her to think about the protagonist's predicament, that "she felt free and then all of a sudden it just came collapsing down on her." She adds, "there are some aspects in my life that came to mind"; although this is not specific, but rather "just the whole idea of how fast life can change." This reader is thus also point-driven, but in a way that seems to illuminate her experience and sense of her own life. Unlike the first reader, however, this commentary shows a reader who seems motivated by a particular concern, that of independence. From her first comment on wishing to be alone to the final comment on life (that it can change suddenly, as it does in the story), this reader adopts Louise's point of view, and seems able to use this narrative experience figuratively in order to reflect on her own stance towards life. Again, the narrative twists in three of the four episodes seem central to this process.

Several other readers show a similar process: a personal concern is evoked by the story, and this then develops alongside the story across several comments, and perhaps at times enables a convergence with the story when the character's and the reader's perspective seem to merge. For example, reader A218 found herself in episode 2 "placing myself in the woman's place. And I found myself picturing myself in a position in that room with a window and the birds and just all that she was seeing." As she put it, "there is kind of a blending of the character and myself." Her concern here is her response to loss, and how far her reaction to grief is the same as the character's, but the larger issue for this reader is, once again, the question of independence. In expressing this near the end of the last comment, she adopts the generalized second person pronoun, which we have seen in many other readers' comments (Kuiken, Miall, and Sikora, 1994), and which usually seems to signify the merging of reader and character: "That individual freedom versus the freedom that comes from loving another person and forgetting and forsaking your own wants and needs."

In summary, the readers described here behave as though each episode has a point, and they often identify the narrative twist as a salient passage for inferring the point, presumably because the twist introduces a new perspective that is, at the same time, fraught with indeterminacy. In so doing, however, readers also tend to be drawn into evoking their own experiences or perspectives and reflecting on their personal stance on the issues they see being raised by the story. The narrative twist seems an effective agent for engaging readers' close attention, principally because in the context of the current episode it seems incongruous, or adds unexpected information. Why would a person just bereaved want to be alone (episode 1)? What lies behind the appearance of repression in her face (episode 2)? Readers who noticed these passages seem to have been better placed to form a coherent representation of the story overall.

Other readers, in contrast, may respond to particular elements of the story that seem important to them, but appear to develop only a partial representation of the story or may even misrepresent it. For reader A264 the opening episode bring to mind the death of her grandfather when she was aged seven, so her main response is to wonder how "one deals with shock." She has no response to the specific contents of episode 2. The third episode, she suggests "is not so much about death but about love," yet she seems to think this points to "a philosophy called fatalism," adding, "It's really funny how you love a person . . . because you love that person, that sense of bondage can get so heavy." She is alert to the misreading of Louise by her family in the fourth episode: "often we don't really know what really happens in people's minds"; there is, she says, a fine line "between pain and joy, between loss and gain." Her comments capture a part of the story's pathos but neither its overall irony nor its challenge to familiar conceptions of love. The memory of her grandfather appears not to be relevant to her response to the remainder of the story.

For reader A234, the theme of the story is the role of relations and friends during bereavement. Episode 1 reminds her of the deaths she has experienced of grandparents and of a friend. In episode 2 she recognizes Louise's need to be alone, but adds, "all of a sudden you do realize, you know, that there are people that you can talk to and that kind of thing." Episode 3 seems "abstract," and Louise's sense of freedom appears foreign to her: she cannot see herself being made free by someone's death. When she has felt "smothered," she says, "it's been resolved through, you know, conflict resolution and having to sit down and talk things out." Thus, in episode 4, she takes the family point of view: "I can definitely identify with Josephine and trying to get Louise to come out of the room." She may have misread the ending of the story: "I . . . don't know of much joy that comes from dying" (which seems to echo the narrator's final phrase, "joy that kills").

These readers, and others like them, tend to characterize the episodes only partially or not at all, and they rarely notice or comment upon the narrative twists. While the readers we have just described are clearly point-driven readers (Vipond and Hunt, 1984), the points they elaborate encompass only a part of the story's meaning, or, as in the last instance, import a point that reflects the reader's own preoccupations rather than being derived from the story. More effective readers, the evidence suggests, tend both to respond to what is distinctive in each episode and to be influenced by the narrative twists that each episode contains. This makes it more possible for the reader to experience the modifying processes that a literary story makes possible. As we saw, for reader A240 this involved first an affirmation of her own bodily-felt sense of independence, then, as she recalled her shock at the end of the story, "just the whole idea of how fast life can change."

As the earlier review showed, episodes can be characterized by a number of convergent criteria: by unity of action (goal and outcome), as a phase in a character's predicament, by coherent location in place and time, and above all by feeling. To this analysis I have added the role of the narrative twist occurring at or near the end of an episode, serving to intensify or redirect the issues raised, and itself characterized by a distinct development in readers' feeling. Above all, episodes provide the phases during which issues of concern to readers are managed and developed: if readers experience the modifying of feelings or concerns about the self as a result of literary reading, it is in the transitions between one episode and the next that we are likely to find such changes—between the twist at the end of one episode and the onset of the scenario provided by the next. In studying the cognitive challenges of reading narrative, especially readers' concerns about a story, how it relates to their own experiences, and the emotional resonance it has for readers, the analysis of the episodes of a story may thus provide a valuable framework for identifying the key developments in the responses of readers.

•CHAPTER NINE•

Literariness: Are There Neuropsychological Indicators?

9.1 Literary Reading

In her memoirs the novelist Paula Fox (2003) reports that at the age of 15 she first read a novel by D. H. Lawrence, *Sons and Lovers*.* She was attending a boarding school in Montreal that year. She tells us that

> As I read the novel, I sank into the world of Paul Morel. The text ignited a latent sense in me of the desirability of self-knowledge. There were other realities in life beside my own. I had not really thought about my life. I began to glimpse at the most elementary level fragments of my own reality. The novel calmed my turbulence, eased my restlessness and shame. (p. 199)

This is all she has to say, yet her comments capture, I suggest, at least three features of the experience of reading that we can postulate as distinctively literary. Through reading we extend the reach of self-knowledge; the experience of reading involves feeling; and reading is anticipatory, allowing us to sense some future understanding. It is this combination of three components, self-reference, feeling, and anticipation that appear characteristic of literary reading—yet in themselves they do not constitute literariness.

As she reads the novel, Fox tells us that she "sank into the world of Paul Morel." Central to her account is her sense during reading of "other realities in life beside my own"; the process of reading involves decentering, an ability to focus on the not-self. This capacity for disinterested appreciation is, I will suggest, a key element of aesthetic response, part of our neuropsychological structure. But once the not-self, or external realm has been understood, its energies

---

* This chapter was previously published in Danish in *Kritik*, 174, 2005, 64–72.

become available as a metaphor to recenter the self. As Fox puts it, having engaged with realities outside her own life through Lawrence's novel, she "began to glimpse at the most elementary level fragments of my own reality." Thus art is not assimilated to the realm of the self as other experiences may have been prior to the encounter with the work of art; on the contrary, the self is extended to accommodate what was previously an unknown way of relating to the world (cf. the two possibilities outlined by De Certeau, 1984, p. 166). It is notable that Fox finds this a calming experience, presumably a release from the self-absorbing emotions of restlessness and shame: her reading has opened channels for the energies of new feelings and modes of self-reflection that were unavailable before.

I will employ the term *literariness* to refer to the combination of formal qualities in the literary text and the array of responses these initiate that we can consider decentering (for an appropriate reader at an appropriate time). Literariness is, necessarily, a result of interaction between text and reader, not merely a specific set of formal textual features. Within this framework I will consider three ways in which literariness may be embodied by distinctive neuropsychological processes: the defamiliarization-recontextualization cycle in response to foregrounding; the dynamic structure of narrative episodes in prose and poetry; and the functions of empathy in our response to characters in narrative. For each I will discuss the neuropsychological evidence that appears to support the distinctiveness of the literary experience in question. There are no doubt other processes beyond the three I will discuss, deriving from genre expectations or from other narrative features than empathy with a character, but the three I will discuss already, I believe, mark out a part of what is distinctive in the response to literary narrative.

Thus the specific conception of literariness I address is that of a shift in feelings and concepts that is brought about by each of the three formal aspects to be discussed. For Paula Fox her reading showed her that "There were other realities in life beside my own." Such realities can be evoked by the encounter with defamiliarizing devices in literary language, by the shift in understanding that characterizes an episode, or by the self-modifying effects of empathy with a character.

By turning to neuropsychological evidence and considering the architecture of the mind, my intention is to provide more reliable support for the arguments about literariness than is available from conventional critical procedures, or even from a review of the cognitive processes thought to be relevant to literary reading (e.g., Stockwell, 2002). I will attempt to establish what neuropsychological processes facilitate the experience of literary reading, and thus ask whether literariness has any basis in a specific, identifiable array of brain functions. Are we, that is, in a position to identify a unique constellation of brain processes underlying the experience of literariness?

9.2 The Defamiliarization-Recontextualization Cycle

One commonly noted feature of literariness is the distinctive stylistic resources on which a writer can draw. In Kate Chopin's "The Story of an Hour" (1894/1999) the bereaved protagonist is sitting alone in her room where she can see through the window "the tops of trees that were all aquiver with the new spring life." This phrase is striking for the repetition of /i/ sounds, and the unusual metric effect given by the series of unstressed syllables following the first stressed syllable of "acquiver"; both effects might be considered to provide aural support for the meaning of the phrase. As we have found in our previous studies (Miall and Kuiken, 1994a) readers tend to notice such effects, even if only by reading the phrases in which they occur more slowly. While in the case of this phrase the meaning at first appears to be purely descriptive, the "new life" which is attributed to the trees will shortly become a central vision of the protagonist for herself as she envisages a life without the oppressive presence of her husband. Thus, while the phrase when first encountered may be defamiliarizing (found striking or evocative), later during reading the conceptual or affective implications of the phrase shift ground and are recontextualized.

As first defined by Roman Jakobson in 1921 (Erlich, 1981, p. 172) *literariness* referred to the linguistic devices said to characterize a literary work. The problem with this approach is that it disregarded the role of the reader: such devices may occur in a newspaper article that no reader would consider literary, although it is likely that in such circumstances features will occur accidentally and not be organized for any specific effect. In the present conception, literariness is considered an interactive process: a reader encounters literary devices during reading (devices can be analysed in the light of foregrounding theory: Van Peer, 1986), finds them striking (i.e., defamiliarizing), and often experiences a distinctive feeling as a result (Miall and Kuiken, 1994a). As our later work suggested, readers who experience such moments of defamiliarization tend to experience a subsequent shift in understanding: this appears to involve a search for meaning guided by the feeling that foregrounding has evoked. A new understanding emerges downstream of the moment of foregrounding, approximately one to two minutes later (Miall and Kuiken, 2001). In other words, the concept or experience that was defamiliarized at the moment of foregrounding becomes recontextualized.

The findings of our studies (Miall and Kuiken, 1994a) and those of van Peer (1986) suggest that foregrounding is recognized by all competent readers, and that the encounter with foregrounded features plays a formative role in the interpretive effort of a reader; in discourse processing terms, literary reading tends to involve schema creation. Although psychological evidence for this cyclical process is now available (Miall and Kuiken, 2001), neuropsychological evidence is less clear: the components of the process clearly depend on right-hemispheric (RH) functions, especially in the prefrontal cortex, which have been well studied; but the cyclical process itself remains elusive. Thus, as Kane (2004) puts it in an important recent article: "over time, evidence has been mounting to show that the right hemisphere controls, or is capable of controlling on its own, a number of very subtle but intriguing 'linguistic' functions . . . which, this paper will attempt to argue, are virtually synonymous with 'poetry' or 'poetic' speech." She goes on to show in detail the evidence for RH involvement in imagery, metaphor, synaesthesia, personification, synecdoche, and other poetic features. Yet she overstates the case when she argues "one could assert that the degree of right-hemispheric involvement in language is what differentiates 'poetic' or 'literary' from 'referential' or 'technical' speech and texts" (p. 22). Not all figurative devices in language are poetic in effect; nor does the understanding of attitude or feeling in spoken language (what is usually called its prosodic aspect) make such language literary. The question at issue, then, is whether the interactive process we have termed the defamiliarization-reconceptualization cycle has neuropsychological correlates beyond those of its constituent linguistic devices (or foregrounding).

Perhaps the most persuasive evidence is provided by the studies of Beeman and his colleagues. In an experimental task that has some processing similarity to the problem of understanding a passage of foregrounding, Bowden and Beeman (1998) showed the advantage of RH at delayed encoding. The task required participants to find a fourth word that would make a familiar word pair with three other presented words: for example, presented with *high*, *district*, and *house*, the participant solves the problem if they can name the word *school*. The task, described as an insight problem, is similar to a standard test for creative thinking, the Remote Associates Test. In the present study, after 15 seconds either the solution word or an unrelated word was presented to either the right or left visual field (i.e., to the left or right hemispheres, respectively). The participant pronounces the word, with the time taken to pronounce the word being measured. It was found that whether the participant has solved the problem or not, the right hemisphere showed greater priming than the left hemisphere for the solution word compared with an unrelated word. In a second experiment, participants pressed a yes or no button to identify a target word as the solution word shown in either the left or right visual field; participants showed a (left visual field) RH advantage for recognizing solutions to unsolved problems. The study suggests that RH has readier access to the (more remote) solution word, but only after an interval of several seconds. In other studies (Beeman and Bowden, 2000) it was shown that RH advantage was present at 7 seconds, but that at earlier intervals (2 or 1.25 seconds) the RH advantage did not appear. This argues that while both hemispheres initially activate the solution, only the RH maintains its activation.

The approach of Beeman and his colleagues is based on the conception that the left hemisphere (LH) is specialized for processing the close associates of a given word or concept, whereas RH is specialized for "coarse" semantic coding such as, for example, connotative or metaphoric meaning, or the novel uses of verbs—associations, in other words, that are more distant. On first presentation, LH is likely to dominate the associates considered; but after an interval of from 7 to 15 seconds RH processing shows an advantage. While the Remote Associates Test is not literary in its effects, it has some parallels to the task facing the reader of a foregrounded passage, such as Chopin's trees "all aquiver with the new spring life." Such a passage is striking because it resists being readily understood: in other words, the close associates of the words being read (LH associates) are inadequate to understanding it. If LH associates limit understanding of "acquiver" to the movement of leaves, the metaphoric extension to the protagonist's predicament remains unrealized at first. Since understanding only emerges over time (as Miall and Kuiken, 2001, showed), it is evident that the RH remote associates are more likely to remain available and to provide the basis for the shift in understanding that will emerge.

This proposed RH advantage is amplified when it is taken together with the additional known RH advantages for phonetic coloration (prosody) and for feeling—the RH is connected with limbic system centres for feeling, notably the hippocampus and amygdala. The hippocampus, for example, according to Epstein (2004) has had two roles assigned to it. The first, following the work of Gray, is "to detect conflicts between competing courses of action," which is consistent with "neuroimaging experiments that show hippocampal activation in response to novelty" (p. 229). Second, the predictive capacities of the hippocampus and their role in memory suggest "the hippocampus is the mechanism that allows stored information about the regularities of the world to be applied to the current substantive thought in order to obtain a subsequent thought that is related to the current thought in a sensible way" (p. 230). In both roles, the hippocampus thus helps resolve the ambiguity or indeterminacy that foregrounding often creates; and it provides resources from long term memory as the basis for recontextualization following the foregrounded moment.

This elaborated conception of RH processing thus provides some basis for confirming the defamiliarization-reconceptualization cycle, with its shift of processing over time from LH to RH. In the literary perspective, the most dramatic example of the disablement of LH associates would be during response to the sublime: here, the delayed emergence of the more remote RH associates would appear to correspond to the experience of suspension during the sublime moment, while the ensuing transcendence of the regular concepts of the understanding is a RH experience. Indeed, the sublime can be seen as a device that partly disables LH responses in favour of RH remote associates which then play a central role rather than being masked as in normal discourse.

9.3 Narrative Episodes

Beyond the defamiliarization-reconceptualization cycle, which can be seen operating in response to foregrounding at the phrase level of a literary text, the *episode* provides another frame within which shifts in feeling and understanding are likely to occur. As I showed in the previous chapter, an episode usually consists of a number of sentences taking up half a page or a page, bounded by continuity in the temporal or spatial setting or both. The most important feature of the episode, however, is that it provides a thematically distinctive topic requiring a shift in the reader's understanding. Episodes often function by introducing and establishing a certain setting or concern, then offering a special twist, or insight, in the final sentence or two. Such a twist has the effect of motivating reader interest in the next episode, which it thus helps to launch.

An example short story that divides clearly into episodes is Chopin's "The Story of an Hour." In the first episode the young Mrs. Louise Mallard is told of the death of her husband in a railway accident, and after weeping at once in response she decides to be alone. In the second episode she sits in her room facing a window through which she can see trees and patches of blue sky and cloud. In the third, a strange sensation gradually overcomes her—she realizes that she is free, and rejoices in the life ahead of her. In the last episode she is persuaded to emerge from her room, but as she comes down the stairs her husband unexpectedly appears through the front door, and at the sight of him she has a heart attack and dies. Each episode has a certain unity given to it not only by its location but by its thematic concerns. Also, at or near the end of each episode we find an important narrative twist that serves to advance our understanding of the main character and her predicament. For example, at the end of episode 1 the narrator mentions Louise's decision to be alone (foreshadowing the recognition of her new status); the last paragraph of 2 notes that the lines of her face "bespoke repression" and her stare the "suspension of intelligent thought, " leaving us to ask what might come to her in her predicament now.

The readers we studied often demonstrated an awareness of episode structures in their responses to this story. The question to be asked here, however, is what neuropsychological functions make the response to the episode possible as a literary experience. A general framework for such an understanding is provided by Grafman (2002), whose account of the prefrontal cortex suggests several of the features necessary for the comprehension of the literary episode. The role of the prefrontal cortex in the online modulation and integration of many central cognitive processes, such as planning, memory, anticipation, etc., has led Grafman to label its represen𝑡ional unit the Structured Event Complex (SEC). According to Grafman the prefrontal cortex, in comparison with other areas of the brain, shows sustained firing of neurons over time, indicating its role in working memory; at the same time, the neurons appear to handle more inputs than other neurons, enabling the prefrontal cortex to integrate signals from a wider range of sources (p. 293). Grafman theorizes that the SEC, which is distinctive to the prefrontal cortex, is "a representation (or set of representations) in action, essentially a representation that, when activated, stays activated over a limited or extended time domain. . . . A representation, when activated, may or may not fit within the typical time window described as working memory. When it does we are conscious of the representation. When it doesn't, we can still process that representation but we may not have direct conscious access to all of its contents" (p. 297–8). This account provides a first approximation to the literary experience of the episode.

Grafman's reference to working memory is a reminder that the retention of cognitive contents in memory is strictly limited (typically seven items plus or minus two), which would appear to provide a boundary to the SEC. However, the prefrontal cortex also plays a key role in the modulation of feeling (Miall, 1995). For instance, in Chopin's story the second episode includes descriptions of the protagonist's perceptions in the room where she has gone to be alone: "The delicious breath of rain was in the air." As a proposition, this is likely to be shunted from working memory before the end of the episode by various other propositions that follow it; the feeling it evokes, however, stands in contrast to the sorrow experienced by the protagonist, and may anticipate a possible alternative to that sorrow, thus it is likely to remain at least in the background of the reader's response until the end of the episode. The feeling imbued by the sentence, in other words, may remain accessible as part of the reader's processing of the episode, even though the reader loses direct conscious access to the sentence itself. Grafman goes on to suggest that SECs that are ill structured require "the subject to adapt to unpredictable events using analogical reasoning or similarity judgment to determine the sequence of actions on-line" (p. 299). Here the likely role of the distinctive RH processing comes into play, as I outlined in the previous section: in Grafman's account, RH "is thought to be specialized for coarse, slower coding, allowing for the processing of information that is more distantly related . . . and could be adept at integrating or synthesizing information across events in time" (p. 301)—for instance, accommodating the "delicious breath of rain" to the ambiguous state of the protagonist later in the same episode by sensing an anticipation of an alternative state (as one of our readers put it at the end of episode 2, "She just begins to experience those feelings that she's trying to repress").

As Mar (2004) points out in his study of the neuropsychology of narrative, Baddeley (2000) has now extended his conception of working memory (WM) to include what he terms an episodic buffer, a unit roughly equivalent to a prose paragraph containing some 15–20 "idea units." In Baddeley's account, "we appear to have evidence for a temporary store that is capable of holding complex information, manipulating it and utilizing it over a time scale far beyond the assumed capacity of the slave systems of WM" (p. 420), i.e., the systems Baddeley has termed the phonological loop and the visuospatial sketchpad. The episodic buffer he proposes is "a process or mechanism for synergistically combining information from various subsystems into a form of temporary representation" (p. 421), involving "more active and attentionally demanding integrative processes" (p. 422). The literary episode is undoubtedly such a process for the reader, although what makes it distinctively literary is most likely the twist or shift in understanding required at or near the end of an episode. Here, the ability of the SEC or episode buffer to accommodate ambiguity or anomaly and to facilitate the creation of a coherent aesthetic experience seems essential; and while the accounts of the SEC and episode buffer do not yet tell us what is distinctively literary in such an experience, they provide a framework that alerts us where to look and what kind of process may be in question.

9.4 Empathy

While the previous two processes I have discussed, the defamiliarization-reconceptualization cycle and the episode, may often involve shifts in self-understanding, probably the greatest challenge to self-understanding occurs when the reader is invited to empathize with a character in a literary text (usually fiction). As Nussbaum has commented, this can be a disturbing experience, since literary reading can challenge our usual self-protective mechanisms: "Literary works that promote identification and emotional reaction cut through those stratagems, requiring us to see and to respond to many things that may be difficult to confront" (6). Readers may find the fictional experiences of others resonant with implications for self understanding. One reader of a Katherine Mansfield story, for example, in which the main character is alarmed by the visit of a funeral procession that arrives at her house in error ("The Wrong House"), commented "It just makes you realize that . . . your own mortality is something that can make you unable to think clearly. . . . While you think you still are alive and well and able to take care of yourself and help others, somebody else has decided that you can't" (Kuiken, Miall, and Sikora, 2004, p. 183). As Iris Murdoch (1970) put it, "In the moral life the enemy is the fat relentless ego" (p. 52); empathy during literary reading can effectively cut across or challenge the ego.

In neuropsychological terms, empathy appears (once again) to depend on right-hemisphere functions. Winner, et al. (1998), found that RH-damaged patients were unable to reliably infer second order beliefs (i.e., what A believes B knows). In a comparable series of right-brain studies, Happé et al. (1999) found that the ability of patients with RH damage (adults with right hemisphere stroke) to understand the point of view of a fictional character was challenged. "In one study using story materials and two using cartoons, patients' understanding of materials requiring attribution of mental states (e.g. ignorance, false belief) was significantly worse than their understanding of non-mental control materials" (p. 211). They propose that "difficulties expressing and recognising emotion are sufficient to account for many of the social and communicative impairments recorded" (p. 214).

While emotion is clearly integral to the capacities in question, the findings of other researchers suggest that the deficit is more specifically in what has been termed Theory of Mind. The specific mechanism that would appear to undergird empathy in literary response is the interaction between the representation of the self, and the representation of the mind of another (fictional) person. According to Vogeley and his colleagues (Vogeley, et al., 2001) these two representations occur in opposite hemispheres. However, while self-perception occurs in the right hemisphere, and perception of others (or Theory of Mind) occurs in the left hemisphere, interaction between them takes place in the right prefrontal cortex. The findings in this study were based on response to stories with different degrees of self or other involvement, while brain regions activated were measured by fMRI.

The approach of Vogeley and his colleagues offers a development of the specific case of negative emotions I have discussed previously (Miall, 1995). As I pointed out, literary texts often deal with predominantly negative situations, enabling a reader to experience negative emotions that are normally repressed as socially unacceptable. As Borod, el al. (2002) have suggested, in conceptualizing the difference between the emotions facilitated by RH and LH, "One explanation involves the operation of social display rules (controlled by the left hemisphere) that normally inhibit the expression of [negative] primary emotions believed to be mediated by the right hemisphere" (p. 25). Thus it is the RH, under appropriate circumstances, that allows experience of negative emotions suppressed by LH. Empathy during literary reading is just such a circumstance, if, as Vogeley, et al. suggest, the interaction of self and other perceptions involves the integrated functioning of both hemispheres. Empathy would thus be required to overcome the role attributed to RH by Ross, Homan, and Buck (1994), who argue that RH "may exert an affective-cognitive influence over the left by suppressing from conscious recall the social emotions surrounding a life event" (p. 12). At the same time, they also suggest that one role of LH is "enhancing socially appropriate and inhibiting socially inappropriate primary emotional displays generated by the right amygdala" (p. 14). Literary reading that involves empathy would thus, in the light of these findings, operate as a powerful incentive to overcome the normal repression of negative emotion in the self-representation system of the RH: this would allow for the archetypal literary experiences, often discussed, of catharsis, or the negative sublime, or the more routine (but still significant) type of self-referential insight of the reader I mentioned above who was moved to reflect on her mortality.

9.5 The Wider Context

While the neuropsychological evidence I have been able to review in the previous three sections points to brain functions that appear to support literary response, there is as yet no direct or unequivocal evidence of the literary processes I have outlined. Recent authors such as Mar (2004) writing on narrative or Kane (2004) on poetic language, have, with the benefit of recent research, been able to point to an array of neuropsychogical components likely to be implicated in the experience of literature, but the unique configuration of brain processes that identifies the literary remains to be established. Possibly this achievement is near at hand, but one clarification that will certainly be required is agreement on what specific experiences constitute literariness. Moreover, capturing in a laboratory setting the kind of experience that, for example, Paula Fox (2003) reports in her reading of D. H. Lawrence, may not be easy. Important theoretical and technical difficulties remain in the way of establishing conclusively what neuropsychological processes appear to characterize literary reading.

My purpose in this chapter has been to draw attention to three processes in particular in which we can identify experiences that are distinctively (if not exclusively) literary, and to consider what neuropsychological functions must be required in order for such experiences to be possible. Such an endeavour must be supplemented in at least two ways in future research: as I outline below, first it will require a better understanding of the temporal modes of literary response; and, second, a broader approach to the aesthetic dimensions of literariness that will accommodate the insights of research into other arts forms, such as music or the visual arts.

Each of the literary processes I outlined earlier involve a temporal dimension, an unfolding of an experience over time that allows both for the instantiation of self-understanding and a shift in the self brought about by the literary devices of defamiliarization, episodic development, or empathy. One of the questions raised by the processes I have discussed is the key role of anticipation, often considered in connection with the so-called frontal lobe syndrome. It has been shown that anticipation is a key component of the processes modulated by the intact prefrontal cortex, and that it is the role of feeling in particular that instantiates and tracks the online anticipatory processes (Miall, 1976, 1995). This has been demonstrated often. For example, Bechara (2004), in studies designed to examine the somatic marker hypothesis of Damasio (1999), refers to the disability produced by a lesion of the prefrontal cortex as a "myopia for the future" (p. 32). He carried out a study of gambling games with cards, using skin conductance response (SCR) as the marker of feeling. Patients with damage in the pre-frontal cortex and normal control subjects both generated SCRs after a choice of good or bad cards; however, normal participants, after becoming more familiar with the game, also began to generate SRC responses *in advance* of choosing cards, whereas the brain-damaged patients never developed such a response. "These results," says Bechara, "provide strong support for the notion that decision-making is guided by emotional signals (or somatic states), which are generated in anticipation of future events" (p. 32).

It seems likely that a similar anticipatory response is called into play during the literary processes I have outlined. In each process a future state of understanding is put in question: the recontextualization that is to follow the defamiliarizing moment, the narrative development that is to follow the twist at or near the end of an episode, or the fate of the character (and its implications for the self) about whom the reader has developed empathic insight. Since feeling itself has an anticipatory component (Miall, 1995; and see Chapter 5), it is evident that the intact right hemisphere and its limbic system connections are the appropriate brain region for the anticipatory function. But more is at stake if a response during reading is to be experienced as literary. Here, some additional suggestions are provided by the work of Davidson and his colleagues (2003). They point out that the prefrontal cortex (PFC) plays a self-directing role, and that recent studies show that the PFC "maintains the representation of goals and the means to achieve them. Particularly in situations that are ambiguous, the PFC sends bias signals to other areas of the brain" (p. 9). In other words, a preferred outcome in the face of conflict is modulated by PFC signals. However, these are affective in nature: "Affect-guided planning and anticipation that involves the experience of emotion associated with an anticipated choice is the hallmark of adapted, emotion-based decision making" (p. 9). They suggest that the role of the amygdala lies "in directing attention to affectively salient stimuli and issuing a call for further processing of stimuli that have major significance for the individual" (p. 15). On the basis of such a structure, it is possible to account for the conflicts in feeling that are involved in the literary processes I have outlined: a signal feature of the defamiliarizing moment, for example, is that the presence of an alliteration or a novel metaphor invokes a feeling that contrasts with and cuts across the prevailing affective tone. As we have shown in more detail elsewhere (Miall and Kuiken, 2002), one of the most characteristic features of literary response is the experience of self-modifying feelings. In such a situation, an existing feeling is recontextualized in relation to an ensuing feeling (as the hubris in a Greek tragedy is modified by the advent of pity and fear, in the classical model of catharsis). Generalizing from this example, we can suggest that the experience of ambiguity, recontextualization, and modifying of feeling is a central characteristic of the literary experience, and that the anticipatory functions of PFC serve to modulate or direct the implications of the feelings in question, doing so in the light of the reader's overall sense of the direction that the text is taking.

This discussion can serve to sketch the outlines of a possible aesthetic model of the literary experience. At the same time, it would be appropriate to ask what continuities this experience might have with the aesthetic experiences that characterize other arts, in the light of the common intuition that an aesthetic dimension embraces all forms of art. Is literature more likely to show features in common with the temporal arts such as dance, music, or film? Or are the aesthetic markers of literary reading also to be found in some form in response to the visual arts? While it would be inappropriate to pursue this issue at length here, the question is raised by two recent studies of the neuropsychology of visual art.

Ramachandran and Hirstein (1999) outline eight features of response to visual art, the most important and original of which is the so-called "peak-shift" effect. Here, in the mammalian brain, attraction to a specific shape is said to prepare for greater attraction to an exaggerated form of the same shape. In the light of this proposal, the authors argue that all visual art works are in some sense cartoons. The other seven principles also involve primarily visual criteria, such as perceptual grouping (or binding), and contrast extraction. It is difficult to see literary equivalents to most of these processes except the last, the metaphoric function of art, and certainly a more general aesthetic principle seems not to be at stake. In the light of the discussion of literary reading I have offered, the commentary of Baars (1999) is striking: the main shortcoming of the approach of Ramachandran and Hirstein, he notes, is the lack of emotional significance. "What is missing" he says, "is a conception of emotional information in art. Beauty comunicates something to us, even if dimly. . . . Art is emotionally informative" (pp. 59–60). Nothing approaching the modifying processes of emotion, therefore, appears to be provided for in their model.

Central to the account of visual art by the neuropsychologist Zeki (1999b) is his description of it as "a search for the constant, lasting, essential, and enduring" (p. 79). While this might remind us of the principles of the eighteenth-century literary critic Dr. Johnson, such principles have long since ceased to determine our understanding of literary response. My approach (which is certainly also open to challenge) has emphasized the value of literary reading to the individual, which may extend to what is lasting and essential to that individual, but not to criteria for what is lasting for all readers. The possible divergence of views on this issue is suggested by a remark of Ellis (1999), writing on the neuropsychological correlates of art. For Ellis experiencing is the aim of art: "to know that a being or experience is unique and fleeting, thus irreplaceable and unduplicated, is different from directly experiencing its uniqueness and fleetingness" (p. 172). What art offers is the direct and perhaps poignant experience of uniqueness—an experience at the opposite pole from Zeki's appeal to the enduring.

The contrast between the accounts of Zeki and Ramachandran and Hirstein and the one offered in the present chapter, between formal qualities and enduring values on the one hand and the self-modifying power of feelings on the other, points to the need for more careful, well-designed studies of the experience of art. That art can be understood in opposed terms is also evident from the philosophers of art I have quoted earlier. For Iris Murdoch (1970) art is "something pre-eminently outside us and resistant to our consciousness. We surrender ourselves to its *authority* with a love which is unpossessive and unselfish" (p. 88). For Felicity Nussbaum (1995), on the other hand, art "inspires distrust of conventional pieties and exacts a frequently painful confrontation with one's own thoughts and intentions" (p. 5). Whether literary reading, as an aesthetic experience, involves the self or is an escape from the self, can perhaps only be settled by empirical methods. In such an endeavour, however, as I have tried to show here, the forms of thought and experience on which we believe art depends can be confirmed in relation to the rapidly developing insights of neuropsychology. As Zeki (1999a) puts it, justifying his own study, "no theory of aesthetics that is not substantially based on the activity of the brain is ever likely to be complete, let alone profound" (p. 1). In the light of what is being discovered about the processes of the brain, then, we must continue to monitor the possibility that new evidence will allow us a greater understanding of the experience of literariness. While neuropsychology as yet provides no direct evidence of the nature of literary reading, it does provide, as I have tried to show, a number of suggestive lines of evidence that provide a foundation for the further examination of the power and significance of literary experience.

• CHAPTER TEN •

The Body in Literature: Metaphor and Feeling

10.1 Bodily Forms of Thought

An inadequate grasp of the role of imagination has vitiated understanding of human cognition in western thinking.* According to Mark Johnson, an "objectivist" tradition of thought from Descartes, through Kant to Frege has overlooked the pervasive structuring of our thought by a range of underlying metaphors. Extending a project initiated with George Lakoff in *Metaphors we Live By* (1980), Mark Johnson's book *The Body in the Mind* (1987) offers the claim that all thinking originates in bodily experience. A range of schemata formed during our early experience manipulating a physical world of surfaces, distances, and forces, lays the foundation of later, more abstract modes of thought. By extension and transformation such "image schemata," as Johnson terms them, determine the processes of rational and propositional thinking. In presenting his argument, Johnson lays special stress on the qualities and dynamics of the image schemata, the (generally unnoticed) metaphoricity of the transformations underlying abstract thought, and the new significance that should be attributed to the imagination, which is the general term Johnson wishes to claim for the mental processes he expounds.

Johnson's work has been largely overlooked so far by students of aesthetics and literary theory, despite the fact that Johnson centres his claims for a reinvigorated understanding of the imagination on Kant's account in the *Critique of Judgement*. In this chapter I will consider the importance of Johnson's insights for understanding literary response. In particular, I will show how a typical procedure of literary texts involves bringing to awareness image schemata of the

---

* This chapter first appeared as "The Body in Literature: Mark Johnson, Metaphor, and Feeling," *Journal of Literary Semantics*, 26, 1997, 191–210. It is reprinted here by kind permission of the publisher, Mouton de Gruyter.

kind that Johnson describes (similar analyses are provided by Lakoff and Turner, 1989; Turner, 1989, 1991). At the same time, several problems in Johnson's account which limit its usefulness will also be examined: an undue reliance upon the spatial properties of schemata; a conflation of dead with live or poetic metaphors; and a neglect of other bodily influences on thought, especially kinaesthetic and affective aspects. These problems, for example, militate against Johnson's attempt to build on Kant's theory of imagination. In comparison with Coleridge, who also attempted to build on Kant, Johnson is unable to overcome the formalism of Kant's theory. Coleridge's account of imagination, I will suggest, provides a better foundation for examining the bodily basis of meaning, while remaining compatible with Johnson's intentions and his more valuable insights. First, I will offer a brief outline of Johnson's project and point to some of its limitations.

10.2 The Body in the Mind

Our bodily interactions with the world around us involve repeated patterns of experience, which, following earlier thinkers such as Kant (1968/1790) and Bartlett (1932), Johnson terms *schemata.* In cognitive psychology, as I noted in Chapter 5, the term *schema* has been applied extensively to account for understanding of conceptual networks, narratives, and many other phenomena: Johnson's use of the term bears little relation to this work, being more comparable to Kant and Bartlett. Johnson's schemata provide the basis for structuring thought at more abstract levels. "I call these patterns 'image schemata'," says Johnson (1987),

> because they function primarily as abstract structures of images. They are gestalt structures, consisting of parts standing in relations and organized into unified wholes, by means of which our experience manifests discernible order. When we seek to comprehend this order and to reason about it, such bodily based schemata play a central role. (p. xix)

The primary focus of Johnson's discussion throughout the book is on the more abstract level at which the schemata operate: he shows how pervasive such schemata are in everyday thought with examples such as "purposes are destinations," and "theories are buildings" (these phrases are only summary statements of elaborate and extensive structures embedded within thought).

Although Johnson offers some account of the origin of schemata in the infant's bodily experience (pp. 13, 15–16), bodily correlates of meaning in later thought are not explored. While he discusses abstract thought at one point as having "emerged" from bodily experience, he also describes it in the same paragraph as a refinement upon bodily experience which "ignores much of what goes into our reasoning" (p. 5). Thus Johnson is perhaps ambiguous on this issue, as one of the book's reviewers noted (Wallace, 1988): it is unclear whether he wishes to claim that all meaning remains within the context of bodily experience, or whether meaning emerges from bodily experience by projection and transformation.

Johnson emphasizes that image schemata are figurative, and analog and non-propositional in nature (p. xx). Schemata should not be seen as either rich, mental images (concrete pictures in the mind); nor are they abstract concepts or propositional structures (p. 23). In fact, his preferred term for understanding how such schemata operate is "metaphor." He argues that the way in which thought is organized is through "metaphorical elaborations of image schemata" which "give rise to form and structure in our experience and understanding" (p. 73). Thus, the OUT or CONTAINER schema which is spatial in origin, projects onto more abstract entities in a statement such as "Tell me your story again, but leave out the minor details" (p. 34). Whereas the original sense of this schema involved a physical object being located "outside," here it is an abstract or logical entity.

Of the specific examples he discusses, almost all appear to involve spatial representations. Johnson defines an image schema as a recurring pattern, but then describes the patterns in spatial terms: they emerge, he says, "chiefly at the level of our bodily movements through space, our manipulation of objects, and our perceptual interactions" (p. 29). Describing his project more generally, he says that he attempts "a kind of 'geography of human experience'" (p. xxxvii); and the examples of schemata he provides throughout the book (see, for example, the list on p. 126) usually necessitate spatial relationships or are interpreted in spatial terms. As Johnson notes in passing, "having some perspective is part of image schemata" (p. 36), which seems to make the spatial a defining quality. Although he introduces the example cited in the previous paragraph as a "nonspatial" extension of the OUT schema, it seems clear that perspective must be involved here too: the statement positions us on the inside of the story, and instructs us to position the "minor details" on the outside. A similar perspective seems integral to his next example: "I give up, I'm getting out of the race." Other qualities are often involved in image schemata, such as balance, pressure, or force; yet these too are generally construed as acting within a spatial context (see, for example, the spatial diagrams used to explicate modal verbs, pp. 51–3).

The ubiquity of the spatial in Johnson's project makes it seem vulnerable to the kind of criticism that Coleridge brought against his eighteenth century predecessors. Coleridge argued against that "despotism of the eye" before which "we are restless because invisible things are not the objects of vision" (Coleridge, 1983, I, 107; on this point see also Jones, 1995). While Johnson insists that image schemata are not mental images, yet they are usually discussed as if they could be visualized in spatial terms. This prominence of the spatial tends to exclude from consideration other types of bodily experience that may be as significant for understanding the development of thought. The kinaesthetic and affective, I will suggest, are especially relevant to a consideration of literary response. The literary domain is particularly suitable for considering their role in thought, since literary texts possess an array of features, such as foregrounding, that systematically organize affective and kinaesthetic responses in the service of the imaginative reconstruction of experience.

Johnson emphasizes that his project involves reinstating the imagination as central to all human cognition (in Chapter 6 he returns to Kant's account in some detail, and seeks to elaborate and correct it). The kind of imagination he has in mind is not, he says, "merely a wild, non-rule-governed faculty for fantasy and creativity" (p. xx). Elsewhere he attempts to summarize Coleridge's account of imagination (p. 68–9), but he does not share Coleridge's interest in pointing to the poetic functions of imagination that Coleridge described; indeed, he seems suspicious of it, assuring us that his account of imagination should not be seen as "imagination in the Romantic sense of unfettered creative fancy" (p. 194). This distinction between an everyday and a "romantic" imagination places unnecessary limits on Johnson's approach, as I will argue below.

However, Johnson also wishes to claim a Coleridgean, transformational power for the image schemata, but he does so by obscuring an important distinction between the metaphoric function of schemata as instruments of everyday thought (what might better be called dead metaphor), and the functioning of poetic metaphors. Johnson's insight is that such metaphoric projections are fundamental to our thought; but to argue that the same projections "make new connections, and remold our experience" (p. 169) is to confuse two different levels of functioning which call for different explanations. As Johnson suggests, the distinction between literal and figurative is perhaps misleading: the literal may be merely what is "conventional" (p. 30). Yet the distinction corresponds to an important psychological difference between instantiation of semantic meaning and awareness of semantic change; or, to put it differently, a contrast of familiar meaning from the defamiliarization of meaning that occurs most notably in literary texts. Johnson (1991) asserts elsewhere that "metaphorical understanding is so pervasive and so deeply constitutive of our intentional interactions within our environment that we are virtually unaware either of its existence or of its metaphorical character." This seems to rule out the more radical metaphor that is characteristic of literary texts. For example, the spatial implications of "rear" or "front" are common in everyday discourse. We no longer notice their figurative origin in such uses as "She was at the front of her class in math"; "He kept at the rear in conversation." If these uses are metaphoric, as Johnson would claim, they have become domesticated, dead metaphors. The process of comprehension clearly differs when the words are used in a context such as this poem by Emily Dickinson: "Remembrance has a Rear and Front—/ 'Tis something like a House –" (Dickinson, 1970, p. 524). In the first examples, the words "rear" and "front" serve merely to locate position on an existing dimension: either eminence in a math class or degree of participation in conversation. In the poem, on the other hand, the words being used figuratively create a dimension for the concept "Remembrance" which is novel. In so doing, Dickinson enables us to see aspects of the concept that we have probably not noticed before.

10.3 The Clerk's Tale

Johnson's primary interest, however, is in the role of image schemata in constructing everyday thought and reasoning. In this respect he provides impressive documentation for their power and pervasiveness. In Chapter 1 he begins his detailed analysis of their presence by examining the schemata underlying a specific passage taken from the report of a legal clerk discussing his response to a certain type of woman. The passage provides important insights into the impulses that may result in rape. The clerk's account reads in part as follows:

> Let's say I see a woman and she looks really pretty, and really clean and sexy, and she's giving off very feminine, sexy vibes. I think "Wow, I would love to make love to her," but I know she's not really interested. It's a tease. A lot of times a woman knows that she's looking really good and she'll use that and flaunt it, and it makes me feel like she's laughing at me and I feel *degraded.* I also feel dehumanized, because when I'm being teased I just turn off.

The clerk then reflects on the double bind this imposes on him, and comments: "Just the fact that they can come up to me and just melt me and make me feel like a dummy makes me want revenge" (p. 6; cited from Beneke, 1982).

Johnson's discussion of the underlying logic of the passage is illuminating. As he points out, the dominant idea motivating the clerk's understanding of his response turns out to be metaphoric: Johnson states this as "PHYSICAL APPEARANCE IS A PHYSICAL FORCE." Johnson shows how this metaphor, and derivatives from it, shape the clerk's discourse. One implication of the clerk's account is the notion that "ANYONE USING A FORCE IS RESPONSIBLE FOR THE EFFECTS OF THAT FORCE" (p. 8). This and other hidden assumptions of his response propel the clerk towards a violent construal of his predicament. Either it requires an act of violence towards himself, suppressing his feelings of sexual desire, resentment, and humiliation—which is the path he actually seems to adopt—or it requires a sexual assault upon the offending woman.

Johnson's discussion in Chapter 1 shows both the strengths and the weaknesses of his approach. While he brings to light a complex metaphoric structure underlying the clerk's discourse, several important questions that have a bearing on Johnson's project are left unconsidered. The analysis overlooks the clerk's motive for construing his response along the metaphoric pathways that Johnson has described, as well as other types of bodily experience that also underlie the clerk's response. Johnson might argue that he is concerned only with the linguistic structuring of the clerk's story, but there is nothing inevitable in the construction given to it by the clerk. Other forces are at work beside the metaphoric which help to determine his discourse. In his book, Johnson sometimes gives the impression that the metaphoric structures that he analyses constitute the basic level at which thought is shaped (for instance, the last part of his discussion of Kant, p. 169, or the definition of non-objectivist meaning given in italics on p. 174). But to understand why particular metaphoric structures appear in thought requires Johnson's account to be supplemented by an examination of the forces that bring them into play in a given context. This in turn bears on Johnson's interest later in the book (in Chapter 4) in how metaphors are created and understood. The clerk's tale illustrates this basic problem.

How does the clerk come to construe his experience in this way? Why is he impelled along the metaphoric path of seeing physical appearance as a physical force, with all its consequences? While we cannot interrogate the clerk himself, it seems probable that the instantiation of this "metaphor" depends upon a specific configuration of bodily feelings. The precipitating cause lies in the clerk's feeling of anomaly: he experiences sexual arousal within a context where expression of such feelings is impermissible. It is an anomaly that calls for metaphor production. Experiencing a force that operates within him to create a conflict between two feelings (sexual arousal and social inhibition), he projects the force on to the woman who appears to be its cause. Locating the force within her (she has "sexy vibes," etc.) instead of within himself, he then sees that force as impacting on him from without. While Johnson is right to note the "logical" shape of the clerk's construal of his experience and to suggest that much of our everyday reasoning shows a similar structuring by metaphor (p. 11), the power of the clerk's tale and its resulting metaphors depend upon its originating feelings. Feeling is, no doubt, a major determinant in the instantiation of many of the metaphoric construals that Johnson discusses.

The power of feeling is indicated in the clerk's case in particular by the number of times he refers to his self-concept. Remarks such as "I feel *degraded*," "I cease to be human," and "they . . . make me feel like a dummy," show that his encounters with such a woman undermine the clerk's image of himself. The passage could be said to enact a conflict between two directions in which his sense of self can develop: either an enabling, aggressive exercise of sexual expression; or an emasculating impairment of his status. The forcefulness of the feelings arises from the significance of the issues raised by the encounter (as Hayles, 1993, has pointed out, Johnson's analysis also overlooks the gender issues it raises). Another dimension of such feelings is apparent in the clerk's use of the term "really clean and sexy." While the narrative is obviously about bodily experience, one important construction not noted by Johnson involves the construct "clean vs. defiled." The clerk's idea of intercourse includes, among other matters, the prospect of degrading the woman's purity. Being physically degraded himself calls for despoiling her physically in revenge. As Ricoeur (1969) notes, the sense of defilement is itself figurative, being based on the literal meaning "stain" or "unclean." But more important, defilement evokes a sense of dread: dread "of a danger which is itself ethical and which, at a higher level of the consciousness of evil, will be the danger of not being able to love any more, the danger of being a dead man in the realm of ends." With such dread, Ricoeur notes, comes the "primordial connection of vengeance with defilement" (pp. 15, 30). Thus the clerk's narrative shows how our body image, the maintenance of purity, is a potentially powerful source of feeling: here it is called into question by the mere presence of a "pretty woman."

This complex of feelings, with its potential consequences for the self-concept, seems to constitute the origin of the clerk's response. And it is from feelings that the metaphoric dimension of the narrative is constructed: the narrative shows the clerk explaining, justifying, and acting upon his feelings in defence of the self. The metaphoric structuring of his discourse (PHYSICAL APPEARANCE IS A PHYSICAL FORCE) comes from the ready availability of this construction in the culture: as Johnson points out, such expressions as "She's *devastating*" and "He is *strikingly* handsome" are common. The clerk's is, one might say, an unthinking, clichéd way of construing experience. It seems likely, indeed, that the clerk himself is unaware of using such a metaphor: for him, the force of the woman's appearance constitutes his reality, which in turn determines how he will understand the alternatives that confront him.

The purpose of the discussion so far, then, has been to show that beneath the metaphoric structure of the clerk's discourse articulated by Johnson, lies a deeper level of structuring, formed by the clerk's feelings and their implications for his self concept. Its metaphoricity is a product of the central anomaly sensed by the clerk; but the specific metaphor he deploys is a "reach-me-down" construct, as Max Black (1954–55, p. 290) put it, available from the culture. I have been concerned to show in particular that the urgency of the clerk's predicament springs from a level more fundamental than the metaphor described by Johnson. The unlawfulness of his desire, and the defilement it incurs, results in the clerk's projection of agency onto the woman, as Johnson shows. The critical issue, however, is how the clerk's metaphor comes to be chosen or produced. Here Johnson's account bypasses important evidence for the role of the feelings and the self—evidence that would help to extend and enrich our understanding of the bodily basis of meaning.

If the clerk's discourse is examined as an example of the structuring of conventional meaning, it is so primarily because the metaphor for which he reaches is a cultural commonplace. The distinction which Johnson claims for his approach involves the major claim that it will rehabilitate the imagination, not in a Romantic sense, but in the sense advanced by Kant, that imagination is an essential power at the basis of all human thought. Yet one significant contribution that imagination can make to human thought is to enable us to transcend conventional meaning, including the automatic (and potentially dangerous) assignment of bodily feelings such as defilement to everyday situations. Unlike the example of the clerk's tale, conventional meaning conveyed through image schemata may be challenged or even overthrown in more powerful kinds of discourse. Specifically, I have in mind the kind of discourse available in literary texts.

Coleridge, whose theory of imagination receives only brief mention in *The Body in the Mind*, argues that at its best imagination "dissolves, diffuses, dissipates, in order to recreate" (Coleridge, 1983, I, 304). To account for a power of this order requires more than the modes of imagination described by Johnson. I will first illustrate the issues by reference to a specific poem. Here, a spatial metaphor, of the kind discussed by Johnson, plays an interesting role; but so do several other features that involve affective and bodily dimensions of meaning. I will then turn to consider the wider implications of the discussion by examining the use to which Johnson puts Kant's aesthetic theory.

10.4 Imagining the Self: Wordsworth's Man of the World

Wordsworth's sonnet "The world is too much with us," first published in 1807, has often been reprinted; it has evidently been considered a powerful poem, providing a challenge to conventional or familiar modes of thinking. The poem as a whole offers a reflection on the relationship we have lost with nature, but an analysis of the first four lines of the poem will be sufficient to show its imaginative power.

> The world is too much with us; late and soon,
> Getting and spending, we lay waste our powers:
> Little we see in nature that is ours;
> We have given our hearts away, a sordid boon!

In certain respects, the poem seems to depend upon a ready understanding of the term "world," which has a sense similar to its meaning in a phrase such as "man of the world." The poem invites us to participate in an act of imagination in which any approval we may feel for the "man of the world" is overthrown. It is possible to see a spatial metaphor, in Johnson's sense, helping to organize a reader's understanding of this shift in sense. A comment that something is "with us" implies physical proximity; but "too much with us" seems to connote the breaching of some boundary of the self, suggesting that "The world" has impinged on the inner terrain of the self. A corresponding idea is offered in the fourth line, where the heart transfers out of the self in being "given away." In this sense the poem deploys Johnson's CONTAINMENT metaphor (pp. 21–3) to striking effect: we see the self as a container whose integrity we have violated. Similarly, "Getting and spending" implies a transfer of goods inwards and money outwards across the boundary of the self. The poem alerts us to the endangered integrity of the self through its imaginative and novel use of the metaphor: we find ourselves implicated in an act of self-betrayal in which "we" (all readers of the poem) have participated.

One significant function of a poem may lie in bringing to consciousness the hidden spatial metaphors that, as Johnson points out, determine the structure and assumptions of much of our everyday thinking. Our normal assumption is perhaps to think of ourselves as "in the world," or to approve of the "man of the world," whose interchange with the material and social aspects of the world is managed in a competent and urbane manner. Wordsworth unsettles this familiar notion by telling us that this world is in us, with harmful consequences; in other words, the container shifts from being the world to being the self. And in this way the poem also seems to suggest that a proper distance of self from the world would protect the self's true interests, although this notion is not explored in the poem explicitly (in the remainder of the poem Wordsworth is more concerned to rehabilitate our relationship with nature).

It is possible to see the container metaphor, then, with its implied derivation from bodily experience, as fundamental to understanding how these lines of the poem function. Other modes of bodily experience, however, are also likely to play a significant role in response to the poem. In this respect, Johnson's account of imagination falls short: being based primarily on spatial accounts of "embodied" thinking it cannot encompass the sensory and affective dimensions that also influence literary response. Yet these aspects of response have as much right to be considered a part of imagination as metaphoric schemata, if the views of Coleridge (perhaps the most important exponent of the imagination) are accepted. Nor does this richer view mean imagination "in the Romantic sense of unfettered creative fancy" (p. 194). As Coleridge (1983) argued, poetry is organized and systematic: it has "a logic of its own, as severe as that of science; and more difficult, because more subtle, more complex, and dependent on more, and more fugitive causes" (I, 9). Among other aspects, the diction and the affective structuring of poetry contribute to its imaginative power in the sense claimed by Coleridge.

Thus in Wordsworth's lines the meaning of the spatial metaphor I pointed to above is amplified by several other important effects. The parallelism of the construction, "late and soon, / Getting and spending," enforces the temporal dimension of our self-violation; the assonance of *e* and *ing* sounds in the second pair of words helps confirm the ceaseless reciprocity of its cause in our material preoccupations. These features, together with the position of the parallelism across the line ending, help create a rising gradient of affective intensity which comes to a focus in the next phrase of the second line, "we lay waste our powers." Here we find assonance, with mutually reinforcing long-*a* sounds, which both echoes the *a* of "late" and anticipates "away" in the fourth line. As well, in the metrical patterning of the line, there are perhaps two adjacent stressed syllables if emphasis in reading is placed upon the word "lay." This serves to emphasize the two *a*-vowels in "lay waste" and hence intensifies our affective response to the idea of wasting the powers of the self. The set of meanings added here include a sense of debasement, which takes on a particularly physical connotation when Wordsworth describes the bargain we have made as "sordid."

As Coleridge's statement on the logic of poetry suggests, the rich meaning of this poem depends upon a range of complex and fugitive causes. Not every reader will be equally sensitive to all of them, no doubt. Yet, as our analysis will have suggested, such effects experienced over several lines of poetry seem to converge on the same underlying meaning. The effects of such poetic diction are, in Mukarovský's (1964, p. 20) terms, systematic and hierarchical. We can claim that assonance and metre in these lines contribute an important sensory component of response: the way the words are articulated in speaking involves subtle physical resonances (Fónagy, 1989) and interconnections that go beyond the effects of normal language use, while the metre draws upon powerful bodily rhythms that tend to pass unnoticed except within such aesthetic domains as poetry or music. Indeed, poetry puts us in touch with this level of our bodily functioning, and in so doing it defamiliarizes the automatic assignment of meaning to experience. The container metaphor, in this poem, is made troubling and questionable for the reader. What *are* we doing in the world if the world is actually "in" us, as Wordsworth suggests?

Wordsworth's poetic discourse can be compared in this respect with the clerk's conventional discourse. The debasement of the self, the "sordid boon," is perhaps the most important idea in these opening lines of the poem. The array of other features, metaphoric and phonetic, are organized to focus on this key idea, imbuing it with feeling. Unlike the clerk's narrative, however, the poem creates a sense of the self as defiled in an unfamiliar domain: we see defilement where we formely saw only the familiar realm of our transactions with the material world. Wordsworth helps us to locate this new sense and give it meaning: out of our cloudy dissatisfactions with the material preoccupations of "getting and spending," shall we say, he condenses a specific attitude, perhaps even a specific bodily unease that is carried by the assonance and other phonetic features of the poem. Brought to consciousness in this way, we also see that the cause lies in us. Unlike the clerk, whose response is predicated on the vengeance to which Ricoeur (1969) points, our response implies ejecting from the self the destructive workings of the world, a type of cleansing or catharsis of the self (p. 41). In fact, the manuscript of the poem shows that Wordsworth originally wrote "selves" in line 4 instead of "hearts," a reading that emphasizes the need for catharsis (Wordsworth, 1983, p. 150). In the remainder of the poem Wordsworth looks, albeit forlornly, to a renewed relationship with nature to achieve this.

The imaginative achievement of this section of the poem, then, lies in reversing our standard assumptions about what it means to be "in the world"; in bringing to consciousness and deploying for unusual ends our spatial metaphor for the self as a container; and, above all, in making felt through a rich weave of poetic devices the debased state of the self. The imagination here, to borrow Coleridge's words, "dissolves and diffuses" the conventional view of our place in the world; it uses poetic devices to defamiliarize it, and to point to an alternative conception of that place. Such an enriched poetic concept, which we have argued is dependent upon sensory and affective meaning, is what Kant calls an "aesthetic idea." However, Kant deals only equivocally with feeling in his third *Critique*, and deals not at all with bodily correlates of meaning. In this respect he provides a questionable basis for building a reinvigorated understanding of imagination. However, the problems that Johnson wishes to resolve in Kant already find an answer in Coleridge: his theory of imagination provides a more powerful and accurate foundation for conceptualizing the role of the body in the mind than Johnson's attempt to build on Kant's formulations in the *Critique of Judgement*.

10.5 Kant and the Disembodied Imagination

In Chapter 6, Johnson appeals to Kant's third *Critique*, arguing that in its account of imagination it provides a basis for extending our understanding of imagination which enlarges the first *Critique*. He focuses specifically on Kant's account of the beautiful. What does it mean to find something, such as a work of art, beautiful? According to Kant, this is an example of the imagination working in a non-rule governed way, unlike its role in mediating between the sensory manifold and concepts in the understanding. In Johnson's summary, we judge objects beautiful when

> they put our imagination in a playful harmony with our intellect or understanding . . . . Thus, we judge objects to be beautiful by a free (non-rule-governed) preconceptual imaginative activity that has a rational character and can lay claim to the agreement of other judges, since it focuses only on the formal features of the object, which imagination allows us all to experience in the same way. (p. 160)

As Johnson observes, Kant seems to be saying that "there is a kind of shared meaning that is not reducible to conceptual and propositional content alone" (p. 161). This is the product of imagination. Kant proposes that works of art embody "aesthetical ideas," whose signifance lies in offering ideas that cannot be brought under a definite concept: they occasion more thought than can be grasped or made clear (p. 162). Johnson expands on Kant's insight, proposing that such thought is pre-conceptual, involving the metaphoric extension of image *schemata*. In understanding a symbol in a poem, says Kant (1968/1790),

> the judgement exercises a double function, first applying the concept to the object of a sensible intuition, and then applying the mere rule of the reflection made upon that intuition to a quite different object of which the first is only the symbol. (§59)

In other words, translating this into the terms for metaphor, we transfer the rule of reflection on a vehicle to reconfiguring the tenor. Johnson claims that Kant's account of this operation is close to what he means by metaphorical projection (p. 164).

What Kant describes here, however, involves the symbolic mode of thought: it works to *defamiliarize* its object (or tenor), just as Wordsworth's poem unsettles our standard notion of being "in the world." In Johnson's book, however, he is primarily concerned with the level of thought at which *familiar* objects and processes are construed (purposes are destinations, theories are buildings). In these instances no other terms are available or occur to mind; no novel meanings are intended. All such terms are "reach-me-down" constructions. While Johnson does mention in passing how such conventional constructions can be invigorated, making dead into live metaphors (e.g., "He prefers massive Gothic theories covered with gargoyles," p. 106), he neither distinguishes adequately the two kinds of metaphor (which have radically different effects), nor does he consider the possibility that many poetic metaphors, unlike the "Gothic theories" example, do not spring from conventional metaphor. (As Neill, 1989, pointed out, Johnson also has difficulty accounting for some conventional metaphors such as "Sally is a block of ice," or "John is bitter," perhaps because they lack the spatial qualities of his standard examples.)

More problematic, Johnson's appeal to Kant bypasses the issue of Kant's formalism. Central to Kant's *Critique* is the disinterested function of the imagination involved in response to both the beautiful and the sublime. For example, it is a condition of the beautiful, says Kant, that the responder "can find as reason for his delight no personal conditions to which his own subjective self might alone be party" (§6). And in the case of the sublime, the mind conceives its powers in purely formal terms as transcending any powers in nature whatever (e.g., §28). The formalism of Kant's account here is integral, not incidental. Johnson attempts to discount it by denying the problem: there is no gap, he asserts, between the formal and material, the rational and the bodily (p. 168).

Where Kant saw an unbridgeable gap, concealing the mystery of how schemata come into being (Kant's notorious observation in the first *Critique* is cited on p. 156), Johnson wishes to see a continuum (p. 170). This is to elide the problem, however, not to resolve it. If a better theory of imagination is to be founded upon bodily meaning, as Johnson proposes, some agency that acts both at the levels of mind and body must be found. Rethinking the disinterest on which Kant insisted offers one possible starting point: it is, moreover, one of the points which distinguishes the theory of imagination that Coleridge formulated, partly out of his dissatisfaction with Kant. In Coleridge's account feelings and the self find a central place.

10.6 Imagination and Feeling: Coleridge's Solution

In letters and notebook entries, particularly in the earlier part of his life (up to about 1810), Coleridge frequently referred to the influence of the body on thinking. Analysing his sense of illness in 1802, for example, he referred to "an undue sensibility of the nervous system, or of whatever unknown parts of our body are the more immediate Instruments of Feeling & Idea" (Coleridge, 1956–71, II, 897). Again, in 1805, in a notebook reflection on love, he remarked "the purest Impulse can introduce itself to our consciousness no otherwise than by *speaking to us* in some bodily feeling" (Coleridge, 1957–2002, II, 2495). And for a while, Coleridge contemplated the possibility that developmentally the sense of touch or feeling lay at the root of the other senses, as well as the growth of the mind (Modiano, 1982).

Thus for Coleridge, unlike in the aesthetics of Kant to which Johnson appeals, there is no dichotomy of body and mind. The body can prompt thought, or can be its instrument. It has a key role in memory: "how imperishable Thoughts seem to be!" said Coleridge, on another occasion; "Renew the state of affection or bodily Feeling, same or similar . . . and instantly the trains of forgotten Thoughts rise from their living catacombs!" (1957–2002, I, 1575) The agent that relates body and mind is feeling: feeling partakes both of bodily states that begin in touch, while at the same time it motivates or even guides processes of thought. The case of the clerk discussed above, whose metaphoric construal is impelled by his feeling of sexual arousal, is a dramatic example of what is undoubtedly a common process. At the same time, this suggests that the role of feeling in the imagination may be of the greatest significance, and that feeling provides the key to the creative power attributed to the imagination by Coleridge.

Johnson's discussions of Coleridge in *The Body in the Mind* do not explore this essential dimension of his theory: rather, Johnson asserts that Coleridge "never supplied . . . an account of the specific nature of this creative, unifying activity of metaphorical imagination" (p. 69). On the contrary, Coleridge provided several accounts in *Biographia Literaria*, his lectures, and elsewhere, of how the imagination works to modify and unify its materials. Two examples will suffice. Images, Coleridge said, "become proofs of original genius only as far as they are modified by a predominant passion; or by associated thoughts or images awakened by that passion" (Coleridge, 1983, II, 23). From the perspective of the reader the effect of this poetic process when focused on the mundane world of objects, is "to represent familiar objects [so] as to awaken in the minds of others a kindred feeling concerning them and that freshness of sensation which is the constant accompaniment of mental, no less than of bodily, convalescence" (1983, I, 81). In the later chapters of the *Biographia*, Coleridge also applies these principles in detailed analyses of specific poems, particularly those of Wordsworth.

The role of feeling in imagination is familiar ground to critics of Coleridge, although his attention to bodily aspects of feeling has received less attention. Also little noted is Coleridge's account of how feeling implicates the self. A notebook remark of 1804 provides the most succinct statement:

> Poetry [is] a rationalized dream dealing . . . to manifold Forms our own Feelings, that never perhaps were attached by us consciously to our own personal Selves. . . . . O there are Truths below the Surface in the subject of Sympathy, & how we *become* that which we understandly [sic] behold & hear, having, how much God perhaps only knows, created part even of the Form. (Coleridge, 1957–2002, II, 2086)

Considering this statement in relation to Wordsworth's poem, for example, illuminates the constructive role of the feelings activated by the "container" metaphor. Wordsworth obliges us to see the self as a container degraded by the world's proximity—a feeling that we may not previously have attached "to our own personal Selves." A similar process is at work through the assonance and the metrical organization of the poem. We become, if only for a moment, the self that Wordsworth makes us understand and hear. If our self concept is at stake, as Wordsworth surely intended it should be, then our response is "interested" in a way that Kant was unable to accept.

Coleridge's view of imagination, as reflected here and in a range of other comments, thus shows that he was able to overcome both the disinterest of Kant's aesthetic theory, and his dichotomy of mind and body. Coleridge attributed to the body, to the feelings, and to the self, essential functions in the process of imaginative thought, although these components of imagination play a less prominent part in his accounts in the *Biographia* of 1817 than they do in the earlier notebook and lecture remarks (Miall, 1991).

Situating Johnson's insights in a Coleridgean context, such as I have (all too briefly) sketched, suggests how image schemata are selected and modified, supplementing Johnson's account of how schemata are metaphorically extended to understand universes of discourse such as the clerk's predicament, or the poem by Wordsworth. As feminist moves towards reconstructing knowledge have suggested, incorporating the body into our discourse is both essential and urgent. The rethinking of "objectivism," which Johnson advocates, is also a principle aim of feminist philosophers such as Alison Jaggar and Susan Bordo (1989). Objectivism, they note, has served to create "dualistic ontologies that sharply separate the universal from the particular, culture from nature, mind from body, and reason from emotion." Moreover, "The body, notoriously and ubiquitously associated with the female, regularly has been cast . . . as the chief enemy of objectivity." The importance of Johnson's book lies in showing how, contrary to objectivism, the body lies at the basis of much of our normal thinking. At the same time, Johnson's account must be extended: the imagination, as Coleridge analysed it, shows us how in literary response conventional applications of metaphoric thinking (which form the substance of Johnson's book) are defamiliarized and their sources revealed. Literary texts, in this view, enable us to recover the bodily and affective sources of our thinking, and to challenge within ourselves the old, damaging, dualistic forms of thought of which Jaggar and Bordo complain. A consideration of Coleridge's accounts of feeling and the body thus opens other productive avenues on the central claim of Johnson's notable book. The implications of this wider theory for developing our understanding of literary response may prove fruitful and far-reaching.

• CHAPTER ELEVEN •

Sounds of Contrast: An Empirical Approach to Phonemic Iconicity

11.1 Sound and Meaning

The eighteenth-century English poet Pope provided the most succinct phonetic theory of poetry: "The sound must seem an Echo to the sense" (*Essay on Criticism*, II, 365).* Since the time of Plato, many commentators have remarked that the sound of a word should suggest its meaning. In the *Cratylus*, Plato (1963) represents Socrates arguing that a legislator must "know how to put the true natural name of each thing into sounds and syllables, and to make and give all names with a view to the ideal name" (389d). Opposed to this view, the linguist Saussure (1974, pp. 67–70) asserted that the sound of language was arbitrary, and most recent literary theorists have tended to agree with him. Yet a number of empirical studies of phonetic symbolism carried out over the last century suggest that hearers may be able to make consistent phonetic discriminations, whether matching phonemic strings from different languages or judging which of two syllables is "light" or "dark." In this chapter I briefly review the empirical studies, but suggest that their atomistic and decontextualized approach, testing responses to small groups of phonemes, is responsible for their inconclusive findings. I outline an alternative approach based on studies incorporating all naturally occurring phonemes in standard English, and show its effectiveness in two respects: first, in measuring contrasts occurring within or between texts, including several literary texts, and second, its power in predicting readers' responses to a modernist short story. While numerous studies in stylistics have been devoted to examining the interpretive meanings suggested by phonetic phenomena, almost no empirical studies with

---

* This chapter is reprinted from *Poetics* Vol. 29: David S. Miall, "Sounds of Contrast: An Empirical Approach to Phonemic Iconicity," 55–70, copyright: 2001, with permission from Elsevier.

readers have been carried out. The present paper thus outlines a new method for empirical examination of phonetic phenomena.

Do the sounds of words convey meaning? The sound of poetry, for example, is often held to be expressive. But as Tsur has pointed out, although an extensive literature is devoted to this topic, "much of it is ad hoc, arbitrary, or skeptical" (Tsur, 1992, p. 1). Do /i/ or /p/ sounds connote smallness or brightness? Does /g/ connote heaviness, and /u/ darkness? This is the hypothesis of phonetic symbolism, i.e., the proposal that specific phonemes encode innate meaning, whether visual, spatial, or kinaesthetic. The most familiar form of sound-meaning is onomatopoeia, the imitation of a natural sound by a word form: for example, the words *hiss*, *miaow*, or *crack* each appear to embody phoneme clusters that sound similar to the event they name. In a recent study of this phenomenon, Hugh Bredin suggested that "onomatopoeia is not a trivial and incidental phenomenon of usage, but answers to a deep-seated need that lies at the heart of the linguistic consciousness. We want language to be onomatopoeic" (Bredin, 1996, p. 560). Similarly, Genette's discussion of the principle of "Cratylism," referred to it as "a myth: it is above all a *seductive* myth" (Genette, 1979, p. 361).

But in the current theoretical climate critics have set their face against such seduction. In his influential essay on stylistics Stanley Fish (1980) objected to any form of stylistics arising from "the desire for an instant and automatic interpretive procedure based on an inventory of fixed relationships between observable data and meanings" (pp. 70–71). While Fish did not deny the existence of formal properties, he went on to argue that we come to them within a framework of meaning already in place: "meanings are not extracted but made and made not by encoded forms but by interpretive strategies that call forms into being" (pp. 172–3). The intuition that sound makes an independent contribution to literary meaning is thus unacceptable to Fish. The intuition, however, is in accord with some substantive phenomena: hearers do make consistent judgements about phonetic meanings under a number of conditions (e.g., Newman, 1933), and analysis of several literary texts has shown arrays of phonetic features that appear to be consistent with their tone (e.g., Fónagy, 1961). As I will suggest, while these studies are suggestive, we lack an integrative framework in which to relate such findings; such a perspective is required in order to examine to what extent systematic sound differences occur in literary texts, and, if so, whether readers are sensitive to them. In the following section a review of prior studies will indicate the basis for developing an integrated perspective on sound meaning in literature. In brief, I will argue that while studies in phonetic symbolism are suggestive, the evidence for innate meaning is inconclusive. I will present an alternative framework that I term *phonemic iconicity*, in which phoneme distributions are shown to systematically embody contrasts of meaning. This approach accounts for the existing findings as well as those to be presented later.

11.2 Studies in Phonetic Symbolism

Onomatopoeia is only one small and perhaps unsystematic dimension of phonemic iconicity, and it was a dimension that Saussure was easily able to dismiss. But his influential claim that the sound of language is arbitrary, or conventional, overlooks a wide range of other types of evidence, some of which have been studied as far back as the ancient linguist Panini (for reviews and additional studies see Brown, 1958; Pinker and Birdsong, 1979; Taylor and Tayor, 1965). In this section, however, I mention only those studies that examined phonemic contrasts, a type of study in which dimensions of meaning (light-dark, small-large) are supposed to be symbolized by particular phonemes.

In order to isolate the tonal qualities of phonemes, the early studies used nonsense syllables. Sapir (1929) carried out a study that examined contrasts between phonemes: he asked participants to classify pairs of verbal items, such as the nonsense words *mil* and *mal*. Asked to say which was light or heavy, respondents showed a high level of agreement. Building on this study, Newman (1933) investigated a wider range of phonemes, obtaining judgements on pairs of nonsense syllables that systematically contrasted short "words" devised from 9 vowels and 21 consonants on the scale small-large. Again, a high level of agreement was obtained, showing a consistent ordering of vowels and consonants from front to back of the oral tract. From this he derived a "magnitude scale" which he tested against a set of actual English words. Using a thesaurus, he extracted a range of words connoting smallness (183 words) and largeness (167 words), and computed the magnitude of each word. But the resulting scale showed almost no difference between the two sets of words, leading him to conclude that the distribution of phonemes in the two categories was "fairly random." The study thus appears to dismiss any more general relation of sound and meaning. A similar study by Bentley and Varon (1933) arrived at the same conclusion: while obtaining consistent results from comparing nonsense monosyllables (e.g., *fim* and *fam*) on several dimensions—small-large, angular-round, hard-soft (Study 4)—they called in question the phenomenon of phonetic symbolism. Simply making a choice about "some sort of difference" doesn't establish the inherent validity of the meaning. While such contrasts may have aesthetic value, they concluded, it cannot be said that "these graded attributes of sound carry in their own right (so to say) a symbolic reference" (p. 85).

A different approach to phonetic symbolism was employed by Tarte and his colleague. Two types of graphical figures, elliptical or triangular, were used to represent sounds considered to be round, sharp, large, or small. In several studies (Tarte & Barritt, 1971) they were able to show that subjects consistently related these shapes to nonsense words consisting of consonant-vowel-consonant (e.g., *wus*, *kas*). For example, large figures were paired with the broad vowel /a/, and small figures with the narrow vowel /i/. In general, triangles were associated with /i/, and ellipses with /u/. In Tarte (1982), nonsense words were paired with tones of different pitch, and judged using semantic differential scales. In both studies a high level of consistency was found in subjects' judgements. They suggest that the sound frequency of vowels is the critical factor in judgements of phonetic symbolism. Tsur (1992, pp. 21–23), on the basis of acoustic analysis, suggests that the position and relation of the first and second formants plays the key role in such perceptions.

In two studies, Taylor (1963) and Taylor and Taylor (1965) reviewed the evidence for phonetic symbolism: this led them to dismiss any underlying physiological or acoustic basis for it. The strong hypothesis of phonetic symbolism suggests a fixed relationship between sound and meaning in any language (Taylor, 1963, p. 200), but in word matching studies across languages results have been contradictory. Participants are given a word or pair of words, and attempt to identify the corresponding words in an unknown language on the basis of sound. While participants appear able to perform this task at above chance levels of correctness (Brown, Black, & Horowitz, 1955), comparisons show that the same phonemes often represent different qualities across the languages studied (Taylor & Taylor, 1962). Studies such as that of Newman (1933), in which participants judge pairs of nonsense words on small-large, or bright-dark dimensions have been more successful, but it is unclear whether the results generalize beyond English.

Taylor and Taylor (1965) compared responses to nonsense syllables in four unrelated languages, and found that while in each language consistent judgements were made, little similarity occurred between languages: for example, a phoneme judged large in one language was judged small in another. Taylor (1963) suggested an alternative explanation for the findings, what she called the "feedback" theory: it is the word meanings in a given language that accustom speakers to associate given sounds with meaning. For example, since a number of English words connoting large size begin with /g/ (grand, great, gross), this leads to the promotion of /g/ for bigness, hence the choice of words beginning with /g/ when largeness is in question. Taylor re-examined Newman's (1933) lists of large and small words: she showed that a significantly higher proportion of large words begin with /g/ or /k/, whereas more smaller than large words begin with /t/ or /n/. In addition Taylor and Taylor (1965) also re-examined the lists for initial vowel differences: they found /I/ and /ɛ/ (small vowels) to predominate in small words, and /u/ and /o/ (large vowels) to predominate in large words. Both findings are statistically significant.

But Taylor and Taylor (1965) make an important distinction between objective and subjective phonetic symbolism. While words of a particular type are found to contain a higher than expected proportion of a certain phoneme (such as Newman's large words that begin with /g/ or /k/), this can have no general significance if hearers are unaware of it: we must also study subjective symbolism and show that such differences have an impact of some kind on hearers or readers. This is a key issue for the present study. While literary studies of stylistic features at the phonetic level are common, and often highly suggestive (e.g., Masson, 1967), critics make no attempt to verify their intuitions with readers.

Whatever its source, however, several other studies point to the validity of phonemic contrasts as an underlying source of meaning. Just as Newman's lists of small and large words are found to be phonetically distinctive when closely examined, so are the differences between men's and women's names. Cutler, McQueen, and Robinson (1990) studied 884 female and 783 male names. Among other differences, they found that more male than female names started with a strong stress; they also found female to be longer than male names. In a study of vowel frequency, female names were shown to contain a significantly higher proportion of the brighter /i/ vowel (usually stressed, as in *Lisa, Mimi*), and fewer of the darker vowels /ɑ/ and /ɔ/. In seeking to explain this finding, they suggest this may be due to the association of the small, bright vowels with the type of sound produced by the smaller vocal tract of the female. No studies of names in other languages have been carried out, as far as I am aware.

A few empirical studies of literary examples have been reported. For example, Fónagy (1961) examined the different tone qualities in a group of Hungarian poems according to topic. In six aggressive and six tender poems by Petöfi, /l/, /m/, and /n/ were more frequent in the tender poems; /k/, /t/, and /r/ predominated in the aggressive poems (a number of other examples are described in his report). Tsur (1996) suggests that the speech sounds acquired later by infants possess greater emotional and aesthetic value (p. 62: cf. Tsur, 1992, pp. 52–58). This helps to account for the power of the frequent nasal vowels and "-eur" word endings that occur in the symbolist poet Baudelaire: these two features are said to be 2.5 times more frequent in a sample of Baudelaire than in a similar size sample from a seventeenth-century poem by the French author Boileau (Tsur, 1996, p. 63). Tsur suggests that in the case of symbolist poetry "the rich precategorical auditory information may get out of control, reverberate at large, and assume the emotive affects of nonreferential sound gestures" (p. 74).

In a more systematic, statistically-based study, Bailey (1971) applied information theory to a group of texts to show whether in certain literary texts some phonemes have a tendency to occur more frequently than expected, when compared with samples of normal prose. A higher than expected frequency of certain phonemes in several poems led him to propose a "prominence index" for phonemes. The frequency of phonemes in a given poem is used to place phonemes in rank order; these ranks are then compared with the ranks in a sample of standard English. Higher frequency of a given phoneme is more likely to be noticed by a reader, especially where a phoneme is relatively rare. This method revealed a high frequency of the low, back vowel /ɔ/ in one text examined. It also revealed meaningful patterns in Dylan Thomas's poem "Fern Hill," such as a preference for voiced over unvoiced consonants. In a second poem, a preference for back over front vowels was demonstrated, which could be related to the aesthetic quality of the poem.

Finally, Lindauer (1988) was able to demonstrate an appreciation of meaning in the titles of short stories in an unknown language. Lindauer suggested that the title of a short story conveys its meaning in part through its sound. Using several different tasks, such as multiple choice, or the matching of pairs of titles, participants unfamiliar with one language compared Hungarian and English versions of titles. Among English-speaking subjects a significantly higher proportion of correct responses was obtained than would be expected by chance: for example, for 28 titles in the multiple choice study, the mean number correct per subject was 17.4 compared with 9.2 incorrect, a significant difference, $p < .01$. Hungarian speakers showed a similar level of response.

This brief review of the main studies in phonetic symbolism shows that the concept has some support. Judgements on dimensions such as small-large are consistent among speakers of English, although speakers of other languages may map different phonemes onto this dimension. But it remains unclear whether symbolism is generated from word meanings in a given language, as Taylor (1963) argued, or is an innate quality of the acoustic components of phonemes, an issue judiciously examined by Tsur (1992). At the same time, several studies have shown systematic differences in phonetic frequencies in poetic texts that correspond with their tone and meaning. The examination of phonetic distributions in the words for smallness or largeness, or in male and female names, also appears to show the effectiveness of phonetic analysis within specific domains. It seems probable, then, that while phonemes have no intrinsic meaning—/i/ is not invariably small or bright—they possess a potential meaning capable of realization when a contrast is in question (/i/ is more likely to contribute to smallness or brightness). In other words, phonemic contrasts can help to motivate meaning in a literary text, as well as direct choices in nonliterary contexts such as the formation of names. No method so far, however, has been proposed for examining phonemic contrasts systematically. In the next section I outline a new method for modelling such contrasts and describe its application to several sample texts.

11.3 Modelling phonemic contrasts

The physiology of pronunciation appears to offer a basis for the meaning dimensions attributed to phonemes. For example, Tsur (1992, pp. 5–6) suggests that the position in the oral tract, that is, the contrast of front and back vowels, underlies such dimensions as bright-dark. Such a dimension is inherent in the typical vowel-space diagram (e.g., Clark & Yallop, 1990, p. 67; O'Grady et al., 1989, p. 30), which displays both a front-back dimension, and a high-low dimension. A similar arrangement is possible for consonants (although this is less commonly displayed graphically, since more variables enter into the question: e.g., voiced vs. unvoiced); but here also, two overall dimensions are evident, front-back and soft-hard.

On the basis of these dimensions, it is possible to place the vowels experimentally into two orders: (1) a front-back ordering with /i/ first in the list and /ʊe/ last, including dipthongs; and (2) an order corresponding to high-middle-low position; given the coarser framework this provides, the vowels at each level are also sorted by their front-back position. Although the position of each vowel in these orderings is not without question, after some trial and error I produced orderings that appear satisfactory, as the analyses to be reported suggest. Each vowel was given a number corresponding to its rank in the two orderings. To foreground the dimensions in question, the ranks range from +9 to +1 for front vowels, and from 0 to –10 for back vowels, with a similar range for high-low. The rank orders are shown in Table 11.1, together with the IPA symbol for each vowel. To facilitate analysis, the vowels were also placed in four groups: two front (high and medium) and two back (medium and low), as shown in the left-hand column of the Table. Two other features of vowels were also considered, given their potential contribution to sound: first, absolute vowel length, which involved identifying such long vowels as /a/ in bard, and /u/ in food, and all the diphthongs; second, the vowel lengthening that occurs before voiced stops and fricatives, known as the vowel shift. Thus two measures based on the frequency of long vowels and the frequency of vowel shifts were devised.

The consonants were also placed in two rank orders, as shown in Table 11.2. Again, the positive ranks are used to indicate front consonants, beginning with /b/, and negative ranks are assigned to back consonants, ending with /k/. The consonants are also placed in four groups, which cut across the two rank orderings: these are (1) unvoiced fricatives and aspirates; (2) voiced fricatives and aspirates; (3) glides, liquids, and nasals; and (4) plosives.

A suite of programs was created to obtain measures of vowel and consonant occurrences in texts. This was achieved as follows. First, the text to be examined was submitted to the Internet facility *Say* (Belinfante, 2000) for phonetic transcription: the program returns a phonetic code based on standard English

Table 11.1 Rank Orderings of 20 Vowels

Group	IPA	Example	Front-back	High-low/ front-back
v-f1	i	bead	9	9
	ɪ	bid	8	7
	e	day	7	5
	ɛ	bed	6	1
v-f2	ɪə	beer	5	-2
	ɛə	bare	4	-1
	æ	bad	3	-7
	ay	eye	2	0
	ɔ	cord	1	-5
	ʌ	bud	0	-3
v-b1	a	bard	-1	-8
	aʊ	cow	-2	-4
	ɗ	cod	-3	-10
	з	bird	-4	4
v-b2	ə	the	-5	3
	ʊ	good	-6	6
	oʊ	go	-7	2
	u	food	-8	8
	ɔɪ	boy	-9	-6
	ʊe	tour	-10	-9

Key to Groups: v-f1: vowels, high front; v-f2: vowels, medium front; v-b1: vowels, medium back; v-b2: vowels, low back.

pronunciation, comprising 20 vowels and 24 consonants. Taking each line of text, the code was then analysed to produce a mean count of vowel lengths (absolute length; vowel shift), and the mean ranks of the two vowel orderings and the two consonant orderings. In other words, the rank of each separate phoneme contributed separately to an overall numerical measure of the phonemes in a given line of text. Although the effect of a phoneme may change according to its context, such changes are probably minimal: the accumulation of separate scores is supported by the finding of Taylor and Taylor (1962) that on a small-large judgement for three letter syllables, no interactions between letters occurred; the best predictor of subjects' judgements was the sum of individual letter scores. Thus the output of the procedure was a set of scores for each line of text. For example, counting the vowels on the front-back dimension, the

Table 11.2 Rank Orderings of 24 Consonants

Group	IPA	Example	front-back	soft-hard
fa-u	f		6	-1
	θ	thin	2	-2
	s		-1	-3
	š	shed	-5	-4
	h		-6	1
	č	etch	-8	-6
fa-v	v		7	4
	ő	then	3	3
	z		0	2
	j	beige	-4	1
	dʒ	edge	-7	-5
g-l-n	w		8	11
	y	yet	-10	10
	l		5	9
	r		4	8
	m		10	7
	n		1	6
	ŋ	sing	-9	5
pl	b		11	-7
	p		9	-10
	d		-2	-8
	t		-3	-11
	g		-11	-9
	k		-12	-12

Key to Groups: fa-v: fricatives and aspirates, voiced; fa-uv: fricatives and aspirates, unvoiced; g-l-n: glides, liquids, and nasals; pl: plosives.

following line from *Paradise Lost* scores a mean rank of 46: "Satan, with thoughts inflamed of highest design" (II, 630), showing that the line is high in front vowels. This line, "If shape it might be called that shape had none" (II, 667), scores -65 on soft-hard consonants, showing that it has a concentration of hard consonants. A second program calculated a score for each line according to the frequency of phonemes in each group, i.e., the number of high front vowels, or the number of unvoiced fricatives and aspirates (eight scores in all). These measures were then applied to several texts and groups of texts to test their validity.

As shown by the analyses of Taylor (1963) and Taylor and Taylor (1965), the list of words for smallness and largeness, which Newman (1933) was unable to distinguish with his measures, were found to be significantly different. They reported that large words begin more often with /g/ or /k/ (hard, back consonants) and contain more back vowels /u/ and /o/. The present measures of phonemic iconicity validate not only these findings, but also show several other distinguishing features. Comparing the same groups of words for smallness (183 words) and largeness (167 words), on *t*-tests for difference (the mean rank data are normally distributed, making this test acceptable), large words contain a higher frequency of vowel shifts (means: Large, 0.395; Small: 0.290), $t(348) = 1.792$, $p < .05$. Small words contain markedly more front vowels (mean ranks: Large: 2.75; Small: 5.0), $t(348) = 2.537$, $p < .005$. No significant difference was found in the consonant rankings. On the phoneme groups, however, several differences in the predicted direction were found. (Since the large words were longer than the small, and the phoneme group data were not normally distributed, data were converted to a measure per phoneme (dividing by frequency) and the Mann-Whitney test of difference was used, with significance assessed by *Z*-score.) On consonant groups, Large words contained more voiced fricatives and aspirates, $Z = 2.95$, $p < .005$, and more unvoiced fricatives and aspirates, $Z = 1.75$, $p < .05$, while Small words contained more plosives, $Z = 2.43$, $p < .01$. On vowel groups, Small words contained more high front vowels, $Z = 1.63$, $p = .05$, while Large words contained more medium back vowels, $Z = 2.16$, $p < .02$ and markedly more low back vowels, $Z = 3.20$, $p < .001$.

The validity of the method was also tested by examining the difference between male and female names, following the report of Cutler, McQueen, and Robinson (1990). Since the extensive list of names they employed was not available, I took names from those given most frequently to babies in the U.S.A. in 1996, a list that provided 50 male and 50 female names (Campbell, 2000). Examination of the mean ranks showed a significant difference on both the rank order vowel and the rank order consonant measures in the predicted direction, as shown in Figure 11.1. Similarly, grouped phoneme data showed female names to contain significantly more glides, liquids, and nasals and more front vowels, but fewer voiced fricatives and aspirates and fewer medium back vowels, as shown in Figure 11.2 (each of these differences is significantly different on a Mann-Whitney test).

The measures thus appear to be supported by these two analyses: they not only confirm previous findings on the phonetic distributions in words for smallness and largeness, and for male and female names, but enable additional detail to be revealed. Two validation tests were then made with literary texts where distinctive phonetic differences would be expected. First, two contrasting passages were taken from Milton's *Paradise Lost.* I compared samples of text from Book II dealing with Hell (Satan's encounter with Sin and Death at the exit from Hell: II, 629–814) and from Book IV offering the first view of Eden (IV, 205–355). If phonemic iconicity is drawn upon to create an underlying tone

Figure 11.1 Phonemic Contrast of 50 Male and 50 Female Names

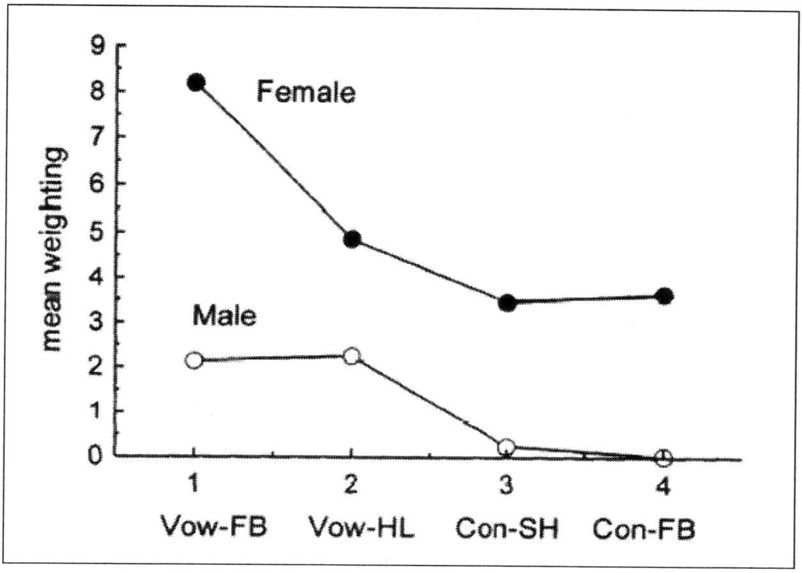

Key. Vow-FB: Vowels front-back; Vow-HL: Vowels high-low; Con-SH: Consonants soft-hard; Con-FB: Consonants front-back.

or mood, then one can expect these two passages to contrast systematically in their use of vowels and consonants: the confinement of Hell should be reflected by a greater proportion of narrow vowels and hard consonants than Eden, which will be characterized by light and space, hence more open vowels and softer consonants. Using the mean ranks of phonemes Hell was found to contain significantly more front vowels than Eden (i.e., the narrow sounds connoting confinement), $t(335) = 2.805$, $p < .005$; at the same time Hell contained significantly more hard consonants than Eden, $t(335) = 2.479$, $p < .02$. In Book II the line with the highest number of hard consonants was 714: "Each cast at th' other as when two black clouds." Lines with a high frequency of soft consonants in Book IV are 207, "In narrow room, Nature's whole wealth, yea more" and 260, "Luxuriant; mean while murmuring waters fall"; and in Book IV a line with a high number of wider, back vowels is 256, "Flowers of all hue, and without thorn the rose." On vowel length, the vowel shift measure showed significantly more longer vowels in Eden in comparison with Hell, $t(335) = 1.822$, $p < .05$ (absolute vowel length was similar in both passages). These findings are supported by several phonetic group measures (making use of Mann-Whitney tests, as data was not normally distributed): Hell contains markedly more high front vowels, $Z = 2.42$, $p < .01$, while Eden contains more medium back vowels, $Z = 1.69$, $p < .05$; there is also a tendency towards more glides, liquids, and nasals in Eden, $Z = 1.34$, $p = .09$, but more unvoiced fricatives and aspirates in

Figure 11.2 Frequencies of Phonemic Groups in 50 Male and 50 Female Names

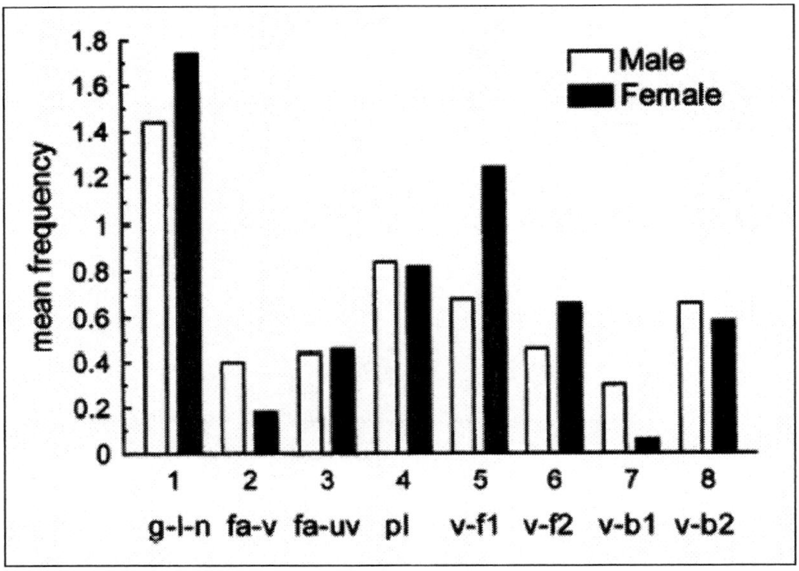

Key. g-l-n: glides, liquids, and nasals; fa-v: fricatives and aspirates, voiced; fa-uv: fricatives and aspirates, unvoiced; pl: plosives; v-f1: vowels, high front; v-f2: vowels, medium front; v-b1: vowels, medium back; v-b2: vowels, low back.

Hell, $Z = 1.55, p = .06$.

The second text to be examined was Coleridge's "Frost at Midnight." In this poem, Coleridge is located in his cottage at midnight where all is silent; he finds the silence disturbing, and this leads to a recollection of his days at school in London where he was unhappy. He continues the poem by anticipating a better future for his child, who will be raised amidst scenes of nature. To analyse the poem phonetically, I categorized the 74 lines of the poem into two types: 22 lines that discuss Coleridge's negative experiences in the present or at school, and the remaining 52 lines that are characterized primarily by positive experiences, either recollections of his home village or his anticipations of the future. Application of the phonetic analysis showed striking contasts in consonant distributions in accord with this analysis: the negative lines contain markedly more back vowels, $t(72) = 3.41$, $p < .005$; from the phonetic groups, glides, liquids, and nasals are more frequent in the positive lines, $Z = 1.67$, $p < .05$, while the negative lines are higher in unvoiced fricatives and aspirates, $Z = 2.11$, $p < .02$ and plosives, $Z = 2.49$, $p < .01$. For example, line 8, classified as negative, "'Tis calm indeed! so calm, that it disturbs," contains several back vowels such as /t/, /k/, and /d/, each of which also occurs in the plosives group. Line 35, in contrast (a positive line), "Lulled me to sleep, and sleep prolonged my dreams," contains a high number of liquids, /l/ and /r/, and front consonants, such as /m/ and /p/. (An extended discussion of the stylistics of this poem is offered in Miall, in press.)

11.4 Readers' Responses to Phonemic Contrasts

If phonetic differences are as systematic as the examples above suggest, then we should also expect to find effects on readers. To study this, I examined phonetic influences in a literary story for which data had already been obtained from readers. The story, "The Trout" by Sean O'Faoláin (1387 words), was divided into 84 segments (roughly one sentence) and coded for the occurrence of foregrounded features in each segment. This involved counting features such as assonance or metrical effects at the phonetic level, grammatical deviations, and semantic effects such as metaphor. A composite foregrounding measure per segment was compiled from these three sources. In a previous study (Miall & Kuiken, 1994a) it was found that readers took longer to read segments high in foregrounding (after controlling for segment length), and they rated such segments higher in affect (i.e., whether the segment aroused feeling in the reader) and in strikingness (whether a given segment stands out as striking in some way). In this first study, 60 readers provided reading time data; of these, 15 readers rated for affect and 15 for strikingness. For the present study, the reader data (mean reading times and ratings per segment) were analysed in relation to the phonetic features of the story in two ways.

First, the mean phonetic ranks and the count of phonetic groups for each segment of the story was obtained. The data from readers was then correlated with each phonetic variable. The data for the first set of analyses is shown in Table 11.3. The data contributing to the correlations with reading time was converted to a measure per syllable in order to control for segment length. Since vowel shift and vowel length can both be expected to contribute to increased reading time, it is not surprising to find a high positive correlation between these measures and reading times. In addition, however, there are strong positive correlations with both of the vowel distribution measures (which, it will be recalled, overlap in part), but a negative correlation with the front-back consonant measure. Thus, while reading this story, readers appear to have lingered more over segments containing front and high vowels and back consonants. In rating for strong affect, on the other hand, segments with front or soft consonants and greater vowel length appear to have been more important; and in rating highly for strikingness, segments with greater vowel length or soft consonants were selected. The possible meaning of these findings will be examined shortly.

The correlations with phoneme groups are shown in Table 11.4. Here it is again apparent that reading times were longer in segments with more front

Table 11.3 Correlations of Reader Data for "The Trout" with Mean Phonetic Variables

	reading time+	affect	strikingness
vowel shift	.309***	.045	.159
vowel length	.536***	.190*	.283***
vowel: F/B	.337***	-.061	.039
vowel: H/L	.316***	.063	.071
conson: F/B	-.295***	.205*	.037
conson: S/H	-.017	.188*	.201*

+Data converted to counts per syllable prior to correlation analysis
*p < .1 **p < .05 *** p < .01 (df 82; two-tailed)

Table 11.4 Correlations of Reader Data for "The Trout" with Phonetic Groups

	reading time+	affect	strikingness
g-l-n	-.195*	.387****	.269***
fa-v	-.370****	.091	.048
fa-uv	.005	-.021	.070
pl	.319****	-.229**	-.132
v-f1	.291***	-.252**	-.238**
v-f2	.211*	.003	-.058
v-b1	-.246**	.121	.213*
v-b1	-.250**	.058	.050

+Data converted to counts per syllable prior to correlation analysis
*p < .1 **p < .05 *** p < .02 ****p < .01 (df 82; two-tailed)

Key. g-l-n: glides, liquids, and nasals; fa-v: fricatives and aspirates, voiced; fa-uv: fricatives and aspirates, unvoiced; pl: plosives; v-f1: vowels, high front; v-f2: vowels, medium front; v-b1: vowels, medium back; v-b2: vowels, low back.

vowels and fewer back vowels; they were also longer in segments high in plosives but low in voiced fricatives and aspirates. In affective terms, readers were most influenced by segments high in glides, liquids, or nasals, and low in plosives and front vowels.

Our previous empirical studies with this story showed that readers were often specially attentive to those passages relating to a particular setting. In the story, Julia, a young girl, finds a live trout in a small hollow of water in a wooded pathway of her garden called the Dark Walk. Of the 84 segments, 32 describe this setting or Julia's behaviour in it as she contemplates the trout's predicament or, towards the end of the story, goes to the Dark Walk at night to rescue the trout. The phonetic differences between the setting and the rest of the story are suggestive. In setting passages, vowel length is significantly longer, as shown by a Mann-Whitney test, $Z = 1.71$, $p < .05$, and there is a higher proportion of front consonants, $Z = 2.483$, $p < .01$; among phoneme groups, setting passages contain significantly more glides, liquids, and nasals, $Z = 2.052$, $p = .02$, and voiced fricatives and aspirates, $Z = 2.534$, $p = < .01$; but these passages are also marginally lower in plosives, $Z = 1.510$, $p = .07$; and contain fewer front vowels, $Z = 1.932$, $p < .05$. A comparison with the ratings for affect and strikingness suggest that it is these qualities in the setting passages to which readers are particularly attentive. Since the story opens with ten segments devoted to the Dark Walk and Julia's behaviour within it, it seems likely that readers soon recognized a specific affective tone associated with the setting; when they encountered this in subsequent setting passages, it helped to make reading more efficient, hence the shorter reading times apparent for each of these phonetic groups, as shown in Table 11.4.

The rating data, analysed in relation to the two types of passage in the story, provides some support for this view. Markedly higher affect ratings were given to setting passages, $Z = 4.142$, $p < .001$, as well as higher strikingness ratings, $Z = 4.276$, $p < .001$. But this latter rating raises the question what relation the phonemic measures have to foregrounding, given our previous finding that elevated levels of foregrounding are associated with longer reading times. While foregrounding is more frequent in setting passages, $Z = 1.65$, $p = .05$, overall the phonemic measures show a relation with foregrounding that cuts across the division of the story into setting and non-setting, as the correlations shown in Table 11.5 suggest. The most notable phonemic components of the passages high in foregrounding are front vowels, back consonants, soft consonants, and plosives.

In brief, the phonemic characteristics of foregrounding, which is defamiliarizing for readers and initiates shifts in story understanding, constitute one tonal quality of "The Trout." The setting passages are distinguished from the rest of the story by a different tonal mix of phonemic features: these in part provide the background of the story, since reading times are generally shorter for passages characterized by this tone. The contrast, then, is between passages found defamiliarizing and those that, once reading is underway, are recognizable and provide an underlying tonal structure to the story. Phonemic patterns, in other words, do influence readers of literary stories, although in different ways according to which aspect of the story is in question.

In conclusion, the findings described here have indicated the presence of phonemic contrasts in several domains: in words for smallness and largeness, in male and female names, and in two literary texts where differences could be expected. In addition, I have shown that readers of a literary story are responsive

Table 11.5 Significant Correlations of Phonetic Measures with Foregrounding in "The Trout"

Mean phonetic ranks:	
front-back vowels	.309***
front-back consonants	-.357***
soft-hard consonants	.327***
Phonetic groups:	
unvoiced fricatives-aspirates	-.190*
plosives	.506***
medium front vowels	.265**
low back vowels	-.343***

*p < .1 **p < .02 ***p < .01 (two-tailed)
Note. Data converted to measures per syllable

to phonemic differences, as their reading times and ratings suggest. Contrary to the earlier studies of phonetic symbolism, and in opposition to a persistent theme in stylistic analysis, phonemes do not appear to possess a fixed quality that can be translated into literary meaning. On the other hand, the physiological dimension of vowels and consonants provides a matrix of potential contrasts, such as high-low, long-short, or bright-dark, which can be realized, as Tsur puts it (1997, p. 286), "when in a specific context the sounds encounter some relevant meaning component." Thus, front vowels are able to connote the confined spaces of Hell in one context, but the feminine qualities of first names in another; plosives tend to characterize words for smallness, but are also prominent in Coleridge's reports of his negative experiences in "Frost at Midnight." The specific qualities that emerge from the array of phonemes in a text depend on the contrasts offered by the text. This, in a word, is why such effects can be described as iconic rather than symbolic, suggesting a relative rather than a fixed meaning.

• CHAPTER TWELVE •

An Evolutionary Framework for Literary Reading

12.1 Evolution and Literature

Every human culture possesses a special mode of verbal behaviour that can be considered "literary," although in most places and at most times this has been an oral rather than a written phenomenon.* However, most current critical theorists appear to accept that "literature," as a body of imaginative writing with distinctive properties, is a rather modern development. Having lasted perhaps some two centuries, it is now in process of being deconstructed following a wide range of historicist and cultural analysis. In short, it is generally held that "literature" emerged in the eighteenth century in order to serve the interests of an emergent middle class culture. As Richard Terry (1997) has suggested, however, the arguments tend to conflate the term "literature" with the concept: citing authors such as Alvin Kernan and Terry Eagleton, he suggests they reveal "slippage from word to concept" (p. 84).

A closely related problem, as Terry's article shows, involves asking when the literary canon came into being. Terry himself argues that the concept of a literary canon emerges around the late sixteenth century, since by this time commentators are privileging a group of creative texts (such as the works of Chaucer, Gower, Spenser, Sidney, and Marlowe) that can be delimited from the noncreative. Willie van Peer (1997) suggests, however, that the processes of canonicity appear to have operated throughout history, as far back as the first "creative" texts on record (Sumerian, c. 3000 BC). The nomination of the term used to label each phenomenon may thus be predated several millenia by the phenomenon itself, that is, by the existence of a select group of texts that tend

* An earlier version of this chapter was first published as "An Evolutionary Framework for Literary Reading" in Gerard Steen & Dick Schram (Eds.), *The Psychology and Sociology of Literature: In Honour of Elrud Ibsch*. Amsterdam: John Benjamins, 2001. I am grateful to the publishers for permission to reprint here.

to outlast the conditions of their production, or by a particular class of texts with special properties and effects.

In this chapter I examine what such an argument implies for literary reading. I will ask whether the experience of the literary may be fundamental to us as a species, and consider whether the proclivity for literary experience fulfils some identifiable and distinctive role. While species-specific traits are commonly thought to require fifty or more generations to develop, the evidence for literature goes back well beyond this; thus the time span for the existence of literature is more than adequate to propose the question: Is literary experience an adaptation, selected by evolutionary pressures because it enhanced survival and reproductive ability? In considering this question, it is important to bear in mind that the conditions under which a trait is manifested now may not provide an accurate guide to how or why the trait was acquired in ancestral conditions. In developed cultures (from Roman to contemporary western civilizations) literary experience has primarily taken the form of reading, which clearly adds a component of learned skills to that experience, likely to have modified it to some degree. Similarly, the powers of literature have at various times been systematically appropriated by religious and secular authorities for their own ends, from Bible rhetoric to modern schoolroom techniques of literary analysis. Indeed, the supposed invention of literature by the middle classes in the eighteenth century has been taken to show that literary experience embodies ideological principles and rests on nothing innate. Disentangling from these cultural formations what may be fundamental to literary experience will hardly be a simple or straightforward task.

In discussing this question, whether literary reading has evolutionary significance, I will limit myself to two issues. In the first main section of the chapter I ask what the evidence is for an innate component of literature. Here I further limit the discussion to the response to literary language, or foregrounding; this stands in for a wider discussion of other distinctive features, such as tropes and narrative forms. In the second section I consider the function of literature as a dehabituating agent; in this light, I then ask what difference an evolutionary perspective might make to our research on reading. The dehabituation theory proposed here offers a formal, testable set of hypotheses for the evolutionary significance of literature, and in this respect it goes beyond the informal, often impressionistic approach of previous critics, while building upon an important suggestion by Ellen Dissanayake.

Dissanayake (1992), who has written extensively on the evolutionary significance of the arts, suggests that works of art promote what we might call a "defamiliarizing" mode of mind, a "making special" (p. 50). In premodern societies this multimodal experience (involving several art forms) prepared the individual for recognizing and participating in an unusual experience: developed at first, perhaps, for encountering the sacred and the rituals that evolved around it, literary experience may have acquired its own specific characteristics, coming in time to incorporate verbal and narrative cues to alert the hearer to adopt a special mode of attention. Dissanayake notes that many cultures make use of specific devices to signal poetic utterance, such as an unusual tone of voice (pp. 113–6). Internalized in the texture of language as foregrounding it is these cues, in part, that we now recognize as giving written literature its distinctiveness as a medium.

Dissanayake's approach suggests a functional approach to the evolutionary significance of the arts, which dehabituation theory is intended to formalize. In contrast, Carroll (1995, 2005) mainly develops a thematic, or content-based approach (see also Storey, 1996; Boyd, 1998). Carroll wishes to ask why literature might be adaptive, why it is produced and consumed. Art matters, he says, because it provides models of reality that help organize human understanding and motivation. This leads to a focus on predominantly thematic issues: to pursue an evolutionary approach, for example, "is to look at narratives or dramatic works for illustrations of some hypothesized universal form of sexual psychology": e.g., sexual competition among males, or male opportunist mating strategies. As a critical approach for the literary scholar it calls for the exercise of some traditional skills: interpretation should involve "tact, intuition, and personal response" (2005, p. 935). Where Carroll comes close to a functional approach he argues that, given the recent evolution of the size of the brain, art may have evolved to solve the problem of possible "confusion and error that accompany the loosening of stereotyped, instinctual responses" (p. 939). In this sense art imposes order or resolves uncertainty. But Carroll's evolutionary approach remains primarily at an interpretive or descriptive level: it is the study of how literature explores human norms and their variations, such that "Depicting and registering the relation between human universals and individual identity is a chief concern for an adaptionist interpretation of literary meaning" (p. 943).

But a content-directed approach, aimed at showing how evolutionary themes underlie the plots and characters of literature, may place too much emphasis on meaning, leading us back to a preoccupation with interpretation. This argument can be illustrated by an analogy. Literature invokes processes in the reader somewhat as a migrating bird depends on its navigational system. The bird does not set out with a fixed goal that it aims to reach: its orientation is guided by reference to such environmental signals as geographical landmarks, terrestrial magnetism, the sun, and stars, all of which provide the bird with a goal-tracking system. It is this content-knowledge that modulates the migratory process of the bird, but in order to understand that process we need to know not what the bird understands about magnetism or the sun but how its systematic use of this information creates a guidance system. Similarly, the literary reader, while knowing there may be a goal to be reached (i.e., an interpretation of a text that is appropriate for that reader), cannot set out knowing in advance what that goal is, in the way that the reader of a repair manual or a chemistry textbook can be goal-oriented; moreover, interpretation may not even be a goal for the reader who reads for the pleasurable experience of reading rather than for meaning. Literary reading is guided, like the migrating bird, by an array of navigational markers, such as the palette of phonetic features, significant tropes, or narrative cues, and it is these that enable readers to attain their goal. Readers do not need knowledge of phonetic tone colours, or even need to be aware of their role during reading. As literary readers, in other words, we deploy a set of "content-sensitive" processes (Tooby and Cosmides, 1992, p. 34) endowed on us by evolution, but fulfil these in ways peculiar to our own needs and historical context.

In the discussion that follows, therefore, I first briefly lay out some evidence for attention to foregrounding, suggesting that this is a distinctive feature of human development from infancy onwards, predating literary experience as such. My comments are intended to be representative, since foregrounding is only one of several formal aspects that should be explored for their evolutionary significance: other major domains of inquiry include figurative structures (analysed, although not in an evolutionary context, by Turner, 1991), and the formal components of narrative (e.g., Fludernik, 1996). Then I examine the "defamiliarizing" process of mind that appears central to literary experience, and consider what evolutionary implications it might possess. I propose that literary experience considered formally can be understood as dehabituating, having emerged in recent human evolution as an adaptive solution to some specific sensory and cognitive limitations in human functioning.

12.2 Form and Foregrounding

The claim that literary texts characteristically exhibit a special use of language, or foregrounding, has been in dispute for several decades, a dispute initiated in particular by Stanley Fish's (1980c) attack on stylistic methods of analysis in a paper first published in 1973. Arguments against literary language have typically taken one of three forms: first, that distinctive features (alliteration, metaphor, etc.) are as common in non-literary as in literary texts; second, that such verbal features provide no formula for reaching an interpretation, i.e., that they are devoid of the kinds of meaning that stylistic critics have attempted to build upon them; or, third, that if we pay attention to foregrounding it is solely because we have been schooled into doing so. Each of these arguments deserves careful consideration (for discussion see Miall and Kuiken, 1998, 1999), but for the present purpose I will point out only that on both sides of the debate the issue of reception has been largely overlooked. Thus, my concern here is with the question, what difference does it make to the reader who encounters such features, whether in a text designated literary or not. For the argument about the existence of literary language to be plausible, we must demonstrate that a distinctive kind of processing during reading corresponds to the presence of foregrounding. If we find evidence of such processing, we have then still to establish whether it is put in place by the reader's literary education or is a sign of an intrinsic capacity for literary response.

On the first issue, we now have some evidence for a distinctive mode of processing. Our studies (Miall and Kuiken, 1994a), which were built in part on those of van Peer (1986), focused on readers' responses to literary short stories in which we had previously analysed the occurrence of foregrounded features. We found that readers typically took longer to read passages containing foregrounding, with longer reading times corresponding to the most highly foregrounded passages. At the same time, readers appeared to consider such passages more striking, productive of more feeling, and more uncertain in relation to the unfolding meaning of the text, as shown by their ratings of each passage. We found some evidence that this first phase of response, which can be termed defamiliarizing, is followed by a constructive process on the part of the reader that appears to centre on the feeling associated with the foregrounded feature: such feeling in time puts in place an alternative framework for interpretation, which contributes to the new perspective opened up by the reading of the story as a whole (cf. Chapter 5; Miall and Kuiken, 2001). It is this phasic process of response, located in relation to specific textual features, that we have proposed as typical of literary reception (Miall and Kuiken, 1999).

What evidence is there, however, that this process is intrinsic rather than induced pedagogically? Two lines of argument can be adduced. First, according to the cultural relativist position espoused by Stanley Fish (1980a), Barbara Herrnstein Smith (1988), and others, the degree to which readers are attentive to foregrounding should be a product of how much literary education they have received. The evidence against this position is not compelling, but serves to call it into question. We compared the responses to foregrounding of advanced students of literature and first year students of psychology who, as we found, had little interest in or experience of literary reading. We found that no difference occurred between the groups in the degree to which lengthened reading times correlated with foregrounding, a finding that showed our non-literary students to be equally attentive to foregrounded passages. In his study of response to foregrounding in several poems, van Peer (1986) similarly found no difference between his three groups of participants, who ranged from students of stylistics to science students with minimal training in literature (pp. 114–5). In a study of response to metaphors in a literary and a newspaper text, Steen (1994) found that expert and less-expert readers (scholars of literature and anthropology, respectively) paid attention to metaphors about equally, with both groups consistently paying more attention to metaphors in the literary text (p. 144). These findings suggest, contrary to the arguments of the cultural critics, that the initial response to foregrounding may be independent of literary training or experience.

A second line of evidence for the literary significance of foregrounding is to be found in genetic studies, which suggest that a sensitivity to such verbal devices may be inborn. For example, in a study I carried out with Ellen Dissanayake (Miall & Dissanayke, 2003), we analysed a recording of a mother's verbal interactions with her 8-week old baby, Liam (recorded at the laboratory of Professor Colwyn Trevarthen at the University of Edinburgh). The mother's language, deployed to engage or sustain her baby's attention, clearly demonstrates a range of foregrounded features including local effects, such as alliteration and assonance, metrical effects, and figurative expressions, as well as larger scale patterns that in poetry would be classified as verse lines and stanzas. What is particularly striking in the interaction is the extent to which high, front phonemes in the mother's speech coincide with maximal attention of the infant, suggesting intimacy, during which the mother addresses the infant directly; in contrast, low, back phonemes occur when the infant is distracted or inattentive, and the mother is more likely to mention the infant's appearance or surroundings. Since the infant at this age has no semantic grasp of language, his attention is mediated by the purely aural pattern of repetitions and differences produced by the mother: in both, a mutual response process is evoked that appears to be characterized by subtle kinaesthetic and affective modulations in the infant that are attuned to within a third of a second.

Once the infant himself begins to generate language a notable feature of spontaneous speech is, once again, a type of language rich with foregrounding. The most detailed available study is that of a boy of two and a half years whose spontaneous language play after he was put to bed was recorded and analysed by his mother, the linguist Ruth Weir (1962), in *Language in the Crib.* Weir shows in detail the array of non-referential features in the child's soliloquies, including alliterations, play with syntax and word forms, and a structure of extended utterances that Weir terms "rondos." The final example transcribed in Weir's book is described by Jakobson, in his prefatory remarks to the book, as a "beautiful poetic composition" (p. 20). In these sequences, as Weir observes in her summary of the study, the child enjoys "play with words, by repetitions of similar sounds, by his rediscovery of what is familiar to him," creating what she calls "a dialogue spoken by a single person" (pp. 144, 146). While the words are derived from the child's daily experience, when alone in his crib the child fashions an aural world out of them whose development is principally dependent on syntactic and aural variation.

Evidence of this kind goes some way toward answering the question, raised by van Peer (1986) in the conclusion of his study, how children come to understand the function of foregrounding. "What is at stake here, is the anthropological status of foregrounding in particular, and of literature in general" (p.

181). At this pre-literary stage in infancy, children's pleasure in wordplay is manifested in numerous forms. In each case, as the first example of the mother's speech shows, verbal texture creates and maintains a special state of being, marked by a distinctive mode of attention and suffused with feelings both bodily and affective. Each state is sufficient to itself, although it undoubtedly contributes toward a repertoire of dispositions of the self—the self in relation to itself and to others. Once literary experience itself becomes possible (beginning, perhaps with the first stories read by parents), it seems likely that such dispositions will be evoked by the same verbal means, but that now they are placed in relation to other states and processes brought into play by the text. In this context a familiar disposition may come to seem less familiar, being subjected to critical revaluation in the light of alternative perspectives. Without the initial responsiveness to the creative power of verbal textures, beginning in the cradle, the variations presented by literary texts would possess no meaning. In brief, while pre-literary experience creates dispositions and states, literary experience begins to frame these in perspective-altering ways.

These examples seem to point to the possibility of an innate capacity for foregrounding, leading to the modifying experiences of literature. We might also consider another type of genetic evidence, that of oral literature, since it seems probable that contemporary examples of such literature are comparable to the pre-literate epoch of all human cultures. The appearance of foregrounding in oral literature cannot be attributed to the practices of a systematic educational programme in literature, although as Ruth Finnegan (1992) makes clear, each culture creates its texts on the basis of a distinctive set of conventions. Such conventions frequently make the use of a specific type of foregrounding obligatory, such as the alliterative patterns of Somali verse (p. 94), or metrical units that create a strict pattern of parallelisms in Toda songs (p. 99), or an organizing metaphor in the Polynesian poem (p. 114). Finnegan suggests that the special diction found in oral literature arises both because it fulfils formal needs, and because it serves to put a "frame" around a poem marking it off from the language of ordinary life (p. 110). Although the palette of foregrounded features varies from one culture to another, its role in the examples cited is evidently important and persuasive, functioning with a power equal to its role in some of the best written poetry of the last few centuries. As Finnegan also points out, however, oral poetry is likely to be a multimodal experience: it is performed, thus achieving through the dramatic role of the speaker with an audience effects that in written literature must depend upon verbal texture alone or its appearance on the page. She also stresses that its functions vary considerably from one culture to another: for example, some poems are said to be communications from a god or from a dead relative; others are interventions in current social relationships designed to influence the standing of the speaker.

Neither oral literature, nor the word play and other early verbal experiences of infants and children, has either a particular function or a single relation to the culture of its participants. We have no reason to think that written literature is significantly different (which makes disputes over whether literature has a transcendental or ideological purpose redundant). What marks each of the examples I have mentioned, including the literary stories that were the focus of the empirical studies I described earlier, is a reception process initiated by and dependent upon foregrounding. In each case, a specific feature—or, more usually, a constellation of features—attracts attention by virtue of its distinctiveness in comparison with other, ordinary uses of language (the meaning of "ordinary" here will be elaborated below). The state of feeling, or disposition, evoked in the hearer appears to be, at least in part, a consequence of the verbal feature. For example, an alliteration of front consonants (liquids or nasals) may invoke a sense of intimacy and affection (as it clearly does in the example of the mother's babytalk); the metre of a song may evoke the lightning speed of the superior hunter in his final chase. Whatever the precise mode of attention, the moment of response to foregrounding promotes a familiar experience to the status of being special (in Dissanayake's terms), and opens it to the possibility of being re-evaluated. In this process, the feeling now in place may outlast its occasion, either allowing it to govern the emergence of some new cognitive formation, or, alternatively, to be relocated within a perspective that will modify understanding of it.

The contrast of a special language containing foregrounded features with "ordinary" language is not uncontentious, however. Whether literary language contains more unusual features such as alliteration or metaphor than other types of language has been disputed, and is evidently not the case with some types of literary texts. Eagleton (1983) sums up his dismissal of the claim by asking us "to face the fact that there is more metaphor in Manchester than there is in Marvell" (p. 6), a clause that, notably, enforces its point by alliteration, unlike the surrounding sentences (presumably a rhetorical flourish intended by Eagleton). The conclusion my discussion points to, however, is that arguments such as Eagleton's miss the point: special uses of language are only special if they are noticed, and, in the case of literature, if they systematically modify the hearer's understanding (this proposal, of course, extends to other forms of modifying understanding, such as narrative). Literary reception, I have suggested, is marked by a special, phasic type of processing, in contrast to the reception of a metaphor in Manchester, which may be incidental to the discourse in which it occurs. A person who uttered a series of metaphors at a bus stop in Manchester would be considered either mad, or engaged in some new kind of performance art. "Ordinary" language requires a type of decorum, one significant feature of which is its avoidance of foregrounded features organized to promote attention to meaning. In the next section I take this contrast between ordinary and literary language as the basis for suggesting where the evolutionary significance of literary response may lie.

12.3 The Dehabituating Role of Literature

Central to the arguments of evolutionary psychology is the claim that whatever psychological mechanisms the human race exhibits now were developed in response to our prehistorical existence as hunter-gatherers in the Pleistocene epoch. Our adaptedness as a species is a reflection of the environment that prevailed some thirty to a hundred thousand years ago, a context that must be considered in attempting to understand any significant human capacity—including that for literature. Thus literature as a response process cannot be understood only in terms of recent cultural developments, or even as a product of middle class ideology across the last two or three centuries. As Bowlby (1974) remarks, we must be attentive to "the fact that not a single feature of a species' morphology, physiology, or behaviour can be understood or even discussed intelligently except in relation to that species' environment of evolutionary adaptedness" (p. 64). Literary reading, in this perspective, must be understood as a response to the ancestral environment and the cognitive, emotional, and social challenges that it posed.

So what kind of adaptation is literary response? How might it promote the inclusive fitness of those early humans who adopted its practice? I will argue that it confers a number of benefits, but that each can be understood in terms of a theory of *dehabituation*. Response to literature promotes an offline tuning of emotional and cognitive schemata, with a particular focus on resetting the individual's readiness for appropriate action. The central observation is that literature facilitates this process through an array of formal features, thus the present account can be seen as a neoformalist theory. In the previous section I advanced a case for foregrounding, but equally important evidence for figurative and narrative structures should also be assessed, structures that contribute equally important formal building blocks to the distinctive properties of literature. Overall, it can be proposed that it is the reception processes initiated by these structures that make literary experience unique. Whereas language in its ordinary uses, as in much everyday conversation, discourse in newspaper journalism, or school textbooks, has the primary function of elaborating information based on prototypical concepts and readers' existing schemata, literary forms disrupt this essential function for reasons which may be equally essential. While effective behaviour, particularly in the ancestral environment, typically depends on rapid assignment of meaning to appearances following their assessment in relation to the interests of the self or the group, the tendency inherent in this facility is to stereotypic concepts and stock responses. Literary experience, which takes place outside the normal demands of daily life, enables stereotypic concepts and responses to be put in question. Through literature readers or hearers may evolve new modes of feeling for the issues that are most central to their experience; as I also suggest below, literature may facilitate the modulation or repair of emotionally negative experiences in particular. By dehabituating, in brief, we prepare ourselves for encountering experience in ways that are potentially (although not necessarily) more productive, thus enhancing the flexibility of our responses to the environment or our social interactions.

Why might the evolutionary approach matter? Speaking most generally, as a mode of inquiry, it enables us to read our present capacities and accomplishments as a solution to past problems. Rooted in capacities that appear to be innate to the human system for the past several thousand years of history (and probably much longer), it suggests a provisional answer to what literary experience might be for. Although the modern literary theorist may accept the truth of the evolutionary argument, however, it may be objected that this is hardly relevant, given the inherent power and prevalance of language and culture now. Hasn't culture developed its own momentum, based on its own laws that now have little or no relation to the ancestral environment? Culture, this argument goes, is built from other cultures; literary texts are made from other texts, and have no substantial relation to the "natural" world. As Roland Barthes (1977) puts it, texts are "woven entirely with citations, references, echoes, cultural languages," their mode of being lying in the "infinite deferment of the signified" (pp. 160, 158). How could an evolutionary psychology have any bearing on literary culture, when culture has long since written over and effaced whatever "natural" functions human beings inherited? Moreover, since we are not born with literary competence, its acquisition must depend not only on developing a competence in language, but also derive from educational and cultural influences in the environment that are not experienced until later childhood: literature, in other words, is entirely a product of the culture and can have nothing "innate" about it. It is in this perspective that the "interpretive community" is emphasized by literary theorists such as Stanley Fish (1980a).

However, the distinction made here between what is due to nature and what to culture is a specious one: every human phenomenon is derived from evolved psychological mechanisms with specialized functions and inherited forms of representation, modified by interaction with a particular local culture and environment. As Bowlby (1974) has noted, "Just as area is a product of length multiplied by width so every biological character whether it be morphological, physiological, or behavioural, is a product of the interaction of genetic endowment with the environment. Terms like innate and acquired must therefore be cast into limbo and a new terminology employed" (p. 38). Evolutionary theorists Tooby and Cosmides (1992) also argue that the distinction is incoherent and "should be consigned to the dustbin of history, along with the search for a biology-free social science" (p. 46). To locate the agency for cultural phenomena outside the person and the rich array of psychological functions that individuals possess in common, they argue, is to mystify the processes in question: there is "no radical discontinuity inherent in the evolution of 'culture' that removes humans into an autonomous realm" (p. 119), as the linguistic premises of poststructuralist theory and its "deferred signified" imply. As Tooby and Cosmides also note, "cognitive architectures that are passive vehicles for arbitrary semiotic systems are not plausible products of the evolutionary process" (p. 109).

Many postmodern accounts of cultural phenomena perpetuate the Cartesian distinction between mind and body, refusing to see the mind as governed by the same principles as the body: "the mind should contain 'mental organs' just as the body does," note Tooby and Cosmides (p. 57). The evidence from evolution suggests that the mind is actually constituted in part by a range of functionally specialized, content-dependent mechanisms, or adaptive specializations (for a recent list, see Buss, 1995, p. 6). It is unlikely that literary response represents an exception: response to literature, in other words, is likely to depend either on an array of domain-specific modules in the mind, or, as may be more probable, constitute in itself a domain-specific module with its own determining mechanisms that underlie its many cultural and historical variations. This does not imply that literature is a closed or fixed system: biological determination does not mean constraint or inflexibility. On the contrary, the domain-specificity of literature is the ground on which has flowered the extraordinary range of literary phenonema apparent across history, while giving literary response a set of core functions that has ensured its central place in human society up to the present era.

Why the literary mechanism represents an effective solution to human adaptive problems can also be understood in terms of our identity, both individual and social. Literary response may represent a solution to social constraints on the expression of emotion (cf. Nesse and Lloyd, 1992), and, in the context of the awareness of contingency, change, and death that first emerged with our ancestors, it offers a medium for reflecting on potential alternative identities. In this respect, also, literature is to be distinguished from ordinary discourse. The primary function of discourse is to instantiate common interpretive schemata, for which emotional response and self-awareness arise only incidentally and are generally stereotypical; but a text that only instantiates a frame with relevant information is not literary. Literature, in contrast, facilitates changes in perception or in the self in its relationship with others, thus enhancing the survival and reproductive ability of the group.

This external factor alone may have been sufficient to favour the selection and perpetuation of the capacity for literature, but literature can also be seen as a solution to an endogenous adaptive problem, that of social constraint, repression, and pathology. What began as a communal experience, especially shared narratives, dramas, and literary components of play or ritual (Dissanayake, 1992, p. 48), may over time have evolved in part to address the singular internal needs of individuals. Literature evolved in particular, perhaps, because it spoke to what was individual in the individual. Where, in other words, powerful feelings, such as love, bereavement, loss, or trauma set the individual apart, forestalling the benefits of solidarity and communication with others, the emotion can be engaged and brought into focus through literary experience. As studies of our own with bereaved participants have suggested, new meanings can then be found that help the individual to accommodate the emotion and come to terms with it. In this way, too, literature enhances our abilities to respond flexibly to experience and thus assists our powers of survival.

Two salient implications for empirical study appear to follow from the evolutionary framework. First, it should be possible to specify dehabituation theory in relation to hypotheses that predict specific aspects of the relationship between literary texts and readers' behavior and that can be tested empirically. Examples of such hypotheses will include:

- Literary texts contain attentional framing devices. Their presence will be signified by increased demands on processing. The discussion offered earlier of foregrounding, whose presence correlated with reading times, is one example of such a device. Another is Johan Hoorn's (1996) neuropsychological study of semantic and phonetic deviation at verse endings, which correlated with increased N400, an electrophysiological measure of unexpected events.
- Increase in stylistic novelty over time is also predicted by dehabituation theory. As Colin Martindale has shown in a number of outstanding studies (e.g., *The Clockwork Muse*, 1990), once a literary style has been established (as, say, at the beginning of the British Romantic period) writers must work progressively harder to create novelty that will attract and hold the attention of readers; they do so by shifting increasingly to the use of primary process thought in their writing.
- Special processing of negative emotions will occur during literary response (a process that we might term catharsis), a hypothesis based on the assumption that adaptive value accrues from attending to negative emotions that tend to be repressed in the familiar social settings for self-expression. In a study in which we compared the valency of judgements for everyday experiences of settings compared with settings in literary stories, we found a significant shift towards negative evaluations in responses to the stories (Corrêa et al., 1998).

Figure 12.1 Levels of Analysis in an Evolutionary Theory of Literature

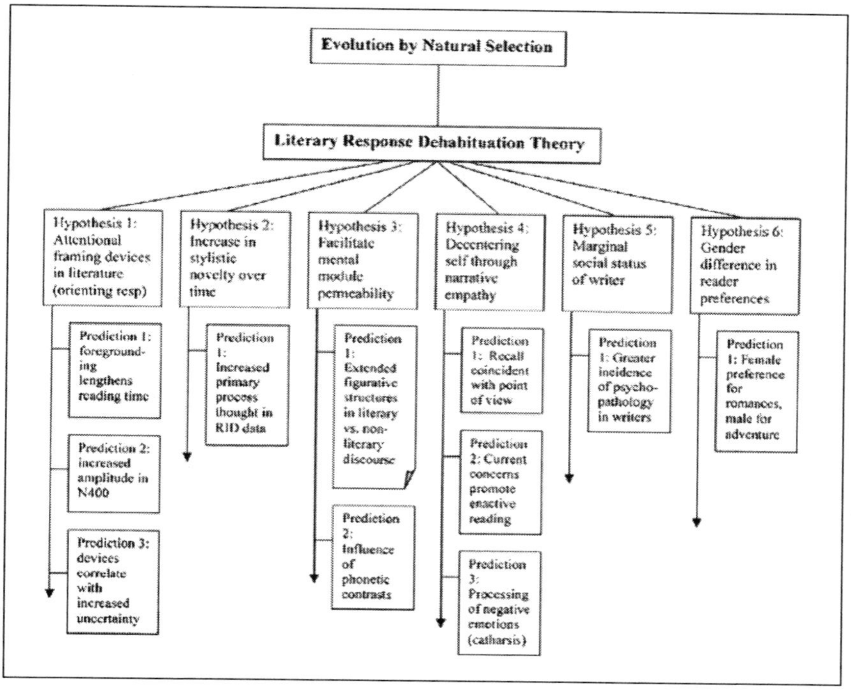

These and other features of the evolutionary approach are summarized in Figure 12.1, which attempts to capture the logic of an empirical research programme as suggested by Buss (1995). Other hypotheses I have included here refer to two well-established findings: the greater incidence of psychopathology in creative writers, perhaps related to their greater exposure to states of cognitive risk (e.g., Jamison, 1993); and the finding of gender differences in preferences for types of reading.

A second implication of the approach taken here is that the readings of literary texts produced by literary scholars, interesting though they may be in themselves, have little value for empirical study, except when they suggest specific hypotheses about literary processing that are amenable to empirical examination. In the terms of neuropsychologist Gerald Edelman (1992), only "population thinking" can account for the selection and development of a species trait: "population thinking states that evolution produces classes of living forms from the bottom up by gradual selective processes over eons of time" (p. 73). For literature, the question is thus what function literary reception may have in populations of readers, not individuals—although the evidence can only be studied as it is manifested within the responses of a range of actual individual readers. This suggests that the current emphasis on critical and historicist interpretations of texts, important though these have sometimes been, has obscured understanding of what may be characteristic and universal in literary response. A population of readings, in contrast, may tell us a great deal about the lawfulness of literary response if the group of responses examined appears to vary systematically in relation to certain significant variables in the text-reader interaction. Thus empirical study of real readers, guided by defensible scientific hypotheses about the adaptive functionality of literature, appears to be the most productive paradigm for future research.

Although the empirical science of literature has been pursued by very few scholars in comparison with the considerable number currently pursuing conventional theoretical and interpretive studies, I argue that the pattern of invariants within the framework of dehabituation theory has the power to offer a foundation for literary studies overall. This will enable literary study to contribute to the integration of the behavioral and social studies for which Tooby and Cosmides (1992) have called. Thus, in the view of it proposed here, empirical literary study is potentially both paradigmatic and unifying.

Appendix

Kate Chopin, "The Story of an Hour" (1894)

Episodes / Paragraphs

E1 /

1. Knowing that Mrs. Mallard was afflicted with a heart trouble, great care was taken to break to her as gently as possible the news of her husband's death.
2. It was her sister Josephine who told her, in broken sentences; veiled hints that revealed in half concealing. Her husband's friend Richards was there, too, near her. It was he who had been in the newspaper office when intelligence of the railroad disaster was received, with Brently Mallard's name leading the list of "killed." He had only taken the time to assure himself of its truth by a second telegram, and had hastened to forestall any less careful, less tender friend in bearing the sad message.
3. She did not hear the story as many women have heard the same, with a paralyzed inability to accept its significance. She wept at once, with sudden, wild abandonment, in her sister's arms. When the storm of grief had spent itself she went away to her room alone. She would have no one follow her.

E2 /

4. There stood, facing the open window, a comfortable, roomy armchair. Into this she sank, pressed down by a physical exhaustion that haunted her body and seemed to reach into her soul.
5. She could see in the open square before her house the tops of trees that were all aquiver with the new spring life. The delicious breath of rain was in the air. In the street below a peddler was crying his wares. The notes of a distant song which some one was singing reached her faintly, and countless sparrows were twittering in the eaves.

6. There were patches of blue sky showing here and there through the clouds that had met and piled one above the other in the west facing her window.
7. She sat with her head thrown back upon the cushion of the chair, quite motionless, except when a sob came up into her throat and shook her, as a child who has cried itself to sleep continues to sob in its dreams.
8. She was young, with a fair, calm face, whose lines bespoke repression and even a certain strength. But now there was a dull stare in her eyes, whose gaze was fixed away off yonder on one of those patches of blue sky. It was not a glance of reflection, but rather indicated a suspension of intelligent thought.

E3 /

9. There was something coming to her and she was waiting for it, fearfully. What was it? She did not know; it was too subtle and elusive to name. But she felt it, creeping out of the sky, reaching toward her through the sounds, the scents, the color that filled the air.
10. Now her bosom rose and fell tumultuously. She was beginning to recognize this thing that was approaching to possess her, and she was striving to beat it back with her will—as powerless as her two white slender hands would have been.
11. When she abandoned herself a little whispered word escaped her slightly parted lips. She said it over and over under her breath: "free, free, free!" The vacant stare and the look of terror that had followed it went from her eyes. They stayed keen and bright. Her pulses beat fast, and the coursing blood warmed and relaxed every inch of her body.
12. She did not stop to ask if it were or were not a monstrous joy that held her. A clear and exalted perception enabled her to dismiss the suggestion as trivial.
13. She knew that she would weep again when she saw the kind, tender hands folded in death; the face that had never looked save with love upon her, fixed and gray and dead. But she saw beyond that bitter moment a long procession of years to come that would belong to her absolutely. And she opened and spread her arms out to them in welcome.
14. There would be no one to live for during those coming years; she would live for herself. There would be no powerful will bending hers in that blind persistence with which men and women believe they have a right to impose a private will upon a fellow-creature. A kind intention or a cruel intention made the act seem no less a crime as she looked upon it in that brief moment of illumination.
15. And yet she had loved him—sometimes. Often she had not. What did it matter! What could love, the unsolved mystery, count for in face of

this possession of self-assertion which she suddenly recognized as the strongest impulse of her being!

16. "Free! Body and soul free!" she kept whispering.

E4 /

17. Josephine was kneeling before the closed door with her lips to the keyhole, imploring for admission. "Louise, open the door! I beg, open the door—you will make yourself ill. What are you doing Louise? For heaven's sake open the door."
18. "Go away. I am not making myself ill." No; she was drinking in a very elixir of life through that open window.
19. Her fancy was running riot along those days ahead of her. Spring days, and summer days, and all sorts of days that would be her own. She breathed a quick prayer that life might be long. It was only yesterday she had thought with a shudder that life might be long.
20. She arose at length and opened the door to her sister's importunities. There was a feverish triumph in her eyes, and she carried herself unwittingly like a goddess of Victory. She clasped her sister's waist, and together they descended the stairs. Richards stood waiting for them at the bottom.
21. Some one was opening the front door with a latchkey. It was Brently Mallard who entered, a little travel-stained, composedly carrying his grip-sack and umbrella. He had been far from the scene of accident, and did not even know there had been one. He stood amazed at Josephine's piercing cry; at Richards' quick motion to screen him from the view of his wife.
22. But Richards was too late.
23. When the doctors came they said she had died of heart disease—of joy that kills.

Bibliography

Andringa, E. (1990). Verbal data on literary understanding: A proposal for protocol analysis on two levels. *Poetics, 19*, 231–257.

——— (1996). Effects of "narrative distance" on readers' emotional involvement and response. *Poetics, 23*, 431–452.

Baars, B. J. (1999). Art must move: Emotion and the biology of beauty. *Journal of Consciousness Studies, 6*, 59–61.

Baddeley, A. (2000). The episodic buffer: A new component of working memory? *Trends in Cognitive Sciences, 4*, 417–423.

Bailey, R. (1971). Statistics and the sounds of poetry. *Poetics, 1*, 16–37.

Barthes, R. (1975). *S/Z*. Trans. R. Miller. London: Jonathan Cape. (Original work published 1970)

——— (1977). Introduction to the structural analysis of narratives. In S. Heath (Ed. and Trans.), *Image-music-text* (pp. 79–124). London: Fontana/Collins.

Bartlett, F. (1932). *Remembering*. Cambridge: Cambridge University Press.

Bawarshi, A. (2000). The genre function. *College English*, 62, 335–360.

Beach, R., and Hynds, S. (1991). Research on response to literature. In R. Barr, M. L. Kamil, P. B. Mosenthal, & P. D. Pearson (Eds.), *Handbook of reading research: Volume II* (pp. 453–489). New York: Longman.

Bechara, A. (2004). The role of emotion in decision-making: Evidence from neurological patients with orbitofrontal damage. *Brain and Cognition, 55*, 30–40.

Beeman, M. J., and Bowden, E. M. (2000). The right hemisphere maintains solution-related activation for yet-to-be-solved problems. *Memory & Cognition, 28*, 1231–1241.

Belinfante, A. (2000). *Say*. http://purl.oclc.org/net/say/ (28 Feb. 2000).

Beneke, T. (1982). *Men on rape*. New York: St. Martin's Press.

Bentley, M., and Varon, E. J. (1933). An accessory study of "phonetic symbolism." *American Journal of Psychology, 45*, 76–86.

Berkowitz, P. (2006). Review of Daphne Patai and Will H. Corral (Eds.), *Theory's empire: An anthology of dissent*. *Policy Review*, Web Special (January 2006) http://www.policyreview.org/135/berkowitz.html (visited February 24 2006)

Birkerts, S. (1994). *The Gutenberg elegies: The fate of reading in an electronic age*, New York: Fawcett Columbine.

Black, J. B. and Bower, G. H. (1980). Episodes as chunks in narrative memory. *Journal of Verbal Learning and Verbal Behavior, 18*, 309–318.

Black, M. (1954–55). Metaphor. *Proceedings of the Aristotelian Society, 55* (New Series), 273–294.

Bock, M. (1986). The influence of emotional meaning on the recall of words processed for form or self-reference. *Psychological Research, 48*, 107–112.

Bock, M. and Klinger, E. (1986). Interaction of emotion and cognition in word recall. *Psychological Research, 48*, 99–106.

Borod, J. C., Bloom, R. L., Brickman, A. M., Nakhutina, L., and Curko, E. A. (2002). Emotional processing deficits in individuals with unilateral brain damage. *Applied Neuropsychology, 9*, 23–36.

Bortolussi, M., and Dixon P. (2003). *Psychonarratology: Foundations for the empirical study of literary response.* Cambridge: Cambridge University Press.

Bourg, T. (1996). The role of emotion, empathy, and text structure in children's and adult's narrative text comprehension. In R. J. Kreuz and M. S. MacNealy (Eds.), *Empirical approaches to literature and aesthetics* (pp. 241–260). Norwood, NJ: Ablex.

Bowden, E., and Beeman, M. J. (1998). Getting the right idea: Semantic activation in the right hemisphere may help solve insight problems. *Psychological Science, 9*, 435–440.

Bower, G. H., and Cohen, P. R. (1982). Emotional influences in memory and thinking: Data and theory. In M. S. Clark and S. T. Fiske (Eds.), *Feeling and cognition: The 17th Annual Carnegie Symposium on Cognition* (pp. 291–331). Hillsdale, N.J.: Lawrence Erlbaum Associates Inc.

Bowlby, J. (1974). *Attachment.* London: Hogarth Press.

Boyd, B. (1998). Jane, meet Charles: Literature, evolution and human nature. *Philosophy and Literature, 22*, 1–30.

Bransford, J. D., & Johnson, M. K. (1972). Contextual prerequisites for understanding: Some investigations of comprehension and recall. *Journal of Verbal Learning and Verbal Behavior, 11*, 717–726.

Bredin, H. (1996). Onomatopoeia as a figure and a linguistic principle. *New Literary History, 27*, 555–569.

Brewer, W. F., & Lichtenstein, E. H. (1981). Event schemas, story schemas, and story grammars. In J. Long, & A. Baddeley (Eds.), *Attention and performance IX* (pp. 363–379). Hillsdale, NJ: Lawrence Erlbaum.

——— (1982). Stories are to entertain: A structural-affect theory of stories. *Journal of Pragmatics, 6*, 473–486.

Brewer, W. F., & Ohtsuka, K. (1988). Story structure and reader affect in American and Hungarian short stories. In C. Martindale (Ed.), *Psychological approaches to the study of literary narratives* (pp. 133–158). Hamburg: Helmut Buske.

Brown, R. (1958). *Words and things.* New York: Free Press.

Brown, R., Black, A. H., & Horowitz, A. E. (1955). Phonetic symbolism in natural languages. *Journal of Abnormal and Social Psychology, 50*, 388–393.

Bruner, J. (1966). *On knowing: Essays for the left hand.* Cambridge, Mass.: Harvard University Press.

Buck, R. (1985). Prime theory: An integrated view of motivation and emotion. *Psychological Review, 92*, 389–413.

——— (1986). The psychology of emotion. In J. E. LeDoux & W. Hirst (Eds.), *Mind and brain: Dialogues in cognitive neuroscience* (pp. 275–300). Cambridge University Press,.

Bürger, P. (1989). Interpretation after Duchamp. In D. Meutsch, & R. Viehoff (Eds.), *Comprehension of literary discourse: Results and problems of interdisciplinary approaches* (pp. 47–55). Berlin & New York: Walter de Gruyter.

Burwick, F. (1991). *Illusion and the drama: Critical theory of the Enlightenment and Romantic era.* University Park, Pennsylvania: Pennsylvania University Press.

Buss, D. (1995). Evolutionary psychology: A new paradigm for psychological science. *Psychological Inquiry, 6*, 1–30.

Campbell, M. (2000). The 50 top baby names in 1996: United States. http://www.behindthename.com/topus1996.html (28 Feb. 2000).

Carroll, J. (1995). *Evolution and literary theory.* Columbia and London: University of Missouri Press.

——— (2004). *Literary Darwinism: Evolution, human nature, and literature.* New York: Routledge.

——— (2005). Literature and evolutionary psychology. In David M. Buss (Ed.), *The handbook of evolutionary psychology* (pp. 931–952). Hoboken, NJ: John Wiley.

Carroll, N. (1997). Art, narrative, and emotion. In M. Hjort & S. Laver (Eds.), *Emotion and the arts* (pp. 190–211). New York: Oxford University Press.

Chatman, S. (1978). *Story and discourse: Narrative structure in fiction and film.* Ithaca: Cornell University Press.

Chein, S. A. (1987). Extending explanation based learning: Failure driven schema refinement. *Proceedings of the 3rd Conference on Artificial Intelligence Applications* (pp. 106–111). Washington, DC: IEEE Computer Society Press.

Chopin, K. (1999). The story of an hour. In G. Geddes (Ed.), *The art of short fiction: Brief edition* (pp. 73–76). Don Mills, Ontario: Addison-Wesley. (Original work published 1894.)

Clark, H., & Haviland, S. (1977). Comprehension and the given-new contract. In R. Freedle (Ed.), *Discourse production and comprehension* (pp. 1–40). Hillsdale, NJ: Erlbaum.

Clark, J., & Yallop, C. (1990). *An introduction to phonetics and phonology.* Oxford: Basil Blackwell.

Cohn, D. (1999). *The distinction of fiction.* Baltimore and London: Johns Hopkins University Press.

Coleridge, S. T. (1956–1971). *Collected letters of Samuel Taylor Coleridge.* E. L. Griggs (Ed.). Oxford: Oxford University Press.

——— (1957–2002). *The notebooks of Samuel Taylor Coleridge*, 5 vols. K. Coburn, et al. (Eds.). London: Routledge.

——— (1983). *Biographia literaria*, 2 vols. J. Engell & W. J. Bate (Eds.). London: Routledge & Kegan Paul. (Original work published 1817.)

Cook, G. (1994). *Discourse and literature.* Oxford: Oxford University Press.

Corrêa A. A., Miall, D. S., and Kuiken, D. (1998). *Response to environments and to literary texts: The role of national identity.* Paper presented at the VIth Biannual Conference of the Association for the Empirical Study of Literature (IGEL), Utrecht, August 26–29.

Culler, J. (1975). *Structuralist poetics: Structuralism, linguistics, and the study of literature.* London: Routledge & Kegan Paul.

——— (1981). *The pursuit of signs: Semiotics, literature, deconstruction.* London: Routledge &

Kegan Paul.

——— (1983). *On Deconstruction: Theory and criticism after structuralism.* London: Routledge & Kegan Paul.

Cupchik, G. C., Leonard, G., Axelrad, E., & Kalin, J. D. (1998). The landscape of emotion in literary encounters. *Cognition and Emotion, 12*, 825–847.

Cupchik, G. C., Oatley, K., & Vorderer, P. (1998). Emotional effects of reading excerpts from short stories by James Joyce. *Poetics, 25*, 363–377.

Currie, G. (1997). The paradox of caring: Fiction and the philosophy of mind. In M. Hjort & S. Laver (Eds.), *Emotion and the arts* (pp. 63–77). New York: Oxford University Press.

Cutler, A., McQueen, J., & Robinson, K. (1990). Elizabeth and John: Sound patterns of men's and women's names. *Journal of Linguistics, 26*, 471–482.

Damasio, A. (1999). *The feeling of what happens: Body and emotion in the making of consciousness.* New York: Harcourt Brace.

——— (2003). *Looking for Spinoza.* Orlando, FL: Harcourt.

Darnton, R. (1990). First steps toward a history of reading. In *The kiss of Lamourette: Reflections in cultural history* (pp. 154–187). New York: W.W. Norton.

Davidson, R. J., Pizzagalli, D., Nitschke, J. B., & Kalin, N, H. (2003). Parsing the subcomponents of emotion and disorders of emotion: Perspectives from affective neuroscience. In R. J. Davidson, K. R. Scherer, & H. H. Goldsmith (Eds.), *Handbook of affective sciences* (pp. 8–24). Oxford: Oxford University Press.

De Beaugrande, R. (1983). Surprised by syncretism: Cognition and literary criticism exemplified by E. D. Hirsch, Stanley Fish, and J. Hillis Miller. *Poetics, 12*, 83–137.

——— (1989). Toward the empirical study of literature: A synoptic sketch of a new "society." *Poetics, 18*, 7–27.

DeJong, G. (1986). An approach to learning from observation. In R.S. Michalski, J.G. Carbonell, & T. M. Mitchell (Eds.), *Machine learning: An artificial intelligence approach,* Vol. II (pp. 571–590). Los Altos, Calif.: Morgan Kaufmann.

Denis, M. (1984). Imagery and prose: A critical review of research on adults and children. *Text, 4*, 381–401.

Derrida, J. (1980). The law of genre. *Critical Inquiry, 7*, 55–81.

Dickinson, E. (1970). *The complete poems.* T. H. Johnson (Ed.). London: Faber & Faber.

Dijkstra, K., Zwaan, R. A., Graesser, A. C., & Magliano, J. P. (1994). Character and reader emotions in literary texts. *Poetics, 23*, 139–157.

Dissanayake, E. (1992). *Homo Aestheticus: Where art comes from and why.* Seattle: Washington University Press.

Dixon, P., & Bortolussi, M. (1996). Literary communication: Effects of reader-narrator cooperation. *Poetics, 23*, 405–430.

——— (2001). Prolegomena for a science of psychonarratology. In W. van Peer and S. Chatman (Eds.), *New perspectives on narrative perspective* (pp. 275–287). Albany, NY: State University of New York Press.

Dixon, P., Bortolussi, M., Twilley, L. C., & Leung, A. (1993). Literary processing and interpretation: Towards empirical foundations. *Poetics, 22*, 5–33.

Doložel, L. (1973). Narrative composition—a link between German and Russian poetics. In S. Bann & J. E. Bowlt (Eds. & Trans.), *Russian Formalism: A collection of articles and texts in translation* (pp. 73–84). New York: Harper & Row.

Dyer, M. G. (1983). The role of feeling in narratives. *Cognitive Science, 7*, 211–242.

Eagleton, T. (1983). *Literary theory: An introduction.* London: Routledge.

Eco, U. (1984). *The role of the reader: Explorations in the semiotics of texts.* Bloomington, IN: Indiana University Press.

Edelman, G. M. (1992). *Bright air, brilliant fire: On the matter of the mind.* New York: Basic Books.

Ellis, J. M. (1997). *Literature lost: Social agendas and the corruption of the humanities.* New Haven: Yale University Press.

Ellis, R. D. (1999). The dance form of the eyes: What cognitive science can learn from art. *Journal of Consciousness Studies, 6*, 161–175.

Epstein, R. (2004). Consciousness, art, and the brain: Lessons from Marcel Proust. *Consciousness and Cognition, 13*, 213–240.

Ericsson, K. A., & Simon, H. A. (1980). Verbal reports as data. *Psychological Review, 87*, 215–251.

——— (1984). *Protocol analysis: Verbal reports as data.* Cambridge, MA: MIT Press.

Erlich, V. (1981). *Russian formalism: History—doctrine*, 3rd ed. New Haven and London: Yale University Press, 1981.

Feagin, S. (1996). *Reading with feeling: The aesthetics of appreciation.* Ithaca and London: Cornell University Press.

Feagin, S. (1997). Imagining emotions and appreciating fictions. In M. Hjort & S. Laver (Eds.), *Emotion and the arts* (pp. 50–62). New York: Oxford University Press.

Fenigstein, A., Scheier, M. F., & Buss, A. H. (1975). Public and private self consciousness: Assessment and theory. *Journal of Consulting and Clinical Psychology, 43*, 522–527.

Finnegan, R. (1992). *Oral poetry: Its nature, significance and social context.* Bloomington, IN: Indiana University Press.

Fish, S. (1980a). *Is there a text in this class? The authority of interpretive communities.* Cambridge, MA: Harvard University Press.

——— (1980b). Literature in the reader: Affective stylistics. In *Is there a text in this class? The authority of interpretive communities* (pp. 21–67). Cambridge, MA: Harvard University Press. (Original work published 1970.)

——— (1980c). What is stylistics and why are they saying such terrible things about it? *Is there a text in this class? The authority of interpretive communities* (pp. 68–96). Cambridge, MA: Harvard University Press. (Original work published 1973.)

——— (1989). *Doing what comes naturally: Change rhetoric, and the practice of theory in literary and legal studies.* Durham, NC: Duke University Press.

Fitterman, L. (1989). 'Book 'em!' *National Post*, Sept 25, p. B11.

Fitts, K., & Lalicker, W. B. (2004). Invisible hands: A manifesto to resolve institutional and curricular hierarchy in English studies. *College English, 66*, 427–451.

Fludernik, M. (1996). *Towards a "natural" narratology.* London & New York: Routledge.

Fokkema, D. W. (1988). On the reliability of literary studies. *Poetics Today, 9*, 529–543.

Fónagy, I. (1961). Communication in poetry. *Word, 17*, 194–218.

——— (1989). The metaphor: A research instrument. In D. Meutsch and R. Viehoff (Eds.), *Comprehension of literary discourse* (pp. 111–130). Berlin & New York: W. De Gruyter.

Fox, P. (2003). *Borrowed finery: A memoir.* London: Flamingo.

Freund, E. (1987). *The return of the reader: Reader-response criticism.* London: Methuen.

Frey, E. (1981). Subjective word frequency estimates and their stylistic relevance in literature. *Poetics, 10*, 395–407.

Frijda, N. H. (1986). *The emotions.* Cambridge: Cambridge University Press.

——— (1988). The laws of emotion. *American Psychologist, 43*, 349–358.

Galda, L. (1983). Research in response to literature. *Journal of Research and Development in Education, 16*, 1–7.

Genette, G. (1979). Valéry and the poetics of language. In J. V. Harari (Ed.), *Textual strategies: Perspectives in post-structuralist criticism* (pp. 359–373). Ithaca: Cornell University Press.

——— (1997). *Paratexts: Thresholds of interpretation.* Trans. J. E. Lewin. Cambridge: Cambridge University Press.

Gerrig, R. J. (1993). *Experiencing narrative worlds.* New Haven: Yale University Press, 1993.

Glucksberg, S., & Keysar, B. (1990). Understanding metaphorical comparisons: Beyond similarity. *Psychological Review, 97*, 3–18.

Goetz, E. T., & Sadoski, M. (1996). Imaginative processes in literary comprehension: Bringing the text to life." In R. J. Kreuz & M. S. MacNealy (Eds.), *Empirical approaches to literature and aesthetics* (pp. 221–240). Norwood, NJ: Ablex, 1996.

Gold, J. (1990). *Read for your life: Literature as a life support system.* Markham, ON: Fitzhenry and Whiteside.

Graesser, A. C. (1981). *Prose comprehension beyond the word.* New York: Springer Verlag.

Graesser, A. C., Kassler, M. A., Kreuz, R. J., & McLain-Allen, B. (1998). Verification of statements about story worlds that deviate from normal conceptions of time: What is true about *Einstein's Dreams*? *Cognitive Psychology, 35*, 246–301.

Graesser, A. C., Person, N., & Johnston, G. S. (1996). Three obstacles in empirical research on aesthetic and literary comprehension. In R. J. Kreuz & M. S. MacNealy (Eds.), *Empirical approaches to literature and aesthetics* (pp. 3–22). Norwood, NJ: Ablex.

Grafman, J. (2002). The Structured Event Complex and the human prefrontal cortex. In D. T. Stuss & R. T. Knight (Eds.), *Principles of frontal lobe function* (pp. 292–310). New York: Oxford University Press.

Graves, B., & Frederiksen, C. H. (1991). Literary expertise in the description of a fictional narrative. *Poetics, 20*, 1–26.

Greenblatt, S. (2003). Introduction. *Profession 2003*, 7–9.

Greenwald, A. G., & Pratkanis, A. R. (1984). The self. In R. S. Wyer & T. K. Srull (Eds.), *Handbook of social cognition*, Vol. 3 (pp.120–178). Hillsdale, N.J.: Lawrence Erlbaum Associates Inc.

Grob, A. (1998). William and Dorothy: A case study in the hermeneutics of disparagement. *ELH, 65*, 187–221.

Groeben, N., & Schreier, M. (1998). Descriptive vs. prescriptive aspects of the concept of literature: The example of the polyvalence convention. *Poetics, 26*, 55–62.

Haberlandt, K. (1980). Story grammar and reading time of story constituents. *Poetics, 9*, 99–116.

Haberlandt, K., Berian, C., & Sandson, J. (1980). The episode schema in story processing. *Journal of Verbal Learning and Verbal Behavior, 19*, 635–650.

Halász, L. (1989). Social psychology, social cognition, and the empirical study of literature. *Poetics, 18*, 29–44.

——— (1991). Emotional effect and reminding in literary processing. *Poetics, 20*, 247–272.

——— (1995). President's address. In G. Rusch (Ed.), *Empirical approaches to literature: Proceedings of the Fourth Biannual Conference of the International Society for the Empirical Study of Literature—IGEL, Budapest, August 1994* (pp. 10–15). Siegen: LUMIS-Publications.

——— (1996). General and personal meaning in literary reading. In R. J. Kreuz & M. S. MacNealy (Eds), *Empirical approaches to literature and aesthetics* (pp. 379–396). Norwood, NJ: Ablex.

Halász, L., Carlsson, M. A., & Marton, F. (1991). Differences in recall and understanding of literary texts read several times. *Spiel, 2*, 235–262.

Halliday, M. A. K. (1978). *Language as social semiotic: The social interpretation of language and meaning*. London: Arnold.

Hanauer, D. (1995a). The effects of educational background on literary and poetic text categorization judgments. In G. Rusch (Ed.), *Empirical approaches to literature: Proceedings of the Fourth Biannual Conference of the International Society for the Empirical Study of Literature—IGEL, Budapest, August 1994* (pp. 338–347). Siegen: LUMIS-Publications.

——— (1995b). Literary and poetic text categorization judgments. *Journal of Literary Semantics, 24*, 187–210.

——— (1996). Integration of phonetic and graphic features in poetic text categorization judgments. *Poetics, 23*, 363–380.

Hansson, G. (1990). Not a day without a book. *Spiel, 9*, 277–293.

Happé, F., Brownell, H., & Winner, E. (1999). Acquired "theory of mind" impairments following stroke. *Cognition, 70*, 211–240.

Harker, W. J. (1996). Toward a defensible psychology of literary interpretation. In R. J. Kreuz & M. S. MacNealy (Eds.), *Empirical approaches to literature and aesthetics* (pp. 645–658). Norwood, NJ: Ablex.

Hauptmeier, H., & Viehoff, R. (1983). Empirical research on the basis of bio-epistemology: A new paradigm for the study of literature? *Poetics Today, 4*, 153–171.

Hayles, N. K. (1993). The materiality of informatics. *Configurations, 1*, 147–170.

——— (2002). *Writing machines*. Cambridge, MA: MIT Press.

Hidi, S., & Baird, W. (1986). Interestingness—A neglected variable in discourse processing. *Cognitive Science, 10*, 179–194.

Hirsch, E. D. (1967). *Validity in interpretation*. New Haven & London: Yale University Press.

Hoffstaedter, P. (1987). Poetic text processing and its empirical investigation. *Poetics, 16*, 75–91.

Hogan, P. C. (1997). Literary universals. *Poetics Today, 18*, 223–249.

——— (2003). *The mind and its stories: Narrative universals and human emotion*. Cambridge: Cambridge University Press.

——— (2004). Literature, God, & the unbearable solitude of consciousness. *Journal of Consciousness Studies, 11*, 116–142.

Holland, N. N. (1968). *The dynamics of literary response*. New York: W. W. Norton.

Hoorn, J. (1996). Psychophysiology and literary processing: ERPs to semantic and phonological deviations in reading small verses. In R. J. Kreuz & M. S. MacNealy (Eds.), *Empirical approaches to literature and aesthetics* (pp. 339–358). Norwood, NJ: Ablex.

Hunt, R. A., & Vipond, D. (1985). Crash-testing a transactional model of literary reading. *Reader: Essays in Reader-Oriented Theory, 14*, 23–39.

——— (1986). Evaluations in literary reading. *Text*, 6, 53–71.

——— (1991). First, catch the rabbit: The methodological imperative and the dramatization of dialogic reading. *Poetics, 20*, 577–595.

Ibsch, E. (1989). "Facts" in the empirical study of literature: The United States and Germany—a comparison. *Poetics, 18*, 389–404.

Ingarden, R. (1973a). *The literary work of art.* Trans. G. G. Grabowicz. Evanston: Northwestern University Press.

———*The cognition of the literary work of art.* Trans. R. A. Crowley & K. R. Olson. Evanston: Northwestern University Press.

Iser, W. (1978). *The act of reading: A theory of aesthetic response.* Baltimore: Johns Hopkins University Press.

——— (1980). The reading process: A phenomenological approach. In J. P. Tompkins (Ed.), *Reader response criticism: From formalism to post structuralism* (pp. 50–69). Baltimore: Johns Hopkins University Press.

Jaggar, A., & Bordo, S. R. (1989). Introduction. *Gender / body / knowledge.* New Brunswick, NJ: Rutgers University Press.

James, H. (1937). *The lesson of the master*, Vol. XV, *The New York Edition.* New York: C. Scribner.

——— (1962). *The art of the novel*, Richard P. Blackmur (Ed.). New York: Charles Scribner's Sons.

Jamison, K. R. (1993). *Touched with fire: Manic-depressive illness and the artistic temperament.* New York: Free Press.

Jauss, H. R. (1982). *Toward an aesthetic of reception* Trans. T. Bahti. Brighton, UK: Harvester Press.

Johnson, M. (1987). *The body in the mind: The bodily basis of meaning, imagination, and reason.* Chicago: Chicago University Press.

——— (1991). Knowing through the body. *Philosophical Psychology, 4*, 3–18.

Johnson-Laird, P. N., & Oatley, K. (1989). The meaning of emotions: Analysis of a semantic field. *Cognition and Emotion, 3*, 81–123.

Jones, M. W. (1995). Inadequacies in current theories of imagination. *The Southern Journal of Philosophy, 33*, 313–333.

Kane, J. (2004). Poetry as right-hemispheric language. *Journal of Consciousness Studies, 11*, 21–59.

Kant, I. (1968). *Critique of judgement.* Trans. J. Haden. New York: Hafner. (Original work published 1790.)

Keen, S. (in press). *Empathy and the novel.* Cambridge: Cambridge University Press.

Kintgen, E. R. (1983). *The perception of poetry.* Indiana University Press.

Kintsch, W. (1980). Learning from text, levels of comprehension, or: Why anyone would read a story anyway. *Poetics, 9*, 87–98.

——— (1998). *Comprehension: A paradigm for cognition.* Cambridge: Cambridge University Press.

Kintsch, W., & van Dijk, T. A. (1978). Toward a model of text comprehension and production. *Psychological Review*, *85*, 363–394.

Kleinginna, P. R., & Kleinginna, A. M. (1981). A categorized list of emotion definitions, with suggestions for a consensual definition. *Motivation and Emotion*, *5*, 345–379.

Klemenz-Belgardt, E. (1981). American research on response to literature: The empirical studies. *Poetics*, *10*, 357–380.

Klinger, E. (1978). Modes of normal conscious flow. In K. S. Pope & J. L. Singer (Eds), *The stream of consciousness: Scientific investigations into the flow of human experience* (pp. 225–258). New York: John Wiley.

——— (1978). The flow of thought and its implications for literary communication. *Poetics*, *7*, 191–205.

Kneepens, E. W. E. M., & Zwaan, R. A. (1994) Emotions and literary text comprehension. *Poetics*, *23*, 125–138.

Kooy, M. J. (2000). Special issue: After romantic ideology. *Romanticism on the Net*, 17 (February 2000) http://www.erudit.org/revue/ron/2000/v/n17/005907ar.html (visited February 24 2006)

Krook, D. (1988). "As a man is, so he sees": The reader in Henry James. *Neophilologus*, *72*, 300–315.

Kuiken, D., & Miall, D. S. (1995). Procedures in think aloud studies: Contributions to the phenomenology of literary response. In G. Rusch (Ed.), *Empirical approaches to literature: Proceedings of the Fourth Biannual Conference of the International Society for the Empirical Study of Literature - IGEL, Budapest, August 1994* (pp. 50–60). Siegen: LUMIS-Publications.

——— (2001). Numerically aided phenomenology: Procedures for investigating categories of experience. *FQS. Forum: Qualitative Social Research*, 2.1, February 2001. http://qualitative-research.net/fqs-texte/1–01/1–01kuikenmiall-e.htm

Kuiken, D., Miall, D. S, and Sikora, S. (2004). Forms of self-implication in literary reading. *Poetics Today*, *25*, 171–203.

Kuiper, N. A., & Rogers, T. B. (1979). Encoding of personal information: Self-other differences. *Journal of Personality and Social Psychology*, *37*, 499–514.

Lakoff, G., & Johnson, M. (1980). *Metaphors we live by*. Chicago: Chicago University Press.

Lakoff, G., & Turner, M. (1989). *More than cool reason: A field guide to poetic metaphor.* Chicago: Chicago University Press.

Langer, J. A. (1990). The process of understanding: Reading for literary and informative purposes. *Research in the Teaching of English*, *24*, 229–260.

Larsen, S. F., & Seilman, U. (1988). Personal remindings while reading literature. *Text*, *8*, 411–429.

Larsen, S. F., László, J., & Seilman, U. (1991). Across time and place: Cultural-historical knowledge and personal experience in appreciation of literature. In E. Ibsch, D. Schram, & G. Steen, G. (Eds.), *Empirical studies of literature: Proceedings of the Second IGEL-Conference, Amsterdam 1989* (pp. 97–103). Amsterdam & Atlanta, GA: Rodopi.

László, J. (1988). Literary text, literary context, and reader expectations. In C. Martindale (Ed.), *Psychological approaches to the study of literary narratives* (pp. 205–226). Hamburg: Helmut Buske.

——— (1990). Images of social categories vs. images of literary and non-literary objects. *Poetics, 19*, 277–291.

László, J., & Larsen, S. F. (1991). Cultural and text variables in processing personal experiences while reading literature. *Empirical Studies of the Arts, 9*, 23–34.

Lazarus, R. S. (1984). On the primacy of cognition. *American Psychologist, 39*, 124–129.

LeDoux, J. (1996). *The emotional brain: The mysterious underpinnings of emotional life.* New York: Simon & Schuster.

Lehnert, W. G. (1981). Plot units and narrative summarization. *Cognitive Science, 4*, 293–331.

Lehnert, W. G., & Vine, E. W. (1987). The role of feeling in narrative structure. *Cognition and Emotion, 1*, 299–322.

Leventhal, H., & Scherer, K. (1987). The relationship of emotion to cognition: A functional approach to a semantic controversy. *Cognition and Emotion, 1*, 3–28.

Levinson, J. (1997). Emotion in response to art: A survey of the terrain. In M. Hjort & S. Laver (Eds.), *Emotion and the arts* (pp. 20–34). New York: Oxford University Press.

Lightman, A. (1993). *Einstein's dreams.* New York: Warner.

Lindauer, M. (1988). Physiognomic meanings in the titles of short stories. In C. Martindale (Ed.), *Psychological approaches to the study of literary narratives* (pp. 74–95). Hamburg: Helmut Buske.

Livingstone, P., & Mele, A. R. (1997). Evaluating emotional responses to fiction. In M. Hjort & S. Laver (Eds.), *Emotion and the arts* (pp. 157–176). New York: Oxford University Press.

Long, D., & Graesser, A. C. (1991). Differences between oral and literary discourse: The effects of pragmatic information on recognition memory. In E. Ibsch, D. Schram, & G. Steen (Eds.), *Empirical studies of literature: Proceedings of the Second IGEL-Conference, Amsterdam 1989* (pp. 105–109). Amsterdam & Atlanta, GA: Rodopi.

Mackey, M. (2002). *Literacies across media: Playing the text.* London: Routledge/Falmer.

Magliano, J. P., & Graesser, A. C. (1991). A three-pronged method for studying inference generation in literary text. *Poetics, 20*, 193–232.

Mailloux, S. (1982). *Interpretive conventions: The reader in the study of American fiction.* Ithaca: Cornell University Press.

Mandler, J. M. (1984). *Stories, scripts, & scenes: Aspects of schema theory.* Hillsdale, N.J.: Lawrence Erlbaum Associates Inc.

Mansfield, K. (1945). The wrong house. In *Collected stories of Katherine Mansfield* (pp. 675–678). London: Constable.

Mar, R. A. (2004). The neuropsychology of narrative: Story comprehension, story production and their interrelation. *Neuropsychologia, 42*, 1414–1434.

Martindale, C. (1990). *The clockwork muse: The predictability of artistic change.* New York: Basic Books.

——— (1996). Empirical questions deserve empirical answers. *Philosophy and Literature, 20*, 347–361.

Martindale, C., & Dailey, A. (1995). I. A. Richards revisited: Do people agree in their interpretations of literature? *Poetics, 23*, 299–314.

Masson, D. I. (1967). Vowel and consonant patterns in poetry. In S. Chatman & S. R. Levin (Eds.), *Essays on the language of literature* (pp. 3–18). Boston: Houghton Mifflin.

Meutsch, D. (1989). How to do thoughts with words II: Degrees of explicitness in think-aloud during the comprehension of literary and expository texts with different types of readers. *Poetics*, *18*, 45–71.

Meutsch, D., & Schmidt, S. J. (1985). On the role of conventions in understanding literary texts. *Poetics*, *14*, 551–574.

Miall, D. S. (1976). Aesthetic unity and the role of the brain. *Journal of Aesthetics and Art Criticism*, *35*, 57–67.

——— (1986a). Authorizing the reader. *English Quarterly*, *19*, 186–195.

——— (1986b). Emotion and the self: The context of remembering. *British Journal of Psychology*, *77*, 389–397.

——— (1987). Metaphor and feeling: The problem of creative thought. *Metaphor and Symbolic Activity*, *2*, 81–96.

——— (1988). Affect and narrative: A model of response to stories. *Poetics*, *17*, 259–272.

——— (1989). Beyond the schema given: Affective comprehension of literary narratives. *Cognition and Emotion*, *3*, 55–78.

——— (1990). Readers' responses to narrative: Evaluating, relating, anticipating. *Poetics*, *19*, 323–339.

——— (1991). Construing experience: Coleridge on emotion. *The Wordsworth Circle*, *22*, 35–39.

——— (1993). Constructing understanding: Emotion and literary response. In D. Bogdan & S. B. Straw (Eds.), *Constructive reading: Teaching beyond communication* (pp. 63–81). Portsmouth, NH: Boynton/Cook.

——— (1995). Anticipation and feeling in literary response: A neuropsychological perspective. *Poetics*, *23*, 275–298.

——— (1996). Empowering the reader: Literary response and classroom learning. In R. J. Kreuz and M. S. MacNealy (Eds.), *Empirical approaches to literature and aesthetics* (pp. 463–478). Norwood, NJ: Ablex.

——— (1998). The hypertextual moment. *English Studies in Canada*, *24*, 157–174.

——— (2001). Sounds of contrast: An empirical approach to phonemic iconicity. *Poetics*, *29*, 55–70.

——— (2004). Episode structures in literary narratives. *Journal of Literary Semantics*, *33*, 111–129.

——— (in press). "Too soon transplanted": Coleridge and the forms of dislocation. In W. van Peer (Ed.), *The quality of literature. Studies in literary evaluation.* Amsterdam & Philadelphia: John Benjamins.

Miall, D. S., & Dissanayake, E. (2003). The poetics of babytalk. *Human Nature*, *14*, 337–364.

Miall, D. S., & Kuiken, D. (1994a). Foregrounding, defamiliarization, and affect: Response to literary stories. *Poetics*, *22*, 389–407.

——— (1994b). Beyond text theory: Understanding literary response. *Discourse Processes*, *17*, 337–352.

——— (1998). The form of reading: Empirical studies of literariness. *Poetics*, *25*, 327–341.

——— (1999). What is literariness? Three components of literary reading. *Discourse Processes*, *28*, 121–138.

——— (2001). Shifting perspectives: Readers' feelings and literary response. In W. van

Peer & S. Chatman (Eds.), *New perspectives on narrative perspective* (pp. 289–301). New York: SUNY Press, 2001.

——— (2002). A feeling for fiction: Becoming what we behold. *Poetics, 30*, 221–241.

Miller, J. H. (1980). The figure in the carpet. *Poetics Today, 1*, 107–118.

Modiano, R. (1982). Coleridge's views on touch and other senses. *Bulletin of Research in the Humanities, 81*, 28–41.

Mukařovský, J. (1964). Standard language and poetic language. In P. L. Garvin (Ed.), *A Prague School reader on esthetics, literary structure, and style* (pp. 17–30). Washington, DC: Georgetown University Press. (Original work published 1932.)

Murdoch, I. (1970). *The sovereignty of good.* London: Routledge and Kegan Paul.

Nauta, W. J. H. (1971). The problem of the frontal lobe: A reinterpretation. *Journal of Psychiatric Research, 8*, 167–187.

Neill, A. (1989). Review article. *British Journal of Aesthetics, 29*, 90–92.

Nell, V. (1988). *Lost in a book: The psychology of reading for pleasure.* New Haven & London: Yale University Press.

Nesse, R. M., & Lloyd, A. T. (1992). The evolution of psychodynamic mechanisms. In Barkow, J., Cosmides, L., & Tooby, J. (Eds.), *The adapted mind: Evolutionary psychology and the generation of culture* (pp. 601–624). New York: Oxford University Press.

Newman, S. (1933). Further experiments in phonetic symbolism. *American Journal of Psychology, 45*, 53–75.

Nisbett, R. E., & Wilson, T. D. (1977). Telling more than we know. *Psychological Review, 84*, 231–259.

Nussbaum, M. C. (1986). *The fragility of goodness: Luck and ethics in Greek tragedy and philosophy.* New York: Cambridge University Press.

——— (1995). *Poetic justice: The literary imagination and public life.* Boston: Beacon Press.

——— (2001). *Upheavals of thought: The intelligence of emotions.* Cambridge: Cambridge University Press.

O'Faoláin, S. (1980–82). The trout. In *The collected stories of Seán O'Faoláin*, Vol. I (pp. 383–386). London: Constable.

O'Grady, W., Dobrovsky, M., & Aronoff, M. (1989). *Contemporary linguistics: An introduction.* New York: St. Martin's Press.

Oatley, K. (1999). Meetings of minds: Dialogue, sympathy, and identification, in reading fiction. *Poetics, 26*, 439–454.

——— (2002). Emotions and the story worlds of fiction. In T. C. Brock, J. J. Strange, & M. C. Green (Eds.), *Narrative impact: Social and cognitive foundations* (pp. 39–69). Mahwah, NJ: Erlbaum.

——— (2004). From the emotions of conversation to the passions of fiction. In A. S. R. Manstead, N. Frijda, & A. Fischer (Eds.), *Feelings and emotions: The Amsterdam Symposium* (pp. 98–115). Cambridge: Cambridge University Press.

Oatley, K., & Gholamain, M. (1987). Emotions and identification: Connections between readers and fiction. In M. Hjort & S. Laver (Eds.), *Emotion and the arts* (pp. 263–281). New York: Oxford University Press.

Oatley, K., & Johnson-Laird, P. N. (1987). Towards a cognitive theory of emotions. *Cognition and Emotion, 1*, 29–50.

Olsen, G. M., Mack, R. L., & Duffy, S. A. (1981). Cognitive aspects of genre. *Poetics, 10*, 283–315.

Perry, M. (1979). Literary dynamics: How the order of a text creates its meanings. *Poetics Today*, *1*, 35–61.

Pinker, S., & Birdsong, D. (1979). Speakers' sensitivity to rules of frozen word order. *Journal of Verbal Learning and Verbal Behavior*, *18*, 497–508.

Plato (1963). *Cratylus*. (B. Jowett, Trans.). In E. Hamilton & H. Cairns (Eds.), *The collected dialogues of Plato, including the letters* (pp. 421–474). Princeton, NJ: Princeton University Press.

Purves, A. C., & Beach, R. (1972). *Literature and the reader*. Urbana, IL: National Council of Teachers of English.

Rabinowitz, P. J. (1996). Reader response, reader responsibility: *Heart of Darkness* and the politics of displacement. In R. C. Murfin (Ed.), *Joseph Conrad: Heart of Darkness*, 2nd edition (pp. 131–147). Boston, New York: Bedford/St. Martin's.

——— (1998). *Before Reading: Narrative conventions and the politics of interpretation.* Columbus: Ohio State University Press.

Ramachandran, V. S., & Hirstein, W. (1999). The science of art: A neurological theory of aesthetic experience. *Journal of Consciousness Studies*, *6*, 15–51.

Reading at risk: A survey of literary reading in America (2004). Washington, DC: National Endowment for the Arts.

Reddy, W. M. (2001). *The navigation of feeling: A framework for the history of emotions.* Cambridge: Cambridge University Press.

Reformatsky, A. A. (1977). An essay on the analysis of the composition of the Novella. In S. Bann & J. E. Bowlt (Eds. & Trans.), *Russian Formalism: A collection of articles and texts in translation* (pp. 85–101). New York: Harper & Row. (Original work published 1922)

Richards, I. A. (1929). *Practical criticism*. London: Routledge & Kegan Paul.

Ricoeur, P. (1969). *The symbolism of evil*. Boston: Beacon Press.

——— (1970). *Freud and philosophy: An essay on interpretation*. Trans. D. Savage. New Haven: Yale University Press.

Rimmon-Kenan, S. (1983). *Narrative fiction: Contemporary poetics*. London and New York: Methuen.

Rogers, T. B., Kuiper, N. A. & Kirker, W. S. (1977). Self reference and the encoding of personal information. *Journal of Personality and Social Psychology*, *35*, 677–688.

Rose, J. (1992). Rereading the English Common Reader: A preface to a history of audiences. *Journal of the History of Ideas*, *53*, 47–70.

——— (2001). *The intellectual life of the British working class*. New Haven and London: Yale University Press.

Rosenberg, J. (1996). The structure of hypertext activity. *Hypertext '96*. New York: ACM. http://www.cs.unc.edu/~barman/HT96/P17/SHA_out.html (site visited June 30th 2004)

Rosenblatt, L. M. (1937). *Literature as exploration*. New York: Appleton-Century-Crofts.

Ross, E. D., Homan, R. W., & Buck, R. (1994). Differential hemispheric lateralization of primary and social emotions: Implications for developing a comprehensive neurology for emotions, repression, and the subconscious. *Neuropsychiatry, Neuropsychology, and Behavioral Neurology*, *7*, 1–19.

Rouse, J. (2004). Review article: After theory, the next new thing. *College English*, *66*, 452–465.

Rumelhart, D. E., & Norman, D. A. (1978). Accretion, tuning, and restructuring: Three modes of learning. In J. W. Cotton & R. L. Klatzsky (Eds.), *Semantic factors in cognition* (pp. 37–53). Hillsdale, N.J.: Lawrence Erlbaum Associates Inc.

Rumelhart, D. E., & Ortony, A. (1977). The representation of knowledge in memory. In R. C. Anderson, R. J. Spiro, & W. E. Montague (Eds.), *Schooling and the acquisition of knowledge* (pp. 99–135). Hillsdale, N.J.: Lawrence Erlbaum Associates Inc.

Ryff, C. D., & Singer, B. H. (2003). The role of emotion on pathways to positive health. In R. J. Davidson, K. R. Scherer, & H. Hill Goldsmith (Eds.), *Handbook of affective sciences* (pp. 1083–1104). Oxford: Oxford University Press.

Sapir, E. (1929). A study in phonetic symbolism. *Journal of Experimental Psychology, 12*, 225–239.

Saussure, F. de (1974). *Course in general linguistics.* Trans.W. Baskin. London: Fontana/Collins.

Schachter, S., & Singer. J. (1962). Cognitive, social and physiological determinants of emotional state. *Psychological Review, 69*, 379–399.

Schmidt, S. J. (1980). Fictionality in literary and non-literary discourse. *Poetics, 9*, 525–546.

——— (1982). *Foundations for the empirical study of literature: The components of a basic theory.* Trans. R. de Beaugrande. Hamburg: Helmut Buske Verlag.

——— (1983). The empirical science of literature ESL: A new paradigm. *Poetics, 12*, 19–34.

Schmidt, S. J., and Groeben, N. (1989). How to do thoughts with words: On understanding literature. In D. Meutsch, D., & R. Viehoff (Eds.), *Comprehension of literary discourse: Results and problems of interdisciplinary approaches* (pp. 16–46) Berlin & New York: Walter de Gruyter.

Scholes, R. E. (1998). *The rise and fall of English: Reconstructing English as a discipline.* New Haven: Yale University Press.

Seilman, U. & Larsen, S. F. (1989). Personal resonance to literature: A study of remindings while reading. *Poetics, 18*, 165–177.

Semino, E. (1997). *Language and world creation in poems & other texts.* London: Longman.

Serres, M. (1995). *The natural contract.* Trans. E. M. & W. Paulson. Ann Arbor: University of Michigan Press.

Shavit, Z. (1991). Canonicity and literary institutions. In E. Ibsch, D. Schram, & G. Steen (Eds.), *Empirical studies of literature: Proceedings of the second IGEL-Conference, Amsterdam 1989* (pp. 231–238). Amsterdam & Atlanta, GA: Rodopi.

Shklovsky, V. (1965). Art as technique. In L. T. Lemon & M. J. Reis (Eds. & Trans.), *Russian formalist criticism: Four essays.* Lincoln, NE: University of Nebraska Press. (Original work published 1917.)

Smith, B. H. (1988). *Contingencies of value: Alternative perspectives for critical theory.* Cambridge, MA: Harvard University Press.

Sontag, S. (1983). Against interpretation. In *A Susan Sontag reader* (pp. 95–104). Harmondsworth, UK: Penguin Books. (Original work published 1964.)

Spiro, R. (1982). Long-term comprehension: Schema-based versus experiential and evaluative understanding. *Poetics, 11*, 77–86.

Steen, G. (1994). *Understanding metaphor in literature.* London: Longman.

Steen, G., & Gavins, J. (2003). *Cognitive poetics in practice.* London: Routledge.

Steig, M. (1989). *Stories of reading: Subjectivity and literary understanding.* Baltimore: Johns Hopkins University Press.

Stephenson, N. (1992). *Snow crash.* New York: Bantam.

Sternberg, M. (1978). *Expositional modes and temporal ordering in fiction.* Baltimore: Johns Hopkins University Press.

Stockwell, P. (2002). *Cognitive poetics: An introduction.* London: Routledge.

Storey, R. (1996). *Mimesis and the human animal: On the biogenetic foundations of literary representation.* Evanston, IL: Northwestern University Press.

Tan, E. S. (1994). Story processing as an emotion episode. In H. van Oostendorp & R. A. Zwaan (Eds.), *Naturalistic text comprehension* (pp. 165–188). Norwood, NJ: Ablex.

Tarte, R. D. (1982). The relationship between monosyllables and pure tones: An investigation of phonetic symbolism. *Journal of Verbal Learning and Verbal Behavior, 21*, 352–360.

Tarte, R. D., & Barritt, L. S. (1971). Phonetic symbolism in adult native speakers of English: Three studies. *Language and Speech, 14*, 158–168.

Taylor, I. K. (1963). Phonetic symbolism re-examined. *Psychological Bulletin, 60*, 200–209.

Taylor, I. K., and Taylor, M. M. (1962). Phonetic symbolism in four unrelated languages. *Canadian Journal of Psychology, 16*, 344–356.

——— (1965). Another look at phonetic symbolism. *Psychological Bulletin, 64*, 413–427.

Terry, R. (1997). Literature, aesthetics, and canonicity in the eighteenth century. *Eighteenth-Century Life, 21*, 80–101.

Todorov, T. (1973). The structural analysis of literature: The tales of Henry James. In D. Robey (Ed.), *Structuralism: An Introduction* (pp. 73–103). Oxford: Clarendon Press..

Tompkins, J. P. (1980). The reader in history: The changing shape of literary response. In J. P. Tompkins (Ed.), *Reader-response criticism: From formalism to post-structuralism* (pp. 200–232). Baltimore: Johns Hopkins University Press.

Tooby, J., & Cosmides, L. (1990). The past explains the present: Emotional adaptations and the structure of ancestral environments. *Ethology and Sociobiology, 11*, 375–424.

——— (1992). The psychological foundations of culture. In J. Barkow, L. Cosmides, and J. Tooby (Eds.), *The adapted mind: Evolutionary psychology and the generation of culture* (pp. 19–136). New York: Oxford University Press.

Tsur, R. (1992). *What makes sound patterns expressive? The poetic mode of speech perception.* Durham & London: Duke University Press.

——— (1996). Rhyme and cognitive poetics. *Poetics Today, 17*, 55–87.

——— (1997). Sound affects of poetry: Critical impressionism, reductionism and cognitive poetics. *Pragmatics & Cognition, 5*, 283–304.

Turner, M. (1989). *Death is the mother of beauty: Mind, metaphor, criticism.* Chicago: Chicago University Press.

——— (1991). *Reading minds: The study of English in the age of cognitive science.* Princeton: Princeton University Press.

Van den Broek, P., Rohleder, L., & Narváez (1996). Causal inferences in the comprehension of literary texts. In R. J. Kreuz & M. S. MacNealy (Eds.), *Empirical approaches to literature and aesthetics* (pp. 179–200). Norwood, NJ: Ablex.

Van Dijk, T. A. (1979). Cognitive processing of literary discourse. *Poetics Today, 1*, 143–159.

——— (1980). *Text and context: Explorations in the semantics and pragmatics of discourse.* London: Longman.

Van Peer, W. (1986). *Stylistics and psychology: Investigations of foregrounding.* London: Croom Helm, 1986.

——— (1990). The measurement of metre: Its cognitive and affective functions. *Poetics, 19,* 259–275.

——— (1997). Two laws of literary history: Growth and predictability in canon formation. *Mosaic, 30,* 113–132.

Verdaasdonk, H. (1982). Conceptions of literature as frames? *Poetics, 11,* 87–104.

Viehoff, R. (1995). Literary genres as cognitive schemata. In G. Rusch (Ed.), *Empirical approaches to literature: Proceedings of the Fourth Biannual Conference of the International Society for the Empirical Study of Literature—IGEL, Budapest, August 1994* (pp. 72–76). Siegen: LUMIS-Publications.

Viehoff, R., & Andringa, E. (1990). Literary understanding as interaction: Some aspects, some hints, some problems. *Poetics, 19,* 221–230.

Vipond, D., & Hunt R. A. (1984). Point-driven understanding: Pragmatic and cognitive dimensions of literary reading. *Poetics, 13,* 261–77.

——— (1989). Literary processing and response as transaction: Evidence for the contribution of readers, texts, and situations. In D. Meutsch, & R. Viehoff (Eds.), *Comprehension of literary discourse: Results and problems of interdisciplinary approaches* (pp. 155–174). Berlin & New York: Walter de Gruyter.

Vogeley, K., Bussfeld, P., Newen, A., Herrmann, S., Happé, F., & Falkai, P., et al. (2001). Mind reading: Neural mechanisms of Theory of Mind and self-perspective. *Neuroimage, 14,* 170–181.

Vosniadou, S., & Brewer, W. F. (1987). Theories of knowledge restructuring in development. *Review of Educational Research, 57,* 51–67.

Wallace, R. J. (1988). Review article. *Philosophical Books, 29,* 225–227.

Walton, K L. (1990). *Mimesis as make-believe: On the foundations of the representational arts.* Cambridge, MA: Harvard University Press.

Weir, R. (1962). *Language in the crib.* The Hague: Mouton.

White, R. (1992). The figure in the carpet of James's temple of delight. *Henry James Review, 13,* 27–49.

Williams, H. M. (1798). *A tour in Switzerland; or, A view of the present state of the government and manners of those cantons: With comparative sketches of the present state of Paris,* 2 vols. London: G. G. and J. Robinson.

Williams, M. A. (1984). Reading "The Figure in the Carpet": Henry James and Wolfgang Iser. *English Studies in Africa, 27,* 107–120.

Wimsatt, W. K., & Beardsley, M. (1954). The affective fallacy. In W. Wimsatt, *The verbal icon* (pp. 21–39). London: Methuen. (Original work published 1946)

Winner E., Brownell, H., Happé, F., Blum, A., & Pincus, D. (1998). Distinguishing lies from jokes: Theory of mind deficits and discourse interpretation in right hemisphere brain-damaged patients. *Brain and Language, 62,* 89–106.

Woolf, V. (1944). *A haunted house.* London: The Hogarth Press.

Wordsworth, W. (1983). *Poems, in two volumes, and other poems, 1800–1807,* ed. J. Curtis. Ithaca: Cornell University Press.

Yanal, R. J. (1999). *Paradoxes of emotion and fiction.* University Park, PA: Pennsylvania

University Press.

Yekovich, F. R., & Thorndyke, P. W. (1981). An evaluation of alternative functional models of narrative schema. *Journal of Verbal Learning and Verbal Behavior, 20*, 454 469.

Zajonc, R. B. (1980). Feeling and thinking: Preferences need no inferences. *American Psychologist, 35*, 151–175.

——— (1984). On primacy of feeling. In K. R. Scherer & P. Ekman (Eds), *Approaches to emotion* (pp. 259 270). Hillsdale, N.J.: Lawrence Erlbaum Associates Inc.

Zajonc, R. B., Murphy, S. I., & McIntosh, D. N. (1993). Brain temperature and subjective emotional experience. In M. Lewis & J. M. Haviland (Eds.), *Handbook of emotions* (pp. 209–220). New York: Guildford Press.

Zeitz, C. M. (1994). Expert-novice differences in memory, abstraction, and reasoning in the domain of literature. *Cognition and Instruction, 12*, 277–312.

Zeki, S. (1999a). *Inner vision: An exploration of art and the brain.* Oxford; New York: Oxford University Press.

——— (1999b). Art and the brain. *Journal of Consciousness Studies, 6*, 76–96.

Zöllner, K. (1990). 'Quotation analysis' as a means of understanding comprehension processes of longer and more difficult texts. *Poetics, 19*, 293–322.

Zwaan, R. A. (1991). Some parameters of literary and news comprehension: Effects of discourse-type perspective on reading rate and surface structure representation. *Poetics, 20*, 139–156.

——— (1993). *Aspects of literary comprehension.* Amsterdam & Philadelphia: John Benjamins.

——— (1994). Effect of genre expectations on text comprehension. *Journal of Experimental Psychology: Learning, Memory, Cognition, 20*, 920–933.

——— (1999). Embodied cognition, perceptual symbols, and situation models. *Discourse Processes, 28*, 81–88.

Zwaan, R. A., Magliano, J. P., & Graesser, A. C. (1995). Dimensions of situation model construction in narrative comprehension. *Journal of Experimental Psychology: Learning, Memory, and Cognition, 21*, 386–397.

Zwaan, R. A., & Radvansky, G. A. (1998). Situation models in language comprehension and memory. *Psychological Bulletin, 123*, 162–185.

Zwaan, R. A., & van Oostendorp, H. (1993). Do readers construct spatial representations in naturalistic story comprehension? *Discourse Processes, 16*, 125–143.

Index

•C•

•D•

•E•

•F•

•G•

•H•

•M•

•N•

•O•

•P•

•R•

•S•

•T•

•U•

•V•

•W•

•Y•

•Z•